DATE DUE

Court and Constitution
in the Twentieth Century
A MODERN INTERPRETATION

By William F. Swindler
Magna Carta: Legend and Legacy
Court and Constitution in the 20th Century
   I. *The Old Legality, 1889–1932*
   II. *The New Legality, 1932–1968*
   III. *A Modern Interpretation*
Principles of Constitutional Law (in preparation)
Sources and Documents of United States Constitutions
   (editor; 10 volumes)

Court and Constitution in the Twentieth Century

A MODERN INTERPRETATION

by William F. Swindler

We, the People of the United States . . .
do ordain and establish this Constitution
for the United States of America.
PREAMBLE

THE BOBBS-MERRILL COMPANY, INC.

INDIANAPOLIS AND NEW YORK

To the Memory of My Father

Contents

Preface

By amendment and judicial interpretation—both processes reflecting the changing climate of American political conviction—the Constitution of the United States has been progressively modified in its meaning for successive generations of the people of the nation. In the case of formal amendments, the impact these have made on the Constitution as a whole may readily enough be correlated with contemporary political, social and economic issues in national life. In the case of changes in judicial interpretation, the impact may be even more significant, but the forces motivating the changes may be less evident (even though they are likely to be the same).

Most particularly has this been true in the case of the challenges presented by, and the efforts to respond to, the intellectual stresses of the Constitution's second century, beginning in 1889. The age dominated by *laissez-faire* jurisprudence, introduced in the late eighties and collapsing in the depression decade of the thirties, and the new constitutionalism which took its place in the course of the New Deal and the years which followed, have been described in the two volumes of this writer's *Court and Constitution in the 20th Century*. The purpose of the present supplementary volume is to provide a concise interpretation of the Constitution itself in the light of these developments, both for the readers of these two volumes and for those who may wish a separate summary of the subject as a guidebook.

More than a decade has elapsed since the twelfth edition of what used to be the standard reference on this subject—Edward S. Corwin's *The Constitution and What It Means Today.** While there have been some occasional efforts to fill the need for an updated version, none (including Corwin) has been prepared with the conscious plan of interpreting the text of the document pri-

---

* A new, thirteenth edition is being published as this volume goes to press.

marily in terms of the Supreme Court opinions of the past three decades, which in turn have refuted much of the judicial dogma of the prior years of the twentieth century. If it should happen that the Court of the immediate future should depart significantly from some of the positions taken after the great turning point of 1937, such a summary may be even more useful as a standard of comparison.

The alternative for one seeking the text of the Constitution as it has been judicially interpreted is to consult exhaustive annotations such as *The Constitution of the United States of America,* periodically edited under the direction of the Legislative Reference Service of the Library of Congress. Aside from this estimable (and formidable) single volume, there are the professional lawyers' editions which appear as parts of the Federal Code Annotated or the United States Code Annotated. These compendious editions, of course, serve a different need from the need of the average layman, or even lawyer, for a relatively concise résumé of the current understanding of the Constitution. Indeed, and with due deference to the editions described above, it is sometimes difficult to discern this understanding amid the all-inclusive citations which appear therein.

Beyond the formal judicial construction of the text of the Constitution, however, an interpretation such as this must take into account the philosophical implications of the changes in construction for this period. Here, too, the alternative to a concise statement is a reference work of some magnitude—Professor Bernard Schwartz's five volumes of commentary, subdivided into *The Powers of Government* (New York, 2 vols., 1963), *The Rights of Property* (New York, 1965) and *The Rights of the Individual* (New York, 2 vols., 1968). To attempt to cover, in a condensation such as the present one, all or even much of the ground covered in these sweeping studies is manifestly impossible; and yet, since it is obvious that the constitutional construction of the post-1937 era does require a jurisprudential framing, some attention must be given to the subject herein.

Jurists and scholars have regularly called attention to the changing issues and principles emerging from the turbulence of the last three-quarters of a century and have sought to restate constitutional theory as affected by these changes. These commentaries, as much as the formal construction, must be recognized as part of the interpretative process. The concept of the legislative function, which switched intellectual poles in 1937; the galvanizing of the "equal protection" doctrine; the growth of what Professor Arthur Selwyn Miller calls "unitary Federalism"; the pros and cons of "incorporation" of the Bill of Rights into the Fourteenth Amendment—all of these are elements of modern constitutional theory which must find some place, however small, within this interpretation.

"What, then, came of it at last?" one may ask after reading of the constitutional disputes of the period since 1889, or since 1937. The answer might be in the form of another question: Would the man in the street, or the man on the bench, read certain clauses of the Constitution the same way in 1973 as in 1937 or in 1889? The obviously negative answer to this question suggests the answer to the other. For, although Justice Oliver Wendell Holmes's aphorism about experience as the growth of the law has become threadbare from quotation, it is nowhere more applicable than to changing constitutional dogma.

In 1889 the most articulate leaders of American affairs spoke with unhesitating confidence of the validity of *laissez-faire,* and the majority of the Court echoed these convictions. In 1937 disillusionment with the idea was all but complete, and at the eleventh hour the Court accepted the fact that both the economic argument and the judicial interpretation based on it had proved bankrupt. Constitutional law since then has been a construction of a whole new jurisprudence.

Hence the present interpretation: Today's Constitution, so fundamentally affected by the developments of the past three decades, not only in law but in all phases of American life, requires an interpretation which has taken these developments into account. That is the rationale, and hopefully the product, of the present writing.

WILLIAM F. SWINDLER

Williamsburg, Virginia
January 1973

Plan of the Book

There are, in effect, two separate commentaries on the Constitution in the pages which follow. The first, occupying pages 4–55, is a literal reprint of the original text, divided into historical periods and with accompanying background notes which illustrate the changing character of the document over parts of three centuries. There is, first, the text of the Constitution as produced by the Convention of 1787. This is followed by fifteen proposed (and twelve adopted) Amendments by which the nation made essential adjustments in the new governmental machinery which had been put into operation. Then come the four proposed (and three adopted) Amendments of the Civil War and Reconstruction era, followed by the twentieth-century Amendments grouped into two general classes—the five proposed (and four adopted) Amendments of the first quarter of the century and the seven adopted between 1932 and 1970.

The second commentary or interpretation, occupying the major part of the book, is a clause-by-clause analysis of the Constitution in terms of the most recent decisions of the Supreme Court. Where, as in certain instances, the judicial understanding of a clause remains unchanged from its nineteenth-century interpretation, this is made clear. The main emphasis of this portion of the book, however, is on recent decisions—i.e., post-1937—which have expressed the contemporary Court's view of the passage in the text. Where this refutes an earlier twentieth-century (e.g., *laissez-faire*) interpretation, or where there is a persuasive dissenting or concurring view, this has also been called to the reader's attention.

Because this does not purport to be a comprehensive documentary history of the Constitution, the annotations are necessarily selective. However, every significant case since 1889 has been included in the interpretation, as well as earlier key cases which are essential to an accurate presentation of judicial construction. Thus the text with its background notes, and the text as commented on by the opinions of the twentieth-century Court, are intended to form two parts of a whole. Taken together, they will, hopefully, illustrate for contemporary readers how the Constitution as a text has evolved and how its judicial interpretation has reached its present posture.

PART I

The Text of the Constitution

With Background Notes

Outline of Contents

The Original Constitution

Introductory Note

The Constitutional Convention assembled in Philadelphia May 25, 1787, and finally rose from its work on September 17 of the same year. State conventions were then called over the course of the next several months to consider the question of adoption. The chronology of action by these conventions is as follows: *Delaware,* December 7, 1787; *Pennsylvania,* December 12, 1787; *New Jersey,* December 18, 1787; *Georgia,* January 2, 1788; *Connecticut,* January 9, 1788; *Massachusetts,* February 6, 1788; *Maryland,* April 28, 1788; *South Carolina,* May 23, 1788; *New Hampshire,* June 21, 1788.

These nine being sufficient to ratify the new Constitution, it was nominally approved to go into effect on the action of New Hampshire. However, the political importance of two remaining states of the expiring Confederation made it a practical necessity that their affirmative actions also be obtained. These were: *Virginia,* which ratified on June 25, 1788, and *New York,* which ratified on July 26, 1788.

With eleven of the thirteen original states thus having adopted the new form of national government, the last session of the Continental Congress made provision for the election of officers to take over the following year. On February 4, 1789, the Electoral College met and declared George Washington to have been chosen President. March 4 was the date set for the opening of the first Congress, but the slowness of members to assemble delayed the opening; Washington himself was not sworn in as President until April 30. Thereupon, two of the three branches of the new government were operational, but the third—the judiciary—had to await legislative action organizing it, and this eventually came in the form of the Judiciary Act of September 24, 1789. The Supreme Court of the United States opened its first term on February 1, 1790.

Belatedly, ratification formalities were performed by *North*

Carolina on November 21, 1789, and by *Rhode Island* on May 29, 1790. The first new state—*Vermont*—established the precedent for admission to the Federal union by ratifying the Constitution on January 10, 1791, as part of its process of qualification for Congressional action.

The Product of the Convention of 1787

PREAMBLE

We, the People of the United States, in Order to form a more perfect Union, establish Justice, insure domestic Tranquillity, provide for the common defence, promote the general Welfare, and secure the Blessings of Liberty to ourselves and our Posterity, do ordain and establish this Constitution for the United States of America.

ARTICLE I

Section 1. All legislative Powers herein granted shall be vested in a Congress of the United States, which shall consist of a Senate and House of Representatives.

Section 2. The House of Representatives shall be composed of Members chosen every second Year by the People of the several States, and the Electors in each State shall have the Qualifications requisite for Electors of the most numerous Branch of the State Legislature.

No Person shall be a Representative who shall not have attained to the age of twenty five Years, and been seven Years a Citizen of the United States, and who shall not, when elected, be an Inhabitant of that State in which he shall be chosen.

[Representatives and direct Taxes shall be apportioned among the several States which may be included within this Union, according to their respective Numbers, which shall be determined by adding to the whole Number of free Persons, including those bound to Service for a Term of Years, and excluding Indians not taxed, three fifths of all other Persons.][1] The actual Enumeration shall be made within three Years after the first Meeting of the Congress of the United States, and within every subsequent Term of ten Years, in such Manner as they shall by Law direct. The

Number of Representatives shall not exceed one for every thirty Thousand, but each State shall have at Least one Representative; [and until such enumeration shall be made, the State of New Hampshire shall be entitled to chuse three, Massachusetts eight, Rhode-Island and Providence Plantations one, Connecticut five, New-York six, New Jersey four, Pennsylvania eight, Delaware one, Maryland six, Virginia ten, North Carolina five, South Carolina five, and Georgia three.][2]

When vacancies happen in the Representation from any State, the Executive Authority thereof shall issue Writs of Election to fill such Vacancies.

The House of Representatives shall chuse their Speaker and other Officers; and shall have the sole Power of Impeachment.

Section 3. The Senate of the United States shall be composed of two Senators from each State, [chosen by the Legislature thereof,][3] for six Years; and each Senator shall have one Vote.

Immediately after they shall be assembled in Consequence of the first Election, they shall be divided as equally as may be into three Classes. The Seats of the Senators of the first Class shall be vacated at the Expiration of the second Year, of the second Class at the Expiration of the fourth Year, and of the third Class at the Expiration of the sixth Year, so that one third may be chosen every second Year; [and if Vacancies happen by Resignation, or otherwise, during the Recess of the Legislature of any State, the Executive thereof may make temporary Appointments until the next Meeting of the Legislature, which shall then fill such Vacancies.][4]

No Person shall be a Senator who shall not have attained to the Age of thirty Years, and been nine Years a Citizen of the United States, and who shall not, when elected, be an Inhabitant of that State for which he shall be chosen.

The Vice President of the United States shall be President of the Senate, but shall have no Vote, unless they be equally divided.

The Senate shall chuse their other Officers, and also a President pro tempore, in the Absence of the Vice President, or when he shall exercise the Office of President of the United States.

The Senate shall have the sole Power to try all Impeachments. When sitting for that Purpose, they shall be on Oath or Affirmation. When the President of the United States is tried the Chief Justice shall preside: And no Person shall be convicted without the Concurrence of two thirds of the Members present.

Judgment in Cases of Impeachment shall not extend further than to removal from Office, and disqualification to hold and enjoy any Office of honor, Trust or Profit under the United States: but the Party convicted shall nevertheless be liable and subject to Indictment, Trial, Judgment and Punishment, according to Law.

Section 4. The Times, Places and Manner of holding Elections for Senators and Representatives, shall be prescribed in each State by the Legislature thereof; but the Congress may at any time by Law make or alter such Regulations, except as to the Places of chusing Senators.

The Congress shall assemble at least once in every Year, and such Meeting shall be [on the first Monday in December,]5 unless they shall by Law appoint a different Day.

Section 5. Each House shall be the Judge of the Elections, Returns and Qualifications of its own Members, and a Majority of each shall constitute a Quorum to do Business; but a smaller Number may adjourn from day to day, and may be authorized to compel the Attendance of absent Members, in such Manner, and under such Penalties as each House may provide.

Each House may determine the Rules of its Proceedings, punish its Members for disorderly Behaviour, and, with the Concurrence of two thirds, expel a Member.

Each House shall keep a Journal of its Proceedings, and from time to time publish the same, excepting such Parts as may in their Judgment require Secrecy; and the Yeas and Nays of the Members of either House on any question shall, at the Desire of one fifth of those Present, be entered on the Journal.

Neither House, during the Session of Congress, shall, without the Consent of the other, adjourn for more than three days, nor to any other Place than that in which the two Houses shall be sitting.

Section 6. The Senators and Representatives shall receive a Compensation for their Services, to be ascertained by Law, and paid out of the Treasury of the United States. They shall in all

Cases, except Treason, Felony and Breach of the Peace, be privileged from Arrest during their Attendance at the Session of their respective Houses, and in going to and returning from the same; and for any Speech or Debate in either House, they shall not be questioned in any other Place.

No Senator or Representative shall, during the Time for which he was elected, be appointed to any civil Office under the Authority of the United States, which shall have been created, or the Emoluments whereof shall have been encreased during such time; and no Person holding any Office under the United States, shall be a Member of either House during his Continuance in Office.

Section 7. All Bills for raising Revenue shall originate in the House of Representatives; but the Senate may propose or concur with amendments as on other Bills.

Every Bill which shall have passed the House of Representatives and the Senate, shall, before it become a Law, be presented to the President of the United States; If he approve he shall sign it, but if not he shall return it, with his Objections to that House in which it shall have originated, who shall enter the Objections at large on their Journal, and proceed to reconsider it. If after such Reconsideration two thirds of that House shall agree to pass the Bill, it shall be sent, together with the Objections, to the other House, by which it shall likewise be reconsidered, and if approved by two thirds of that House, it shall become a Law. But in all such Cases the Votes of both Houses shall be determined by Yeas and Nays, and the Names of the Persons voting for and against the Bill shall be entered on the Journal of each House respectively. If any Bill shall not be returned by the President within ten Days (Sunday excepted) after it shall have been presented to him, the Same shall be a Law, in like Manner as if he had signed it, unless the Congress by their Adjournment prevent its Return, in which Case it shall not be a Law.

Every Order, Resolution, or Vote to which the Concurrence of the Senate and House of Representatives may be necessary (except on a question of Adjournment) shall be presented to the President of the United States; and before the Same shall take Effect, shall be approved by him, or being disapproved by him, shall be repassed by two thirds of the Senate and House of Representatives, according to the Rules and Limitations prescribed in the Case of a Bill.

Section 8. The Congress shall have Power To lay and collect Taxes, Duties, Imposts and Excises, to pay the Debts and provide for the common Defence and general Welfare of the United States; but all Duties, Imposts and Excises shall be uniform throughout the United States;

To borrow Money on the credit of the United States;

To regulate Commerce with foreign Nations, and among the several States, and with the Indian Tribes;

To establish an uniform Rule of Naturalization, and uniform laws on the subject of Bankruptcies throughout the United States;

To coin Money, regulate the Value thereof, and of foreign Coin, and fix the Standard of Weights and Measures;

To provide for the Punishment of counterfeiting the Securities and current Coin of the United States;

To establish Post Offices and post Roads;

To promote the Progress of Science and useful Arts, by securing for limited Times to Authors and Inventors the exclusive Right to their respective Writings and Discoveries;

To constitute Tribunals inferior to the supreme Court;

To define and punish Piracies and Felonies committed on the high Seas, and Offences against the Law of Nations;

To declare War, grant Letters of Marque and Reprisal, and make Rules concerning Captures on Land and Water;

To raise and support Armies, but no Appropriation of Money to that Use shall be for a longer Term than two Years;

To provide and maintain a Navy;

To make Rules for the Government and Regulation of the land and naval Forces;

To provide for calling forth the Militia to execute the Laws of the Union, suppress Insurrections and repel Invasions;

To provide for organizing, arming, and disciplining, the Militia, and for governing such Part of them as may be employed in the Service of the United States, reserving to the States respectively, the Appointment of the Officers, and the Authority of training the Militia according to the discipline prescribed by Congress;

To exercise exclusive Legislation in all Cases whatsoever, over such District (not exceeding ten Miles square) as may, by Cession of Particular States, and the Acceptance of Congress, become the Seat of the Government of the United States, and to exercise like Authority over all Places purchased by the Consent of the Legislature of the State in which the Same shall be, for the Erection of Forts, Magazines, Arsenals, dock-Yards, and other needful Buildings;—And

To make all Laws which shall be necessary and proper for carrying into Execution the foregoing Powers, and all other Powers vested by this Constitution in the Government of the United States, or in any Department or Officer thereof.

Section 9. The Migration or Importation of such Persons as any of the States now existing shall think proper to admit, shall not be prohibited by the Congress prior to the Year one thousand eight hundred and eight, but a Tax or duty may be imposed on such Importation, not exceeding ten dollars for each Person.

The Privilege of the Writ of Habeas Corpus shall not be suspended, unless when in Cases of Rebellion or Invasion the public Safety may require it.

No Bill of Attainder or ex post facto Law shall be passed.

No Capitation, or other direct, Tax shall be laid, unless in Proportion to the Census of Enumeration herein before directed to be taken.

No Tax or Duty shall be laid on Articles exported from any State.

No Preference shall be given by any Regulation of Commerce or Revenue to the Ports of one State over those of another; nor shall Vessels bound to, or from, one State, be obliged to enter, clear or pay Duties in another.

No Money shall be drawn from the Treasury, but in Consequence of Appropriations made by Law; and a regular Statement and Account of the Receipts and Expenditures of all public Money shall be published from time to time.

No Title of Nobility shall be granted by the United States: And no Person holding any Office of Profit or Trust under them, shall, without the Consent of the Congress, accept of any present, Emolument, Office, or Title, of any kind whatever, from any King, Prince or foreign State.

Section 10. No State shall enter into any Treaty, Alliance, or Confederation; grant Letters of Marque and Reprisal; coin Money; emit Bills of Credit; make any Thing but gold and silver Coin a Tender in Payment of Debts; pass any Bill of Attainder, ex post facto Law, or Law impairing the Obligation of Contracts, or grant any Title of Nobility.

No State shall, without the Consent of the Congress, lay any Imposts or Duties on Imports or Exports, except what may be absolutely necessary for executing its inspection Laws: and the net Produce of all Duties and Imposts, laid by any State on Imports or Exports, shall be for the Use of the Treasury of the United States; and all such Laws shall be subject to the Revision and Controul of the Congress.

No State shall, without the Consent of Congress, lay any Duty of Tonnage, keep Troops, or Ships of War in time of Peace, enter into any Agreement or Compact with another State, or with a foreign Power, or engage in War, unless actually invaded, or in such imminent Danger as will not admit of delay.

ARTICLE II

Section 1. The executive Power shall be vested in a President of the United States of America. He shall hold his Office during the Term of four Years, and, together with the Vice President, chosen for the same Term, be elected, as follows:

Each State shall appoint, in such Manner as the Legislature thereof may direct, a Number of Electors, equal to the whole Number of Senators and Representatives to which the State may be entitled in the Congress: but no Senator or Representative, or Person holding an Office of Trust or Profit under the United States, shall be appointed an Elector.

[The Electors shall meet in their respective States, and vote by Ballot for two Persons, of whom one at least shall not be an Inhabitant of the same State with themselves. And they shall make a List of all the Persons voted for, and of the Number of Votes for each; which List they shall sign and certify, and transmit sealed to the Seat of the Government of the United States, directed to the President of the Senate. The President of the Senate shall, in the Presence of the Senate and House of Representatives, open all the Certificates, and the Votes shall then be counted. The Person having the greatest Number of Votes shall be the President, if such Number be a Majority of the whole Number of Electors appointed; and if there be more than one who have such Majority, and have an equal Number of Votes, then the House of Representatives shall immediately chuse by Ballot one of them for President; and if no Person have a Majority, then from the five highest on the List the said House shall in like Manner chuse the President. But in chusing the President, the Votes shall be taken by States, the Representation from each State having one Vote; a quorum for this Purpose shall consist of a Member or Members from two thirds of the States, and a Majority of all the States shall be necessary to a Choice. In every Case, after the Choice of the President, the Person having the greatest Number of Votes of the Electors shall be the Vice President. But if there should remain two or more who have equal Votes, the Senate shall chuse from them by Ballot the Vice President.][6]

The Congress may determine the Time of chusing the Electors, and the Day on which they shall give their Votes; which Day shall be the same throughout the United States.

No Person except a natural born Citizen, or a Citizen of the United States, at the time of the Adoption of this Constitution, shall be eligible to the Office of President; neither shall any person be eligible to that Office who shall not have attained to the Age of thirty five Years, and been fourteen Years a Resident within the United States.

[In Case of the Removal of the President from Office, or of his Death, Resignation, or Inability to discharge the Powers and Duties of the said Office, the Same shall devolve on the Vice President, and the Congress may by Law provide for the Case of Removal, Death, Resignation or Inability, both of the President and Vice President, declaring what Officer shall then act as President, and such Officer shall act accordingly, until the Disability be removed, or a President shall be elected.][7]

The President shall, at stated Times, receive for his Services, a Compensation, which shall neither be encreased nor diminished during the Period for which he shall have been elected, and he shall not receive within that Period any other Emolument from the United States, or any of them.

Before he enter on the Execution of his Office, he shall take the following Oath or Affirmation:—"I do solemnly swear (or affirm) that I will faithfully execute the Office of President of the United States, and will to the best of my Ability, preserve, protect and defend the Constitution of the United States."

Section 2. The President shall be Commander in Chief of the Army and Navy of the United States, and of the Militia of the several States, when called into the actual Service of the United States; he may require the Opinion, in writing, of the principal Officer in each of the executive Departments, upon any Subject relating to the Duties of their respective Offices, and he shall have Power to grant Reprieves and Pardons for Offenses against the United States, except in Cases of Impeachment.

He shall have Power, by and with the Advice and Consent of the Senate, to make Treaties, provided two thirds of the Senators present concur; and he shall nominate, and by and with the Advice and Consent of the Senate, shall appoint Ambassadors, other public Ministers and Consuls, Judges of the supreme Court, and all other Officers of the United States, whose Appointments are not herein otherwise provided for, and which shall be established by Law: but the Congress may by Law vest the Appointment of such inferior Officers, as they think proper, in the President alone, in the Courts of Law, or in the Heads of Departments.

The President shall have Power to fill up all Vacancies that may happen during the Recess of the Senate, by granting Commissions which shall expire at the End of their next Session.

Section 3. He shall from time to time give to the Congress Information of the State of the Union, and recommend to their Consideration such Measures as he shall judge necessary and expedient; he may, on extraordinary Occasions, convene both Houses, or either of them, and in Case of Disagreement between them, with Respect to the Time of Adjournment, he may adjourn them to such Time as he shall think proper; he shall receive

Ambassadors and other public Ministers; he shall take Care that the Laws be faithfully executed, and shall Commission all the Officers of the United States.

Section 4. The President, Vice President and all Civil Officers of the United States, shall be removed from Office on Impeachment for, and Conviction of, Treason, Bribery, or other high Crimes and Misdemeanors.

ARTICLE III

Section 1. The judicial Power of the United States, shall be vested in one supreme Court, and in such inferior Courts as the Congress may from time to time ordain and establish. The Judges, both of the supreme and inferior Courts, shall hold their Offices during good Behaviour, and shall, at stated Times, receive for their Services, a Compensation, which shall not be diminished during their Continuance in Office.

Section 2. The judicial Power shall extend to all Cases, in Law and Equity, arising under this Constitution, the Laws of the United States, and Treaties made, or which shall be made, under their Authority;—to all Cases affecting Ambassadors, other public Ministers and Consuls;—to all Cases of admiralty and maritime Jurisdiction;—to Controversies to which the United States shall be a Party;—to Controversies between two or more States;—between a State and Citizens of another State;[8]—between Citizens of different States;—between Citizens of the same State claiming Lands under Grants of different States, and between a State, or the Citizens thereof, and foreign States, Citizens or Subjects.

In all Cases affecting Ambassadors, other public Ministers and Consuls, and those in which a State shall be Party, the supreme Court shall have original Jurisdiction. In all the other Cases before mentioned, the supreme Court shall have appellate Jurisdiction, both as to Law and Fact, with such Exceptions, and under such Regulations as the Congress shall make.

The Trial of all Crimes, except in Cases of Impeachment, shall be by Jury; and such Trial shall be held in the State where the said Crimes shall have been committed; but when not committed within any State, the Trial shall be at such Place or Places as the Congress may by Law have directed.

Section 3. Treason against the United States, shall consist only in levying War against them, or in adhering to their Enemies, giving them Aid and Comfort. No Person shall be convicted of Treason unless on the Testimony of two Witnesses to the same overt Act, or on Confession in open Court.

The Congress shall have Power to declare the Punishment of Treason, but no Attainder of Treason shall work Corruption of Blood, or Forfeiture except during the Life of the Person attainted.

ARTICLE IV

Section 1. Full Faith and Credit shall be given in each State to the public Acts, Records, and judicial Proceedings of every other State. And the Congress may by general Laws prescribe the Manner in which such Acts, Records and Proceedings shall be proved, and the Effect thereof.

Section 2. The Citizens of each State shall be entitled to all Privileges and Immunities of Citizens in the several States.

A Person charged in any State with Treason, Felony, or other Crime, who shall flee from Justice, and be found in another State, shall on Demand of the executive Authority of the State from which he fled, be delivered up, to be removed to the State having Jurisdiction of the Crime.

[No Person held to Service or Labour in one State, under the Laws thereof, escaping into another, shall, in Consequence of any Law or Regulation therein, be discharged from such Service or Labour, but shall be delivered up on Claim of the Party to whom such Service or Labour may be due.][9]

Section 3. New States may be admitted by the Congress into this Union; but no new State shall be formed or erected within the Jurisdiction of any other State; nor any State be formed by the Junction of two or more States, or Parts of States, without the Consent of the Legislatures of the States concerned as well as of the Congress.

The Congress shall have Power to dispose of and make all needful Rules and Regulations respecting the Territory or other Property belonging to the United States; and nothing in this Constitution shall be so construed as to Prejudice any Claims of the United States, or of any particular State.

Section 4. The United States shall guarantee to every State in this Union a Republican Form of Government, and shall protect each of them against Invasion; and on Application of the Legislature, or of the Executive (when the Legislature cannot be convened) against domestic Violence.

ARTICLE V

The Congress, whenever two thirds of both Houses shall deem it necessary, shall propose Amendments to this Constitution, or, on the Application of the Legislatures of two thirds of the several States, shall call a Convention for proposing Amendments, which, in either Case, shall be valid to all Intents and Purposes, as Part of this Constitution, when ratified by the Legislatures of three fourths of the several States, or by Conventions in three fourths thereof, as the one or the other Mode of Ratification may be proposed by the Congress; Provided [that no Amendment which may be made prior to the Year One thousand eight hundred and eight shall in any Manner affect the first and fourth Clauses in the Ninth Section of the first Article; and][10] that no State, without its Consent, shall be deprived of its equal Suffrage in the Senate.

ARTICLE VI

All Debts contracted and Engagements entered into, before the Adoption of this Constitution, shall be as valid against the United States under this Constitution, as under the Confederation.

This Constitution, and the Laws of the United States which shall be made in Pursuance thereof; and all Treaties made, or which shall be made, under the Authority of the United States, shall be the supreme Law of the Land; and the Judges in every State shall be bound thereby, any Thing in the Constitution or Laws of any State to the Contrary notwithstanding.

The Senators and Representatives before mentioned, and the Members of the several State Legislatures, and all executive and judicial Officers, both of the United States and of the several States, shall be bound by Oath or Affirmation, to support this Constitution; but no religious Test shall ever be required as a Qualification to any Office or public Trust under the United States.

ARTICLE VII

The Ratification of the Conventions of nine States, shall be sufficient for the Establishment of this Constitution between the States so ratifying the Same.

1. Changed by Amendment XIV, §2.
2. Obsolete.
3. Changed by Amendment XVII, §1.
4. Changed by Amendment XVII, §2.
5. Changed by Amendment XX, §2.
6. Superseded by Amendment XII.
7. Modified by Amendment XXV.
8. *Cf.* Amendment XI.
9. Superseded by Amendment XIII.
10. Obsolete.

Note: The "Original Meaning" and the Constitution as Amended

One of the most persistent arguments between strict constructionists and broad or liberal constructionists of the Constitution concerns what the former insist on calling the "original meaning" of the document—or the "original meaning" of any particular Amendment (e.g., the Fourteenth). Beyond dispute, the starting point in constitutional interpretation is the framework of contemporary circumstances in which any passage in the Constitution or its Amendments was drafted: "The necessities which gave birth to the Constitution, the controversies which preceded its formation, and the conflicts of opinion which were settled by its adoption, may properly be taken into view for the purpose of tracing to its source any particular provision of the Constitution, in order thereby to be enabled to correctly interpret its meaning."[1]

Especially where there is any ambiguity concerning a specific clause or article, a judicial inquiry into the known condition of affairs at the time of its drafting and adoption is proper.[2] The Court is disposed to take notice of the legislative history and the circumstances which led to an Amendment's adoption where a question of construction arises within recent memory of the adoption.[3] But as early as 1884 the Court warned that there was "danger of giving too much weight . . . to the debates and votes," when substantial intervals of time had changed conditions and attitudes; whereas, a century before, when the Constitution was drafted, there had been strong public hostility to a national power of incorporation (the subject of this particular litigation), by the last part of the nineteenth century such a power had been clearly established.[4]

Specific words and concepts in the Constitution—and particularly in the Bill of Rights (e.g., "ex post facto," "infamous crime," etc.)—are defined in terms of the understanding of the contemporary common law;[5] but in recent years the Court has given fresh viability to certain phrases (e.g., "bill of attainder")[6] and has at least considered argument for the broadening of the scope of other provisions (e.g., "cruel and unusual punishment").[7] There is also the question of whether specific words and phrases in the Constitution are limited to their contemporary meaning at the time of adoption, when the common law both in England and the United States has undergone substantial change with reference to these meanings.[8]

Throughout its history the Court has consistently held that the Constitution as amended must be construed as a whole.[9] As a literal concept (which is, however, beside the point), therefore, the "original meaning" of the Constitution of 1787 was modified in 1791 when the Bill of Rights was finally adopted—and has changed sixteen more times with Amendments XI through XXVI. "In determining whether a provision of the Constitution applies to a new subject matter, it is of little significance that it is one with which the framers were not familiar," said Chief Justice Stone in 1941.[10]

In 1905 the Court undertook to enunciate a general rule of construction when it said: "The Constitution is a written instrument. As such, its meaning does not alter. That which it meant when adopted it means now. Being a grant of powers to a government its language is general, and as changes come in social and political life it embraces in its grasp all the conditions which are within the scope of the powers in terms conferred. In other words, while the powers granted do not change, they apply from generation to generation to all things to which they are in their nature applicable. This in no manner abridges the fact of its changeless nature and meaning. Those things which are within its grants of power, as those grants were understood when made, are still within them, and those things not within them remain still excluded."[11]

Whatever the foregoing language meant, the Court reiterated this as a general principle in 1926: While the meaning of the constitutional language never varies, the scope of the application may expand or contract to deal with new and different conditions.[12] Moreover, when the words of the instrument are susceptible of two or more possible meanings, the Court will be presumed to seek the meaning which will effectuate rather than defeat the constitutional purpose.[13]

From the foregoing commentaries it is fairly obvious that judicial determination of when and to what degree conditions have changed, warranting a broadened applicability of a constitutional provision, is a value judgment or a policy decision. And this is the real crux of the matter of strict versus broad construction. Because the accelerated rate of constitutional interpretation coincided with the development of economic jurisprudence revolving about the Fourteenth Amendment and in support of a *laissez-faire* economy, the strict constructionists relying on the rules of decision laid down in that era have tended to be political and economic conservatives. They have sought to perpetuate these rules of decision by appeal to *stare decisis**—a common-law doctrine that need not necessarily apply to constitutional law.[14] (It is, indeed, something of an irony of history that the diminution of the force of *stare decisis* in constitutional law began at the height of the *laissez-faire* dominance of judicial thought, with *Pollock v. Farmers' Loan & Trust Co.* in 1895.)[15]

The doctrine of *stare decisis* has, in fact, been in decline since the great constitutional revolution in 1937.[16] So has the plea of "original meaning." In 1954, in rejecting the argument that public-school education, and hence the question of its segregation or desegregation, was unknown to the framers of the Fourteenth Amendment, Chief Justice Warren observed: "In approaching this problem, we cannot turn the clock back to 1868 when the

---

* "To stand by the decisions," the so-called doctrine of the controlling force of precedents.

Amendment was adopted, or even to 1896 when *Plessy v. Ferguson*[17] was written. We must consider public education in the light of its full development and its present place in American life throughout the nation. Only in this way can it be determined if segregation in public schools deprives these plaintiffs of the equal protection of the laws."[18]

The issue of "original meaning" has yielded place in the present generation to the dialogue over "judicial restraint" versus "activism." For Justice Felix Frankfurter, as for Justice Oliver Wendell Holmes before him, the essence of the liberalization of constitutional law in the latter years of the New Deal was the abandoning of the basic premise that legislative power was to be defined narrowly. Once the scope of legislative power was defined as broadly as any language of the Constitution would admit, in Frankfurter's view it was thereafter the primary responsibility of Congress (or the state legislatures) to exercise the power as its judgment might dictate. The activist rejoinder to this dogma has been that, in the face of legislative inaction to enforce recognized individual rights of general validity, the applicable constitutional provision (most commonly in recent years, the "equal protection" clause of the Fourteenth Amendment) may be treated as self-executing, or at least as negating existing rules of law which burden the enjoyment of the rights.[19]

Since the second century of the Constitution began in 1889, judicial interpretation has been divided between the successive dominance of two philosophies—the *laissez-faire* jurisprudence of the half century extending to 1937 and the broad constructionism of the three decades following.[20] To establish the jurisprudential foundation for freedom of private enterprise from all but minimal government regulation and surveillance, the *laissez-faire* Court in the years 1889–1937 had to overturn a certain number of earlier precedents and to establish in a long series of cases the judicial doctrine which Holmes declared represented the "personal economic predilections" of the majority on the bench. When, in the decade of the Great Depression, it became manifest that the doctrine of *laissez-faire* was bankrupt, it followed that the body of decisional law based on the premise of its unqualified validity would become suspect and systematically thereafter negated.

Yet it would be an oversimplification to define continuing

constitutional doctrine of the twentieth century as a succession of pendulum swings. If the judicial conservative of today is still bound to "stand by the decisions" of the Court, the decisions are virtually certain to be those of the past three decades rather than the contrasting decisions of the half-century before that.[21] Holmes, who may properly be described as the first twentieth-century man on the bench, continually admonished his colleagues that it was not the wisdom of legislative action but solely its constitutional permissibility with which judicial review was to be concerned,[22] and the members of the modern Court have consistently acceded to that view. In the final analysis, it is not "original meaning" but what Justice Jackson called "the great silences of the Constitution" to which the Court of the past thirty years has addressed itself.

1. *Knowlton v. Moore*, 178 U.S. 521 (1917).
2. *South Carolina v. United States*, 199 U.S. 457 (1905); and *cf. Twining v. New Jersey*, 211 U.S. 78 (1908).
3. *Brushaber v. Union Pac. R. Co.*, 240 U.S. 1 (1916).
4. *Legal Tender Case*, 110 U.S. 444 (1884); and *cf. Maxwell v. Dow*, 176 U.S. 601 (1900); *United States v. Wong Kim Ark*, 169 U.S. 699 (1898); *Downes v. Bidwell*, 182 U.S. 254 (1901).
5. *Ex Parte Grossman*, 267 U.S. 527 (1925); *Schick v. United States*, 195 U.S. 68 (1904); and *cf. Grosjean v. American Press Co.*, 297 U.S. 233 (1936).
6. Beginning with *United States v. Lovett*, 388 U.S. 303 (1946).
7. *Cf. North Carolina v. Pearce*, 395 U.S. 711 (1969); *Boykin v. Alabama*, 395 U.S. 238 (1969); *Robinson v. California*, 370 U.S. 660 (1962).
8. *Cf.* the discussion on this subject in *Hurtado v. California*, 110 U.S. 531 (1884).
9. *Cf. Marbury v. Madison*, 1 Cranch (5 U.S.) 137 (1803); *Proutt v. Starr*, 188 U.S. 543 (1903).
10. *United States v. Classic*, 313 U.S. 299 (1941).
11. *South Carolina v. United States*, 199 U.S. 457 (1905).
12. *Euclid v. Ambler Realty Co.*, 272 U.S. 365 (1926).
13. *United States v. Classic*, 313 U.S. 299 (1941).
14. *Cf.* the detailed analysis of overruled cases in Justice Brandeis's dissent in *Burnet v. Coronado Oil & Gas Co.*, 285 U.S. 393, 405–11 (1932); Justice Jackson's supplementary list in *Helvering v. Griffiths*, 318 U.S. 371, 401 (1943); and the two views of the consequence of this trend in Justice Reed's majority opinion and Justice Roberts's dissent in *Smith v. Allwright*, 321 U.S. 649, 655, 669 (1944).
15. *Pollock v. Farmers' Loan & Trust Co.*, 157 U.S. 429 (1895).
16. *Cf.* note 14 *supra*.
17. *Plessy v. Ferguson*, 163 U.S. 537 (1896), upholding the constitutionality of segregated transportation in Louisiana and initiating the "separate but equal" doctrine. The case is remembered today for the eloquent dissent by the first Justice Harlan: "Our Constitution is color blind." 163 U.S. at 559.

18. *Brown v. Board of Education,* 347 U.S. 483 (1954).
19. *Cf.* Swindler, "The Warren Court: Completion of a Constitutional Revolution," 23 *Vanderbilt L. Rev.* 205 (1970).
20. *Cf.* generally the text of the two volumes in Swindler, *Court and Constitution in the 20th Century* (New York, 1969, 1970).
21. *Cf.* Swindler, *loc cit.,* note 19 *supra.*
22. *Cf. Adair v. United States,* 208 U.S. 161 (1908); *Hammer v. Dagenhart,* 247 U.S. 251 (1918); *Abrams v. United States,* 250 U.S. 616 (1919); and other opinions throughout Holmes's tenure.

Adjusting the New Process of Government

Introductory Note

Nearly three hundred proposals for amendment of the Constitution were urged on Congress at its first session under the new government in 1789. A substantial number had been formulated by states as a condition of ratification of the original instrument the previous year. Massachusetts had suggested nine, South Carolina four, New Hampshire twelve, Virginia twenty, New York thirty-two, North Carolina twenty-six and Rhode Island twenty-one.[1] Many of these were, of course, repetitious, and many of them dealt with subject matter that had already been debated at length in the Convention of 1787. Over the years, if anything, the volume was steadily to increase; by the time of the Ninetieth Congress, more than six thousand proposals for change had been introduced—and in the vast majority of instances forgotten.[2]

While it was obvious that recent memory of arbitrary government by Crown officers had inspired the demand for certain Amendments which ultimately became the Bill of Rights—similar bills had appeared in some of the Revolutionary state constitutions—it was at least arguable in 1789 that such Amendments were irrelevant since little of the power of Federal government was assumed to reach the individual. The guarantee of personal rights against government was presumed to be a responsibility of the states. In No. 84 *Federalist,* Alexander Hamilton pointed out that in any case the most fundamental guarantees to be analogized from the English constitution were already to be found in the product of 1787: the preservation of the writ of *habeas corpus,* the prohibition of bills of attainder, the guarantee of jury trial in criminal cases; and the limitation of acts of treason to the levying of war against the United States or giving aid and comfort to its enemies.[3] To list rights to be enjoyed, Hamilton feared, would be to encourage the denial of unlisted rights (a danger which the Ninth Amendment sought to anticipate).[4] Hamilton concluded:

> It has been several times truly remarked, that bills of rights are in their origin, stipulations between kings and their subjects, abridgements of prerogatives in favor of privilege, reservations of rights not surrendered to the prince. Such was *Magna Charta,* obtained by the Barons, sword in hand, from king John. Such were the subsequent confirmations of that charter by subsequent princes. Such was the *petition of right,* assented to by Charles the First, in the beginning of his reign. Such also was the declaration of right presented by the lords and commons to the prince of Orange in 1688, and afterwards thrown into the form of an act of parliament, called the bill of rights. It is evident, therefore, that according to their primitive signification, they have no application to constitutions confessedly founded upon the power of the people, and executed by their immediate representatives and servants. Here, in strictness, the people surrender nothing, and as they retain everything, they have no need of particular reservations. "We the people of the United States, to secure the blessings of liberty to ourselves and our posterity, do *ordain* and *establish* this constitution for the United States of America." Here is a better recognition of popular rights than volumes of those aphorisms which make the principle figure in several of our state bills of rights sound better in a treatise of ethics than in a constitution of government.[5]

Although Hamilton's argument was eloquent—and, indeed, the provisions in some state bills of rights were more in the nature of general policy statements rather than the stipulation of specific guarantees—he was arguing against the trend of public opinion whose rationale in the American Revolution was the inalienable nature of "rights of Englishmen" expressed in the Parliamentary enactments of the English Revolution a century before. The First Continental Congress in its resolutions of grievances in 1774 had reiterated these: the right of peaceable assembly and petition, the guarantees of law and custom established in the mother country at the time of colonization, protection against unreasonable search and seizure, the right to jury trial, and the like.[6]

It was, therefore, a recognition of the basic premise on which the War of Independence had been fought that underlay the demand for a Bill of Rights in the new Constitution. James Madison accordingly introduced a series of bills into the opening session of the First Congress embodying the most universally demanded guarantees; the floodgates thus opened, scores of other proposals on the same subject were offered by other Congressmen. Out of these were ultimately drafted the twelve which were submitted to the people in the summer of 1789; by December 1791 ten of these had been ratified by the necessary three-fourths of the states and thus became the American Bill of Rights. (See tables at end of text for order of ratification of these and other proposed Amendments.)

Text of Twelve Proposed Amendments

[AMENDMENT I]

[After the first enumeration required by the first article of the Constitution, there shall be one Representative for every thirty thousand, until the number shall amount to one hundred, after which the proportion shall be so regulated by Congress, that there shall be not less than one hundred Representatives, nor less than one Representative for every forty thousand persons, until the number of Representatives shall amount to two hundred; after which the proportion shall be so regulated by Congress, that there shall be not less than two hundred Representatives, nor more than one Representative for every fifty thousand persons.]

[AMENDMENT II]

[No law varying the compensation for the services of the Senators and Representatives shall take effect, until an election of Representatives shall have intervened.]

AMENDMENT I

Congress shall make no law respecting an establishment of religion, or prohibiting the free exercise thereof; or abridging the freedom of speech, or of the press; or the right of the people peaceably to assemble, and to petition the Government for a redress of grievances.

AMENDMENT II

A well regulated Militia, being necessary to the security of a free State, the right of the people to keep and bear Arms, shall not be infringed.

AMENDMENT III

No Soldier shall, in time of peace be quartered in any house, without the consent of the Owner, nor in time of war, but in a manner to be prescribed by law.

AMENDMENT IV

The right of the people to be secure in their persons, houses, papers, and effects, against unreasonable searches and seizures, shall not be violated, and no Warrants shall issue, but upon probable cause, supported by Oath or affirmation, and particularly decribing the place to be searched, and the persons or things to be seized.

AMENDMENT V

No person shall be held to answer for a capital, or otherwise infamous crime, unless on a presentment or indictment of a Grand Jury, except in cases arising in the land or naval forces, or in the Militia, when in actual service in time of War or public danger; nor shall any person be subject for the same offence to be twice put in jeopardy of life or limb; nor shall be compelled in any criminal case to be a witness against himself, nor be deprived of life, liberty, or property, without due process of law; nor shall private property be taken for public use, without just compensation.

AMENDMENT VI

In all criminal prosecutions, the accused shall enjoy the right to a speedy and public trial, by an impartial jury of the State and district wherein the crime shall have been committed, which district shall have been previously ascertained by law, and to be informed of the nature and cause of the accusation; to be confronted with the witnesses against him; to have compulsory process for obtaining witnesses in his favor, and to have the Assistance of Counsel for his defence.

AMENDMENT VII

In Suits at common law, where the value in controversy shall exceed twenty dollars, the right of trial by jury shall be preserved, and no fact tried by a jury, shall be otherwise re-examined in any Court of the United States, than according to the rules of the common law.

AMENDMENT VIII

Excessive bail shall not be required, nor excessive fines imposed, nor cruel and unusual punishments inflicted.

AMENDMENT IX

The enumeration in the Constitution, of certain rights, shall not be construed to deny or disparage others retained by the people.

AMENDMENT X

The powers not delegated to the United States by the Constitution, nor prohibited by it to the States, are reserved to the States respectively, or to the people.

Note: Sources of the Bill of Rights

As Table I indicates, the first of the twelve proposed Amendments fell two votes short of ratification, while the second fell four short. Although the subject matter of these proposals was not philosophically related to the remaining ten, they all reflected the concern of the eighteenth century with the problems of making federalism work. The first proposal reflected the fear that representation in Congress would not keep pace with the growth of population. By the second quarter of the nineteenth century, however, the greater fear of centralized government became an argument for permanently limiting the number of Representatives. In 1821 Senator Philip P. Barbour of Virginia warned that the longer the lower House was permitted to grow with population, "you give to it more the form and eventually more of the character of a National in contradistinction to a Federal Government."[7]

A related state concern, at the possibility of self-aggrandizement on the part of Congress, was reflected in the second proposal. The original Constitution had left to the discretion of Congress the fixing of compensation for its members; but when the First Congress in fact set a very modest *per diem* stipend, it may have taken away the force of the argument in favor of the second proposed Amendment. Without a sense of urgency, any campaign which might tacitly have been waged for the first two measures inevitably languished, and although there was no time limit for the proposals' lying before the states,[8] the natural focus of attention on the Bill of Rights and the more explicit issues presented by the Eleventh and Twelfth Amendments in the ensuing decade soon dropped these original proposals from public attention.

This note does not purport to summarize or to supplement the substantial interpretative commentary which already exists on the Bill of Rights. It is sufficient, as illustrating the development of the text of the Constitution, to indicate the general sources of the major provisions in the first eight of these Amendments, viz.:

In several instances, and most strikingly in the case of the First Amendment, the guarantee in the Federal Bill of Rights was more explicit than the equivalent provision in any of the states or in English law. On freedom of expression, either by speech or by print, many existing state declarations either fell into Hamilton's denigrated category of generalities—e.g., Virginia's "That the freedom of the press is one of the great bulwarks of liberty, and can never be restrained but by despotick governments"—or qualified the guarantee by reciting the limits imposed by the law of libel.[9] Statutory reform of the common law of libel, establishing truth of publication as a defense, did not come into English law until 1792.

The twentieth-century Court developed distinct bodies of

case law respecting the "free exercise" of religion and the prohibition of "establishment" of religion by government action. English law, and the law of most of the colonies in the last quarter of the eighteenth century, emphasized religious toleration rather than religious freedom—adherence to certain religious sects automatically created a civil disability in many instances. As for the establishment concept, it persisted in various forms in various states for some years after the Revolution. The Rhode Island "charter of liberties" in 1663 was unique in its sweeping declaration of religious liberty, and the charters of West New Jersey and Pennsylvania were more broadly tolerant than most; but it was not without reason that Thomas Jefferson was to consider his authorship of the Virginia statute on religious liberty in 1776 to be an accomplishment equal in magnitude to the drafting of the Declaration of Independence.

On the other hand, some of the provisions in the Bill of Rights—including the freedom-of-assembly guarantee in the First Amendment—were directly traceable to the provisions in the English constitution which the American Revolutionists had insisted were part of their rights as Englishmen. A number of the guarantees hammered out in the Parliamentary battles with the Stuarts in the seventeenth century—the provisions of due process from Magna Carta and against the private quartering of troops, both from the Petition of Right; the Habeas Corpus Act; and the Bill of Rights of 1689—had been incorporated into the fundamental laws of several colonies, and even when later nullified by Parliament or the Crown they had remained inalienable in the view of the colonists.[10]

The right to bear arms had been confirmed (for Protestants) in the English Bill of Rights as well as in the constitutions of Massachusetts, North Carolina, Pennsylvania, Vermont and Virginia. Quartering of troops, in addition to being prohibited in the Petition of Right, was forbidden by the constitutions of Delaware, Maryland, Massachusetts and New Hampshire. Unreasonable searches and seizures were explicitly prohibited, together with the general warrant, in half of the states.

As for due process, it lay at the heart of the Fifth Amendment as it lay at the heart of Magna Carta itself, the texts inviting a dramatic comparison:

Magna Carta, c. 29	*Amendment V*
No freeman shall be taken, imprisoned, disseised, outlawed, or in any way destroyed, nor will we proceed against him or prosecute him, except by the lawful judgment of his peers, and by the law of the land.	No person shall be held to answer for a capital, or otherwise infamous crime, unless on a presentment or indictment of a grand jury . . . nor shall any person . . . be deprived of life, liberty, or property, without due process of law. . . .

The words were echoed in the opening provision of the Massachusetts Body of Liberties adopted in 1641:

> No mans life shall be taken away, no mans honour or good name shall be stayned, no mans person shall be arested, restrayned, banished, dismembred, or any ways punished, no man shall be deprived of his wife or children, no mans goods or estaite shall be taken away from him, nor any way indammaged under coulor of law or Countenance of Authoritie, unless it be by vertue or equitie of some expresse law of the Country waranting the same. . . .

The equivalent of the Sixth Amendment—in some instances more liberally explicit—appeared in the constitutions of half a dozen states. Delaware's Declaration of Rights stipulated: "That in all prosecutions for criminal offenses, every man hath a right to be informed of the accusation against him, to be allowed counsel, to be confronted with the accusers or witnesses, to examine evidence on oath in his favour, and to a speedy trial by an impartial jury, without whose unanimous consent he ought not to be found guilty." The Pennsylvania constitution added the provision against self-incrimination, and New Hampshire retained the provision of Chapter 14 of the Magna Carta for trials by juries of the vicinage.

Jury trials in civil cases, the burden of Amendment VII, had been the subject *in haec verba* of several bills of rights. Similarly, the language of Amendment VIII was taken verbatim from half a dozen state constitutions.

The last two Amendments, like the first two which failed of adoption, reflected the lingering concern of the states at the powers they were vesting in the new central government. Hamilton, Madison and others had all warned that the enumeration of certain rights in the first eight Amendments could be taken to imply the limiting of government authority only in respect of these rights, under the old common-law rule *expressio unius est exclusio alterius.** The Ninth Amendment sought to negate the applicability of this rule and the Tenth to reiterate the limited and delegated nature of the government power in general.

Text of Three Proposed Amendments

AMENDMENT XI

The Judicial power of the United States shall not be construed to extend to any suit in law or equity, commenced or prosecuted against one of the United States by Citizens of another State, or by Citizens or Subjects of any Foreign State.

AMENDMENT XII

The Electors shall meet in their respective states and vote by ballot for President and Vice-President, one of whom, at least, shall not be an inhabitant of the same state with themselves; they shall name in their ballots the person voted for as President, and in distinct ballots the person voted for as Vice-President, and they shall make distinct lists of all persons voted for as President, and of all persons voted for as Vice-President, and of the number of votes for each, which lists they shall sign and certify, and transmit sealed to the seat of the government of the United States, directed to the President of the Senate;—The President of the Senate shall, in the presence of the Senate and House of Representatives, open all the certificates and the votes shall then be counted;—The person having the greatest number of votes for President, shall be the President, if such number be a majority of the whole number of Electors appointed; and if no person have such majority, then from the persons having the highest numbers not exceeding three on the list of those voted for as President, the House of

---

* Liberally translated, "The expression of one [provision in a statute] infers the exclusion of another [not expressed]."

Representatives shall choose immediately, by ballot, the President. But in choosing the President, the votes shall be taken by states, the representation from each state having one vote; a quorum for this purpose shall consist of a member or members from two-thirds of the states, and a majority of all the states shall be necessary to a choice. And if the House of Representatives shall not choose a President whenever the right of choice shall devolve upon them, before the fourth day of March next following, then the Vice-President shall act as President, as in the case of the death or other constitutional disability of the President—The person having the greatest number of votes as Vice-President, shall be the Vice-President, if such number be a majority of the whole number of Electors appointed, and if no person have a majority, then from the two highest numbers on the list, the Senate shall choose the Vice-President; a quorum for the purpose shall consist of two-thirds of the whole number of Senators, and a majority of the whole number shall be necessary to a choice. But no person constitutionally ineligible to the office of President shall be eligible to that of Vice-President of the United States.

[AMENDMENT XIII]

[If any citizen of the United States shall accept, claim, receive or retain any title of nobility or honour, or shall, without the consent of Congress, accept and retain any present, pension, office or emolument of any kind whatever, from any emperor, king, prince or foreign power, such person shall cease to be a citizen of the United States, and shall be incapable of holding any office of trust or profit under them, or either of them.]

*Note: Judicial and Political Issues
and the Amendment Process*

The three proposed Amendments which followed the adoption of the Bill of Rights reflected the final adjustments to the new Federal government which seemed necessary to the post-Revolutionary generation. Amendment XI specifically nullified the Supreme Court ruling on state suability in *Chisholm v. Georgia;*[11] Amendment XII undertook to correct a breakdown in the process of electing the President and Vice President which came about with the Jefferson–Burr deadlock in 1800 and resulted in the anomaly of having in the Vice Presidency a man vehemently opposed to the program contemplated by the incoming President. The proposed Thirteenth Amendment, submitted in 1810, reflected the waves of xenophobia produced by the Napoleonic age in Europe.

The question of state suability had been a touchy one in the course of the debates on ratification of the Constitution, and it seemed in 1793 that the worst fears of the states'-rights advocates were confirmed when the Supreme Court, in *Chisholm v. Georgia,* affirmed the right of two residents of South Carolina to maintain a suit on defaulted war debts against the state of Georgia.[12] The Eleventh Amendment, specifically negating the majority holding in *Chisholm,* was swiftly drafted in Congress and rushed through ratification with what Justice Frankfurter later called "vehement speed."[13]

As for the proposed Thirteenth Amendment, a paucity of documentary information exists, but it is known that anti-foreign feeling was at a high pitch in the years leading up to the War of 1812. It was said that the coming of Jerome Bonaparte to Baltimore, and his marriage to a Maryland woman, may have been the type of incident that provoked the constitutional proposal. Relatively trivial though the whole subject was, the proposed Amendment advanced apace and largely *sub silentio* and finally failed of adoption only when the second house of the needed thirteenth state legislature failed to ratify it. Indeed, a report issued that the thirteenth state—South Carolina—had in fact ratified the proposal, and a collection of Federal laws published in 1815 in Philadelphia contained the Amendment as though ratified. So did the "official" edition of the Constitution prepared for the Fifteenth Congress (1817–19), and although on a formal inquiry it was confirmed that South Carolina had in fact not ratified, schoolbooks on American government continued to treat the Amendment as though adopted for the next thirty years.[14]

This somewhat ludicrous turn of constitutional history illustrates the intimate relationship to the document which was maintained during the first two generations of the Republic. An intense public interest in politics, both foreign and domestic, on the part of a political elite concentrated on the Eastern seaboard could, as in the case of the Eleventh Amendment or the proposed Thirteenth Amendment, make it possible to react relatively quickly to situations where it was thought a correction in the Constitution might be urgent. The danger in this circumstance was that it would tend to reduce the Constitution to a code of fundamental laws (as too many state constitutions had become) instead of a broad standard of national government by which fundamental laws could be measured. Fortunately, the rapid geographic expansion of the country in the thirties and forties, diluting the concentrated politico-legal elite which had tended to develop, disposed of this question.

1. The classic study on the subject is H. V. Ames, "The Proposed Amendments to the Constitution of the United States During the First Century of Its History," American Historical Assn. *Report* for 1896 (Washington, 1897), App. A.
2. *Cf.* Appendix B in both volumes of Swindler, *Court and Constitution in the 20th Century* (New York, 1969, 1970).
3. *Cf.* Jacob Cooke, ed., *The Federalist* (Middlebury, Conn., 1961), p. 576.
4. *Id.*, p. 577.
5. *Id.*, p. 578.
6. Acts and Resolves of the First Continental Congress, in *Documents Illustrative of the Formation of the Union of the American States* (Washington, 1927), pp. 1–5.
7. Ames, *op. cit.*, p. 55.
8. *Cf. Coleman v. Miller*, 307 U.S. 433 (1939).
9. *Cf.* Street, *Foundations of Legal Liability* (Northport, New York, 1906), I, Ch. 19.
10. *Cf.* Perry, ed., *Sources of Our Liberties* (Chicago, 1959), *passim.*
11. *Chisholm v. Georgia*, 2 Dall. (2 U.S.) 419 (1793).
12. *Id.*, 479.
13. *Larson v. Dom. & For. Corp.*, 337 U.S. 682, 708 (1949).
14. Ames, *op. cit.*, pp. 186–89.

The Reconstruction Amendments

Introductory Note

Half a century passed, after the projected "titles of nobility" amendment, before any more proposals for change in the Constitution were submitted to the people by Congress. With the deepening crisis of the slavery issue, which even the most thoughtful regional leaders, North and South, believed now could be resolved only by drastic constitutional steps or finally by resort to arms, the first agitation for an Amendment on the subject took the form of advocacy of a provision to perpetuate rather than abolish the "local domestic institution."

In 1861, as frantic efforts were made to stave off secession and Civil War, a variety of proposed Thirteenth Amendments came before Congress. Democratic leaders from Northern and border states were especially zealous in their efforts to relieve Southern alarm at the incoming Republican administration by proposing an Amendment that would bar Congress from exercising any legislative power on the subject. On March 2, 1861, a proposed Amendment to this effect passed both houses of Congress and—in a show of support although it had no legal significance—President James Buchanan added his signature to the measure. Thus another proposed Thirteenth Amendment was submitted to the states; together with the Amendments which followed the Civil War, they dealt not only with the subject of Negro freedoms and rights but in more general terms with a totally new relationship between the Federal government and the people of the United States.

Text of Four Proposed Amendments

[AMENDMENT XIII]

[No amendment shall be made to the Constitution which will authorize or give to Congress the power to abolish or interfere, within any state, with the domestic institutions thereof, including that of persons held to labor or service by the laws of said state.]

AMENDMENT XIII

Section 1. Neither slavery nor involuntary servitude, except as a punishment for crime whereof the party will have been duly convicted, shall exist within the United States, or any place subject to their jurisdiction.

Section 2. Congress shall have power to enforce this article by appropriate legislation.

AMENDMENT XIV

Section 1. All persons born or naturalized in the United States and subject to the jurisdiction thereof, are citizens of the

United States and of the State wherein they reside. No State shall make or enforce any law which shall abridge the privileges or immunities of citizens of the United States; or shall any State deprive any person of life, liberty, or property, without due process of law; nor deny to any person within its jurisdiction the equal protection of the laws.

Section 2. Representatives shall be apportioned among the several States according to their respective numbers, counting the whole number of persons in each State, excluding Indians not taxed. But when the right to vote at any election for the choice of electors for President and Vice President of the United States, Representatives in Congress, the Executive and Judicial officers of a State, or the members of the Legislature thereof, is denied to any of the male inhabitants of such State, being twenty-one years of age, and citizens of the United States, or in any way abridged, except for participation in rebellion, or other crime, the basis of representation therein shall be reduced in the proportion which the number of such male citizens shall bear to the whole number of male citizens twenty-one years of age in such State.

Section 3. No person shall be a Senator or Representative in Congress, or elector of President and Vice President, or hold any office, civil or military, under the United States, or under any State, who, having previously taken an oath, as a member of Congress, or as an officer of the United States, or as a member of any State legislature, or as an executive or judicial officer of any State, to support the Constitution of the United States, shall have engaged in insurrection or rebellion against the same, or given aid or comfort to the enemies thereof. But Congress may by a vote of two-thirds of each House, remove such disability.

Section 4. The validity of the public debt of the United States, authorized by law, including debts incurred for payment of pensions and bounties for services in suppressing insurrection or rebellion, shall not be questioned. But neither the United States nor any State shall assume or pay any debt or obligation incurred in aid of insurrection or rebellion against the United States, or any claim for the loss or emancipation of any slave; but all such debts, obligations and claims shall be held illegal and void.

Section 5. The Congress shall have power to enforce, by appropriate legislation, the provisions of this article.

AMENDMENT XV

Section 1. The right of citizens of the United States to vote shall not be denied or abridged by the United States or by any State on account of race, color, or previous condition of servitude.

Section 2. The Congress shall have power to enforce this article by appropriate legislation.

Note: The "Conspiracy Theory"
and Three Constitutional Decisions

With the adoption of the Reconstruction Amendments, the stage was set for a totally new relationship between the people of the United States and their government. The impact of the Civil War on the structure of American society had been cataclysmic: An entire social and economic system in the South had been wiped out, and in the North an economic system unknown to men of 1861 had evolved in the course of the years of conflict. Transcontinental railroads and business corporations which suddenly extended their influence into scores of American communities replaced the localisms of the antebellum age; Big Business came into being in the postwar decade.

For many Americans, these sweeping social and economic changes created a suspicion of betrayal—a conviction that some alien and disingenuous form of government had been devised without their awareness or consent and fixed on them by some legal legerdemain. In due course the developing jurisprudence of the three new Amendments—and particularly the Fourteenth—was taken as evidence of the "conspiracy." During the first quarter of the twentieth century, constitutional historians developed an elaborate case for the proposition that the draftsmen of the Fourteenth Amendment had deliberately selected general language which could be made to apply by judicial interpretation to a wide variety of corporate interests rather than solely to Negro rights.[1]

There is no denying the fact that Fourteenth Amendment jurisprudence—beginning with the construction favorable to *lais-*

sez-faire concepts in the eighties and nineties—has broadened progressively in the twentieth century until it has become the vital center of modern constitutional theory and law. In the thirties the concept of "substantive due process," as a guarantee in itself, was developed to its ultimate dimension; as *laissez-faire* jurisprudence was renounced by the Court in the latter years of the New Deal, the concept was retained and applied to broad public interests where it had previously been a sanctuary for protected private interests. The progressive extension of provisions of the Bill of Rights to the states through the Fourteenth Amendment began in this same period and continued to the end of the Warren Court. Finally, the activation of a variety of concepts of "equal protection" as a means of asserting general rights of citizens of the United States as against infringement by the states has completed the broadening of Fourteenth Amendment jurisprudence.[2]

All of this had been the product of a judicial and political atmosphere which coalesced in the decade following adoption of the Fourteenth Amendment. Aside from the roughshod methods by which the Amendment itself had been declared adopted (see Table II), the readiness of the Court, with the passing of time, to relegate the original objectives of the Reconstruction Amendments to a secondary status encouraged the application of the Amendment's general language to other subjects. Such a "conspiracy" as may have existed in this period was thus a conspiracy of circumstances[3]—the fortuitous confluence of a drastically changing economy and the need for a doctrine of constitutional permissiveness which would stimulate the full development of this economy.

In any event, three fateful decisions of the Supreme Court in the years between 1873 and 1886 completed the relegation of the matter of Negro rights to a minor position in the jurisprudence of the Reconstruction Amendments and the concomitant development of the Fourteenth into a cornerstone for *laissez-faire* constitutionalism. In the *Slaughterhouse Cases*,[4] it was not alone the majority opinion of Justice Miller but the searching dissents of Justices Field and Bradley which laid the foundation for a separate body of interpretation of the Amendment in the generation to follow. There is also the fact that the issue in the case had nothing to do with Negro rights; it tested the constitutionality of a Louisiana statute granting a twenty-five-year monopoly in slaughterhouse operations in three parishes (counties) of the state.

Justice Miller, speaking for the Court majority, rejected the argument that the state law abridged "privileges and immunities of citizens of the United States."[5] Justice Field, dissenting, contended that the privileges and immunities which "of right belong to the citizens of all free governments" include "the right to pursue a lawful employment in a lawful manner, without other restraint than such as equally affects all persons."[6] Justice Bradley added: "In my view, a law which prohibits a large class of citizens from adopting a lawful employment, or from following a lawful employment previously adopted, does deprive them of liberty as well as property, without due process of law."[7]

Nine years after the *Slaughterhouse Cases,* in oral argument in the case of *San Mateo County v. Southern Pacific R. Co.,* Senator Roscoe Conkling made the famous (and perhaps gratuitous) statement: "At the time the Fourteenth Amendment was ratified, individuals and joint stock companies were appealing for Congressional and administrative protection against invidious and discriminating state and local taxes." He quoted at length from the manuscript journal of the Select Committee of Fifteen which had drafted the Fourteenth Amendment, to underscore his basic contention that the draftsmen had had two objectives in mind—to confirm the rights of "freedmen" and, "far more important . . . to frame an amendment which would secure universal protection in the rights of life, liberty, and property."[8]

By inference rather than direct allegation, Conkling repeatedly pointed out to the Court that the Amendment had been intended to distinguish between "citizens"—Negroes and others—whose "privileges and immunities" were to be protected, and "persons," who could be "legal persons" (i.e., corporations) as well as real persons.[9] It was clear that Conkling's task as counsel for the California railroads was to persuade the Court to accept this as the proper legislative history of the Amendment—and the Court majority, seeking a constitutional rationale to undergird the developing *laissez-faire* capitalism of the age, did indeed accept the argument. Although the *San Mateo* case was dismissed three years later as moot, the Court in a companion case thereafter declared that the definition of "persons" in the Fourteenth Amendment as "legal persons" was settled beyond further argument.[10]

Tenuous as Conkling's theory might have been, the inescapable fact was that it was seized on as the means of enlarging the applicability of the Fourteenth Amendment which had been suggested in the dissenting opinions in the *Slaughterhouse Cases*.[11] With the zeal of the Court of the eighties and nineties to develop a constitutional barrier to interference with the free-enterprise system, the corresponding decline in the effectiveness of the Fourteenth Amendment as a safeguard of civil rights was almost inevitable. That trend had begun in 1883, the year after Conkling's famous oral argument in *San Mateo;* in a series of five cases consolidated from California, Kansas, Missouri, New York and Tennessee, Justice Bradley for an eight-to-one majority declared categorically: "It is state action of a particular character that is prohibited [by the Fourteenth Amendment]. Individual invasion of individual rights is not the subject matter of the Amendment."[12] As a consequence, the Amendment as an effective instrument for the protection of individual rights of citizenship was to be frustrated for sixty-five years, until *Shelley v. Kraemer* would turn the "state action" doctrine against itself.[13]

Thus the Reconstruction Amendments—and particularly the Fourteenth—became the foundation for a jurisprudence of free-enterprise capitalism which developed to all but impregnable dimensions in the next half century. The Great Depression brought both the *laissez-faire* economic base and the jurisprudence supporting it tumbling into ruins; but the intervening course of American history had been fundamentally shaped by the judicial rationale which evolved from the *Slaughterhouse Cases,* the oral argument in *San Mateo* and the *Civil Rights Cases*.[14]

1. *Cf.* Graham, "Conspiracy Theory of the Fourteenth Amendment," 47 *Yale L. J.* 371 (January 1938).
2. *Cf.* Swindler, *The Old Legality*, Ch. 2.
3. *Cf.* Avins, ed., *The Reconstruction Amendments Debates* (Richmond, 1967), pp. 301 ff.
4. *Slaughterhouse Cases,* 16 Wall. (83 U.S.) 36 (1873).
5. *Id.,* at 72 ff.
6. *Id.,* at 83.

7. *Id.,* at 111.
8. *Cf. San Mateo County v. Southern Pac. R. Co.,* 116 U.S. 138 (1885).
9. Oral Argument of Roscoe Conkling, in *San Mateo County v. Southern Pac. R. Co.,* cited in Graham, *loc. cit.,* p. 377.
10. *Santa Clara County v. Southern Pac. R. Co.,* 118 U.S. 394 (1886).
11. *Cf.* Swindler, *The Old Legality,* Ch. 2.
12. *Civil Rights Cases,* 109 U.S. 3 (1883).
13. *Shelley v. Kraemer,* 334 U.S. 1 (1948).
14. Swindler, *The Old Legality,* Ch. 14.

Twentieth-Century Amendments

Introductory Note

As the main table of contents points out, the eleven Amendments of the twentieth century—the number attesting to the accelerating tempo of constitutional change in the present era—may be divided into four groups: four which were adopted in the heyday of the Progressive Movement extending from the administration of Theodore Roosevelt through that of Woodrow Wilson; three which reflected the temper of the New Deal era; two which have had the effect of sharpening the definition of the rights of citizens of the United States; and the Twenty-fifth seeking to insure the continuity and efficiency of national government in an era of personal tensions and continuing national need for swift response to domestic and world issues. The Twenty-sixth, the most recently adopted, is intellectually related to the Twenty-third and Twenty-fourth.

The Progressive Movement generated five proposals for amending the Constitution, all of them in subject matter characteristic of the reform emphases of the movement. The Sixteenth, like the Eleventh and Thirteenth, was a deliberate overturning of a specific Supreme Court holding.[1] The Seventeenth reflected the democratizing credo of government in making the popular election of Senators a means of more direct representation of the people. The Eighteenth marked the high-water mark of agrarian influence on national life; by the time of the repeal of the Amendment in 1933, that influence had already been in long decline. The

Nineteenth, broadening the base of suffrage, was the first major breakthrough in the effort of reformers to establish equality of rights for women in all phases of American life.

The proposed Twentieth Amendment, empowering Congress to regulate child labor, was another attempt to override specific Supreme Court decisions.[2] The languishing of that attempt, and the ultimate constitutional issue presented by the 1940 case of *United States v. Darby*[3] which did override the earlier decisions, is the subject of a final note to the present text of the Constitution.

Text of Five Proposed Amendments

AMENDMENT XVI

The Congress shall have power to lay and collect taxes on incomes, from whatever source derived, without apportionment among the several States, and without regard to any census or enumeration.

AMENDMENT XVII

The Senate of the United States shall be composed of two Senators from each State, elected by the people thereof, for six years; and each Senator shall have one vote. The electors in each State shall have the qualifications requisite for electors of the most numerous branch of the State legislatures.

When vacancies happen in the representation of any State in the Senate, the executive authority of such State shall issue writs of election to fill such vacancies: *Provided,* that the legislature of any State may empower the executive thereof to make temporary appointments until the people fill the vacancies by election as the legislature may direct.

This amendment shall not be so construed as to affect the election or term of any Senator chosen before it becomes valid as part of the Constitution.

AMENDMENT XVIII

Section 1. After one year from the ratification of this article the manufacture, sale, or transportation of intoxicating liquors within, the importation thereof into, or the exportation thereof from the United States and all territory subject to the jurisdiction thereof for beverage purposes is hereby prohibited.

Section 2. The Congress and the several States shall have concurrent power to enforce this article by appropriate legislation.

Section 3. This article shall be inoperative unless it shall have been ratified as an amendment to the Constitution by the legislatures of the several States, as provided in the Constitution, within seven years from the date of the submission hereof to the States by the Congress.

AMENDMENT XIX

The right of citizens of the United States to vote shall not be denied or abridged by the United States or by any State on account of sex.

Congress shall have power to enforce this article by appropriate legislation.

[AMENDMENT XX]

[Section 1. The Congress shall have power to limit, regulate, and prohibit the labor of persons under eighteen years of age.

[Section 2. The power of the several States is unimpaired by this article except that the operation of State laws shall be suspended to the extent necessary to give effect to legislation enacted by the Congress.]

Note: The Child Labor Cases and the Question of Judicial Amendment

The proposed Twentieth Amendment, submitted to the states in June 1924, had been prompted by the adamance of the Court in denying to Congress a power to legislate on the subject of child labor under either the commerce power or the tax power. The elimination of economic exploitation of children was one of the basic credos of the Progressive Movement, ardently advocated through the first four decades of the twentieth century. But the counter-argument was fully as fervent and not confined wholly to doctrinaire reactionaries. Many church leaders had serious reservations about the concept of a constitutional power in government to assume such a role *in loco parentis* as the regulation of children's activities implied. Farm leaders as a group strongly disputed the right of the government to intervene in the utilization of the labor of all members of a family living on a farm, the immemorial obligation of those who sought to make their living from the soil.[4]

Hammer v. Dagenhart,[5] however, was decided on none of these issues. The constitutional question was raised on a statute (the Owen-Keating Act of 1916)[6] under which Congress prohibited the shipment in interstate commerce of goods produced in whole or part by the labor of children under the age of sixteen. Justice Day, speaking for a five-to-four majority of the Court, insisted that the matter of controlling child labor was a purely local question to be dealt with by each state in accordance with its own concept of public policy. The commerce clause, he argued, "was not intended to give to Congress a general authority to equalize" conditions between states which regulated such employment and those which did not.[7] Justice Holmes, in dissent, declared that in his view "the most conspicuous decisions of this Court had made it clear that the power to regulate commerce and other constitutional powers could not be cut down or qualified by the fact that it might interfere with the carrying out of the domestic policy of any state."[8]

Holmes further pointed out: "If there were no Constitution and no Congress, [the states'] power to cross the line would depend upon their neighbors. Under the Constitution such commerce belongs not to the states but to Congress to regulate. It may carry out its views of public policy whatever indirect effect they may have upon the activities of the states. Instead of being encountered by a prohibitive tariff at her boundaries the state encounters the public policy of the United States which it is for Congress to express."[9]

Following the judicial narrowing of the commerce clause in *Dagenhart,* the reformers in Congress turned to the alternative use of the tax power as a means of prohibiting the shipment of products of child labor across state lines. This provision of the Revenue Act of 1919 was challenged in *Bailey v. Drexel Furniture Co.*[10] and held unconstitutional by an eight-to-one majority. Chief Justice Taft, reviewing the long line of cases in which the tax power had been used for regulatory or prohibitory purposes, re-

fused to find an analogy between the type of goods—e.g., colored
oleomargarine, noxious drugs, state banknotes—whose liability to
the use of the tax power had been upheld and the products of
child labor. Taft said:

> The Congressional power over interstate commerce is, within
> its proper scope, just as complete and unlimited as the con-
> gressional power to tax, and the legislative motive in its ex-
> ercise is just as free from judicial suspicion and inquiry. Yet
> when Congress threatened to stop interstate commerce in
> ordinary and necessary commodities, unobjectionable as sub-
> jects of transportation, and to deny the same to the people
> of a state in order to coerce them into compliance with Con-
> gress's regulation of state concerns, the Court said this was not
> in fact regulation of interstate commerce, but rather that of
> state concerns and was invalid. So here the so-called tax is a
> penalty to coerce people of a state to act as Congress wishes
> them to act in respect of a matter completely the business of
> the state government under the Federal Constitution.[11]

Thwarted twice in its efforts to deal with the subject through
a gratuitous finding by the Supreme Court that the subject itself
was limited to state jurisdiction, Congress then turned to the device of a proposed constitutional amendment to override the Court,
as the Sixteenth Amendment had most recently done with reference to the narrow judicial construction of the tax power in
relation to income taxes. After spirited debate, the proposed
Twentieth Amendment was duly submitted—and ran into serious
trouble immediately. By the end of 1925, sixteen states had specifically rejected the proposal, making it impossible to muster a
three-quarters affirmative majority unless at least four states could
somehow be prevailed on to reverse their negative vote.[12]

Thus the proposed Child Labor Amendment created a flurry
of constitutional questions: How long did an Amendment, rejected by more than one-fourth of the states, continue to lie before
the people for action?[13] Could Congress renew its efforts to assert
its authority under the commerce or tax clauses, or was it estopped
by its own decision to attempt to amend the Constitution on the
subject of child labor? And could (or should) the Supreme Court

be expected to reverse itself and thus undermine the doctrine of precedents (*stare decisis*)?[14]

Students of the twentieth-century Court could recall that, before the Sixteenth Amendment was formally submitted to the people, the Court had substantially retreated from the position taken in its 1895 decision against the income tax.[15] During Taft's Presidency, indeed, there had been some sentiment for enacting a new income-tax statute as a means of testing the Court's willingness to reverse itself on the 1895 decision; but the counter-argument had been that Congress would be contributing to an undermining of public confidence in the Court, creating the suspicion that the Court if it reversed itself had yielded to political pressure.[16]

The better course seemed to be the forlorn one, of seeking to win over three-fourths of the states to ratification of the Amendment. In fact, in the course of the early New Deal, a few states did reverse their earlier negative vote; but the prospect of mustering thirty-six affirmative votes in the foreseeable future remained bleak. (See Table III.) Accordingly, the Franklin D. Roosevelt administration elected to raise the issue legislatively, by reasserting its power over child labor through the commerce clause. In the Fair Labor Standards Act of 1938, President Roosevelt reminded Congress that Holmes in his dissent in *Dagenhart* had spoken "for a minority of the Court" but "for a majority of the American people." The resulting legislation virtually reiterated the language of the Webb–Kenyon Act of 1916; both Congress and the Chief Executive clearly recognized that the 1938 statute was an invitation to the Court to reverse itself—and the Court recognized this as well.[17]

In *United States v. Darby* in 1941, Justice Stone said for a unanimous Court: "The conclusion is inescapable that *Hammer v. Dagenhart* was a departure from the principles which have prevailed in the interpretation of the commerce clause both before and since the decision and that such vitality, as a precedent, as it then had has long since been exhausted. It should be, and now is, overruled."[18]

The proposed Child Labor Amendment thus became moot. Other Amendments, in fact, had subsequently been proposed and ratified (see below). Other narrow constructions of the Constitution from the heyday of *laissez-faire,* before and after *Darby,* were similarly overruled. Were these judicial amendments to the Constitution? Or were the cases which they overruled judicial amendments? Or was this, in the final analysis, the ultimate function of judicial review in the peculiarly American context of constitutional interpretation?

Text of Eight Proposed Amendments

AMENDMENT XX

Section 1. The terms of the President and Vice President shall end at noon on the 20th day of January, and the terms of Senators and Representatives at noon on the 3d day of January, of the years in which such terms would have ended if this article had not been ratified; and the terms of their successors shall then begin.

Section 2. The Congress shall assemble at least once in every year, and such meeting shall begin at noon on the 3d day of January, unless they shall by law appoint a different day.

Section 3. If, at the time fixed for the beginning of the term of the President, the President elect shall have died, the Vice President elect shall become President. If a President shall not have been chosen before the time fixed for the beginning of his term, or if the President elect shall have failed to qualify, then the Vice President elect shall act as President until a President shall have qualified; and the Congress may by law provide for the case wherein neither a President elect nor a Vice President elect shall have qualified, declaring who shall then act as President, or the manner in which one who is to act shall be selected, and such person shall act accordingly until a President or Vice President shall have qualified.

Section 4. The Congress may by law provide for the case of the death of any of the persons from whom the House of Representatives may choose a President whenever the right of choice shall have devolved upon them, and for the case of the death of any of the persons from whom the Senate may choose a Vice President whenever the right of choice shall have devolved upon them.

Section 5. Sections 1 and 2 shall take effect on the 15th day of October following the ratification of this article.

Section 6. This article shall be inoperative unless it shall have been ratified as an amendment to the Constitution by the legislatures of three-fourths of the several States within seven years from the date of its submission.

AMENDMENT XXI

Section 1. The eighteenth article of amendment to the Constitution of the United States is hereby repealed.

Section 2. The transportation or importation into any State, Territory or possession of the United States for delivery or use therein of intoxicating liquors, in violation of the laws thereof, is hereby prohibited.

Section 3. This article shall be inoperative unless it shall have been ratified as an amendment to the Constitution by conventions in the several States, as provided in the Constitution, within seven years from the date of the submission hereof to the States by the Congress.

AMENDMENT XXII

Section 1. No person shall be elected to the office of the President more than twice, and no person who has held the office of President, or acted as President, for more than two years of a term to which some other person was elected President shall be elected to the office of the President more than once. But this article shall not apply to any person holding the office of President when this article was proposed by the Congress, and shall not prevent any person who may be holding the office of President, or acting as President, during the term within which this article becomes operative from holding the office of President or acting as President during the remainder of such term.

Section 2. This article shall be inoperative unless it shall have been ratified as an amendment to the Constitution by the legislatures of three-fourths of the several States within seven years from the date of its submission to the States by the Congress.

AMENDMENT XXIII

Section 1. The District constituting the seat of Government of the United States shall appoint in such manner as the Congress may direct:

A number of electors of President and Vice President equal to the whole number of Senators and Representatives in Congress to which the District would be entitled if it were a State, but in no event more than the least populous State; they shall be in addition to those appointed by the States, but they shall be considered, for the purposes of the election of President and Vice President, to be electors appointed by a State; and they shall meet in the District and perform such duties as provided by the twelfth article of amendment.

Section 2. The Congress shall have power to enforce this article by appropriate legislation.

AMENDMENT XXIV

Section 1. The right of citizens of the United States to vote in any primary or other election for President or Vice President, for electors for President or Vice President, or for Senator or Representative in Congress, shall not be denied or abridged by the United States or any State by reason of failure to pay any poll tax or other tax.

Section 2. The Congress shall have power to enforce this article by appropriate legislation.

AMENDMENT XXV

Section 1. In case of the removal of the President from office or of his death or resignation, the Vice President shall become President.

Section 2. Whenever there is a vacancy in the office of the Vice President, the President shall nominate a Vice President who shall take office upon confirmation by a majority vote of both Houses of Congress.

Section 3. Whenever the President transmits to the President pro tempore of the Senate and the Speaker of the House of Representatives his written declaration that he is unable to discharge the powers and duties of his office, and until he transmits to them a written declaration to the contrary, such powers and duties shall be discharged by the Vice President as Acting President.

Section 4. Whenever the Vice President and a majority of either the principal officers of the executive departments or of such other body as Congress may by law provide, transmit to the President pro tempore of the Senate and the Speaker of the House of Representatives their written declaration that the President is unable to discharge the powers and duties of his office, the Vice President shall immediately assume the powers and duties of the office as Acting President.

Thereafter, when the President transmits to the President pro tempore of the Senate and the Speaker of the House of Representatives his written declaration that no inability exists, he shall resume the powers and duties of his office unless the Vice President and a majority of either the principal officers of the executive department or of such other body as Congress may by law provide, transmit within four days to the President pro tempore of the Senate and the Speaker of the House of Representatives their written declaration that the President is unable to discharge the powers and duties of his office. Thereupon Congress shall decide the issue, assembling within forty-eight hours for that purpose if not in session. If the Congress, within twenty-one days after receipt of the latter written declaration, or, if Congress is not in session, within twenty-one days after Congress is required to assemble, determines by two-thirds vote of both Houses that the President is unable to discharge the powers and duties of his office, the Vice President shall continue to discharge the same as Acting President; otherwise the President shall resume the powers and duties of his office.[18]

AMENDMENT XXVI

Section 1. The right of citizens of the United States, who are eighteen years of age or older, to vote shall not be denied or abridged by the United States or by any State on account of age.

Section 2. The Congress shall have power to enforce this article by appropriate legislation.

[AMENDMENT XXVII]

[Section 1. Equality of rights under the law shall not be denied or abridged by the United States or by any State on account of sex.

[Section 2. The Congress shall have the power to enforce, by appropriate legislation, the provisions of this article.

[Section 3. This amendment shall take effect two years after the date of ratification.]

1. *Chisholm v. Georgia*, 2 Dall. (2 U.S.) 419 (1793); *Dred Scott v. Sanford*, 19 How. 393 (1857); *Pollock v. Farmers' Loan & Trust Co.*, 158 U.S. 601 (1895).
2. *Hammer v. Dagenhart*, 247 U.S. 251 (1918); *Bailey v. Drexel Furn. Co.*, 259 U.S. 20 (1922).
3. *United States v. Darby*, 312 U.S. 100 (1941).
4. *Cf.* Swindler, *The Old Legality*, p. 239.
5. *Hammer v. Dagenhart*, 247 U.S. 251 (1918).
6. Ch. 432, 39 Stat. 757.
7. 247 U.S., at 269.
8. *Id.*, at 278.
9. *Id.*, at 281.
10. *Bailey v. Drexel Furn. Co.*, 259 U.S. 20 (1922).
11. *Id.*, at 39.
12. Swindler, *The Old Legality*, p. 239.
13. *Coleman v. Miller*, 307 U.S. 433 (1939).
14. *Cf. Burnet v. Coronado Oil & Gas Co.*, 285 U.S. 393, 405 (1932).
15. Swindler, *The Old Legality*, p. 147.
16. *Id.*, p. 148.
17. *Id.*, p. 240.
18. *United States v. Darby*, 312 U.S. 100 (1941).

TABLE 1
Amendments Proposed or Adopted, 1789–1815

(Roman numeral in brackets refers to rejected Amendment. Figure in parentheses indicates number of states constituting three-quarters majority as of that date.)

States (in order of admission)	[I] (11)	[II] (11)	I–X (11)	XI (12)	XII (13)	[XIII] (13)
Delaware	R 1–28–90	1–28–90	1–28–90	1–23–95	R 1–18–04	2– 2–11
Pennsylvania	9–21–91*	R 3–10–90	3–10–90		1– 5–04	2– 6–11
New Jersey	11–20–89	R 11–20–89	11–20–89		2–22–04	2–13–11
Georgia				11–29–94	5–19–04	12–13–11
Connecticut				5– 8–94	R 5–10–04	R 5– ?–13
Massachusetts				6–26–94		2–27–12
Maryland	12–19–89	12–19–89	12–19–89	12–26–94	12–24–03	12–25–10
South Carolina	1–19–90	1–19–90	1–19–90	12– 4–95	5–15–04	[12– 7–13]†
New Hampshire	1–25–90	R 1–25–90	1–25–90	6–16–94	6–15–04	12–10–12
Virginia	10–25–91	12–15–91	12–15–91	11–18–94	2– 3–04	
New York	3–27–90	3–27–90	3–27–90	3–27–94	2–10–04	R 2–27–12
North Carolina	12–22–89	12–22–89	12–22–89	2– 7–95	12–22–03	12–23–11
Rhode Island	6–15–90	R 6–15–90	6–15–90	3–31–94	3–12–04	R 9–15–14
Vermont		11– 3–91	11– 3–91	11– 9–94	1–30–04	10–24–11
Kentucky				12– 7–94	12–27–03	1–31–11
Tennessee					7–27–04	11–21–11
Ohio					12–30–03	1–31–11

R—rejected.

* prior negative vote was reconsidered this date.

† lower house of legislature failed to act, thus failing to establish three-fourths majority of the states.

Comment on Table 1: Poor communications in the eighteenth and early nineteenth centuries made for some confusion as to the actual voting record on early Amendments. As a consequence, there is some discrepancy between the data cited here, taken from Ames, *Proposed Amendments, etc.,* and such sources as *Documents on the History of the Constitution* (H. Doc. 529, 56th Cong. 2d Sess., 1894), II, pp. 325–90.

Also because of poor communications, Congress received one more ratification than was needed in the cases of the Eleventh and Twelfth Amendments, and was under a misapprehension as to the ratification of the proposed Thirteenth Amendment; see Ames, *op. cit.,* pp. 186–89.

Although ratifications beyond the three-fourths majority have no legal effect, the states of Connecticut, Georgia and Massachusetts in 1939 ratified the Bill of Rights, on the one hundred fiftieth anniversary of the same.

TABLE 2
Civil War and Reconstruction Era Amendments

States (in order of admission)	[XIII] (25)	XIII (27)	XIV (28)	XV (28)
Delaware				R
Pennsylvania		2- 8-65	2-12-67	3-25-59
New Jersey		[1-23-66]*	W [9-11-66]	[2-15-71]*
Georgia		12- 6-65	[7-21-68]*	2- 2-70
Connecticut		5- 4-65	6-30-66	5-19-69
Massachusetts		2- 7-65	3-20-67	3-12-69
Maryland	1-10-62	2- 3-65		R
South Carolina		11-13-65	7- 8-68	3-15-69
New Hampshire		6-30-65	7- 7-66	7- 1-69
Virginia		2- 9-65	[10- 8-69]*	10- 8-69
New York		2- 3-65	1-10-67	W [4-14-69]
North Carolina		12- 4-65	[7- 2-68]*	3- 5-69
Rhode Island		2- 2-65	2- 7-67	1-18-70
Vermont		3- 9-65	10-30-66	10-20-69
Kentucky		R 2-24-65	R 1- 8-67	R
Tennessee		4- 7-65	7-19-66	R
Ohio	5-13-61	2-10-65	W [1-11-67]	1-27-70*
Louisiana		2-16-65	7- 9-68*	3- 5-69
Indiana		2-16-65	1-23-67	5-14-69
Mississippi		R 12- 2-65	[1-17-70]	1-17-70
Illinois		1- 1-65	1-15-67	3- 5-69
Alabama	2-14-62	12- 2-65	[7-13-68]	11-16-69
Maine		2- 7-65	1-19-67	3-11-69
Missouri		2- 6-65	1-26-67	1- 7-70*
Arkansas		4-14-65	4- 6-68	3-15-69
Michigan		2- 2-65	1-16-67	3- 5-69
Florida		[12-28-65]*	6- 9-68	6-14-69
Texas		[2-18-70]	[2-18-70]*	[2-18-70]
Iowa		1-17-66	3- 9-68	2- 3-70
Wisconsin		2-24-65	2-13-67	3- 5-69
California		[12-15-65]		R
Minnesota		2-23-65		1-13-70
Oregon		[12-11-65]	W [9-19-66]	R
Kansas		2- 7-65	1-17-67	1-19-70
West Virginia		2- 3-65	1-16-67	3- 3-69
Nevada		2-16-65	1-22-67	3- 1-69
Nebraska			6-15-67	2-17-70

R—rejected.   W—withdrawn.   * Previously rejected.

Figures in brackets indicate challenged ratifications or ratifications which were of no legal effect because adopted after three-fourths majority obtained. In the case of the Fourteenth Amendment, Congress by resolution denied the effect of the withdrawals of ratification by New Jersey, Ohio and Oregon; when this still left two states necessary to complete ratification, Congress accepted the ratifications of various Southern states not yet restored to the Union.

Comment on Table 2: The exceedingly confused status of ratification of the Reconstruction era Amendments arose in part from the fact that a number of the votes making up the required three-quarters majority had been secured from puppet Reconstruction legislatures in Southern states. Since in most instances these states had not been readmitted to the Union, and their Senators and Representatives seated in Congress, there was a serious doubt as to the validity of these ratifications. Reconstruction Congresses met the problem in three ways: First, they required seceded states to ratify the Fourteenth Amendment (about which there was the greatest doubt) as a condition of readmission. Second, they continued to accept ratifications beyond the nominal three-quarters of the states; these are indicated by the dates in brackets in the columns. Third, by resolution they denied that ratification once voted could be "withdrawn" by a state—another doubtful constitutional proposition.

Several of the states which originally rejected one or more of the Amendments formally ratified them at various dates later in the nineteenth or early in the twentieth centuries. The Amendments may at least be said to have *de facto* ratification as of the present.

TABLE 3

Progressive Era Amendments

States (in order of admission)	XVI (36)	XVII (36)	XVIII (36)	XIX (36)	[XX] (36)
Delaware	2- 3-13		3-18-18		R 2-25-24
Pennsylvania		4- 2-13		6-24-19	R 4- 1-25†
New Jersey		3-17-13		2- 9-20	
Georgia	8- 3-10		6-26-18	R 7-24-19	R 2- 3-24
Connecticut	R	4-18-13			R 2-13-24
Massachusetts		5-22-12	4- 2-18	6-25-19	R 2-16-25
Maryland	4- 8-10		2-13-18	R 2-24-20	R 3-18-27
South Carolina	2-19-10		1-29-18	R 1-29-20	R 12-28-24
New Hampshire		2-19-13	1-15-19	9-10-19	R 3-18-25†
Virginia			1- 8-18	R 2-12-20	R 1-22-26
New York	7-12-11	1-15-13		6-16-19	
North Carolina	2-11-11	1-25-13	1-16-19		R 6-27-24
Rhode Island	R			1- 6-20	
Vermont		2-19-13			R 2- 4-24
Kentucky	2- 8-10		1-14-18	1- 6-20	
Tennessee	4- 7-11	4- 1-13	1-13-19	8-18-20	R 2-24-24
Ohio	1-19-11	2-25-13	1- 7-19	6-16-19	3-22-33
Louisiana	6-28-12		8- 9-18	R 7- 1-20	R 1-21-25
Indiana	1-10-11	2-19-13	1-14-19	1-16-20	R 2- 7-25†
Mississippi	3- 7-10		1- 8-18	R 3-29-20	
Illinois	3- 1-10	2-13-13	1-14-19	6-10-19	9-16-33
Alabama	8-10-09		1-15-19	R 9-22-19	
Maine	3-31-11	2-20-13	1- 8-19	11- 5-19	R 4-10-25
Missouri	3-16-11	3- 7-13	[1-16-19]	7- 3-19	R 3- 3-25
Arkansas	4-22-11*	2-11-13	1-14-19	7-28-19	1-28-24

Table 3 (cont.)

States	XVI	XVII	XVIII	XIX	[XX]
Michigan	2-23-11	1-28-13	1- 2-19	6-10-19	5-10-33
Florida			11-27-18		R 3-15-26
Texas	8-16-10	2- 7-13	3- 4-18	6-28-19	R 2- 4-24
Iowa	2-24-11	1-30-13	1-15-19	7- 2-19	R 2- 5-25†
Wisconsin	5-16-11	2-18-13		6-10-19	R 2-26-24†
California	1-31-11	1-28-13	1-13-19	11- 1-19	1- 8-25
Minnesota	6-11-12	6-10-12		9- 8-19	R 4-14-25
Oregon	1-23-11	1-23-13	1-15-19	1-13-20	1-31-33
Kansas	3- 2-11	1-17-13	1-14-19	6-16-19	R 8- 6-24†
West Virginia	1-31-13	2- 4-13	1- 9-19	3-10-20	12-12-33
Nevada	1-31-11	2- 6-13		2- 7-20	1-29-37
Nebraska	2- 9-11	3-14-13	1-16-19	8- 2-19	
Colorado	2-15-11	2- 5-13	1-15-19	12-15-19	R 2-13-24†
North Dakota	2-17-11	2-14-13	1-28-18	12- 1-19	R 8-23-24
South Dakota	2- 1-11	2-19-13	3-20-18	12- 4-19	R 1-27-24
Montana	1-27-11	1-30-13	2-19-18	8- 2-19	2-11-27
Washington	1-26-11	2- 7-13	1-13-19	3-22-20	2-22-33
Idaho	1-20-11	1-31-13	1- 8-19	2-11-20	R 1-28-25
Wyoming	[2- 3-13]	2- 8-13	[1-16-19]	1-27-20	1-31-51
Utah	R	R 2-26-13	1-16-19	10- 2-19	R 2-26-24
Oklahoma	3-10-10	2-24-13	1- 7-19	2-28-20	
New Mexico	[2- 3-13]	3-13-13		2-21-20	2-12-37
Arizona	4- 3-12	6- 3-12	5-24-18	2-12-20	1-29-25

R—rejected. * Reversing former rejection. † Subsequently reversed.
Figures in brackets indicate vote of no legal effect because three-fourths majority already attained.

TABLE 4
Recent Amendments

States (in order of admission)	XX (36)	XXI (36)	XXII (36)	XXIII (38)	XXIV (38)	XXV (38)
Delaware	1-19-33	6-24-33	4- 2-47	2-20-61	5- 1-63	12- 7-65
Pennsylvania	8-11-32	12- 5-33	4-29-47	2-28-61	3-25-63	8-18-65
New Jersey	3-21-32	6- 1-33	4-15-47	12-19-60	12- 3-62	11-29-65
Georgia	1-23-33		2-17-51			
Connecticut	[1-27-33]	7-11-33	5-21-47	3- 9-61	3-20-63	[2-14-67]
Massachusetts	[1-24-33]	6-26-33		7-22-60	3-28-63	8- 9-65
Maryland	[3-24-33]	10-18-33	[3-14-51]	1-30-61	2- 6-63	3-23-66
South Carolina	3-25-32	R 12- 4-33	[1-13-51]			
New Hampshire	[1-31-33]	7-11-33	4- 1-47	[3-30-61]	6-16-63	6-13-66
Virginia	3- 4-32	10-25-33	5-28-47			3- 8-66
New York	3-11-32	6-27-33	3- 9-48	1-17-61	2- 4-63	3-14-66
North Carolina	1- 5-33	*	[2-28-51]			[3-22-67]
Rhode Island	4-14-32	5- 8-33		3-22-61	2-14-63	1-28-66

Table 4 (cont.)

States	XX	XXI	XXII	XXIII	XXIV	XXV
Vermont	[2- 2-33]	9-23-33	4-15-47	3-15-61	3-15-63	2-10-66
Kentucky	3-17-32	11-27-33			6-27-63	9-15-65
Tennessee	1-20-33	8-11-33	2-20-51	3- 6-61	3-21-63	1-12-67
Ohio	1-23-33	12- 5-33	4-16-47	3-29-61	2-27-63	[3- 7-67]
Louisiana	6-22-32		5-17-50			7- 5-66
Indiana	8-15-32	6-26-33	1-29-51	3- 3-61	2-19-63	
Mississippi	3-16-32		2-12-48			3-10-66
Illinois	4-21-32	7-10-33	4- 3-47	3-14-61	11-14-62	[3-22-67]
Alabama	9-13-32	8- 8-33	[5- 4-51]			[3-14-67]
Maine	4- 1-32	[12- 6-33]	3-31-47	1-31-61	1-16-64	1-24-66
Missouri	[1-23-33]	8-29-33	5-22-47	3-20-61	5-13-63	3-30-66
Arkansas	3-17-32	8- 1-33	2-15-51			
Michigan	3-31-32	4-10-33	3-31-47	3- 8-61	2-20-63	
Florida	[4-26-33]	11-14-33	[4-16-51]		4-18-63	
Texas	9- 7-32	11-24-33	2-22-51			[4-25-67]
Iowa	1-20-33	7-10-33	4- 1-47	3-16-61	4-24-63	1-26-67
Wisconsin	[1-24-33]	4-25-33	4-16-47	2-21-61	3-26-63	7-13-65
California	1- 4-33	7-24-33	4-15-47	1-19-61	2- 7-63	
Minnesota	1-12-33	10-10-33	2-27-51	1-31-61	2-27-63	2-10-67
Oregon	1-16-33	8- 7-33	4- 3-47	1-27-61	1-25-63	2- 2-67
Kansas	1-16-33		4- 1-47	3-29-61	3-28-63	2- 8-66
West Virginia	7-30-32	7-25-33		2- 9-61	2- 1-63	1-20-66
Nevada	[1-26-33]	9- 5-33	2-26-51	2- 2-61	3-19-63	2-10-67
Nebraska	1-13-33		5-23-47	3-15-61	4- 4-63	7-12-65
Colorado	[1-24-33]	9-26-33	4-12-47	2- 8-61	2-21-63	2- 3-66
North Dakota	1- 9-33		2-25-49	3- 3-61	3- 7-63	
South Dakota	1-20-33		1-21-49	2-14-61	1-23-64	[3- 6-67]
Montana	1-13-33	[8-16-34]	1-25-51	2- 6-61	1-28-63	[2-15-67]
Washington	1-19-33	10- 3-33		2- 9-61	3-14-63	1-26-67
Idaho	[1-21-33]	10-17-33	1-30-51	1-31-61	3- 8-63	3- 2-66
Wyoming	1-19-33	5-25-33	2-12-51	2-13-61		1-25-67
Utah	[1-23-33]	12- 5-33	2-26-51	2-21-61	2-20-63	1-17-66
Oklahoma	1-13-33			3-21-61		7-16-65
New Mexico	[1-21-33]	11- 2-33	2-12-51	2- 1-61	3- 5-63	2- 3-66
Arizona	1-13-33	9- 5-33		3-10-61		9-22-65
Alaska				2-10-61	2-12-63	2-18-66
Hawaii				6-23-60	3- 6-63	3- 3-66

R—rejected.   * Voters declined to call convention.

Figures in brackets indicate vote of no legal effect because three-fourths majority already attained.

The latest (Twenty-sixth) Amendment was ratified by the following states: Alabama, Alaska, Arizona, Arkansas, Delaware, Hawaii, Idaho, Illinois, Indiana, Iowa, Kansas, Louisiana, Maine, Maryland, Massachusetts, Michigan, Minnesota, Missouri, Montana, Nebraska, New Hampshire, New Jersey, New York, North Carolina, Ohio, Oklahoma, Oregon, Pennsylvania, Rhode Island, South Carolina, Tennessee, Texas, Vermont, Washington, West Virginia, Wisconsin.

TABLE 5
Recapitulation: Effective Date of Amendments

Amend- ment	Effective Date	Official Publication	Means of Proclamation
I–X	December 15, 1791	1 Stat. 97*	Congressional receipt of 11th ratification
XI	January 8, 1798	1 Stat. 402*	Presidential message
XII	September 25, 1804	2 Stat. 306*	Circular letter of Secretary of State
XIII	December 18, 1865	13 Stat. 567*	Certification by Secretary of State
XIV	July 28, 1868	14 Stat. 358*	do.
XV	March 30, 1870	16 Stat. 1131	do.
XVI	February 25, 1913	37 Stat. 3785	do.
XVII	May 31, 1913	38 Stat. 2049	do.
XVIII	January 29, 1919	40 Stat. 1941	do.
XIX	August 26, 1920	41 Stat. 1823	do.
XX	February 6, 1933	47 Stat. 2569	do.
XXI	December 5, 1933	48 Stat. 1749	do.
XXII	March 1, 1951	16 Fed. Reg. 2019	Certification by Administration of General Services
XXIII	April 13, 1961	26 Fed. Reg. 2808	do.
XXIV	February 4, 1964	29 Fed. Reg. 1717	do.
XXV†	February 23, 1967	32 Fed. Reg. 3287	do.
XXVI	July 5, 1971	36 Fed. Reg. 12725	do.

* Published at time of submission to people.
† Signed by President Johnson, although signature of no legal effect.

PART II

The Twentieth-Century Interpretation

The Original Constitution

Cl. 2. The Power to Borrow
Cl. 3. The Commerce Power
Cl. 4. Uniform Laws on Naturalization and Bankruptcy
Cl. 5. Coinage; Weights and Measures
Cl. 6. Counterfeiting Currency
Cl. 7. The Postal Power
Cl. 8. "Progress of Science and the Useful Arts"
Cl. 9. Creation of Inferior Courts
Cl. 10. Suppression of Piracies
Cl. 11. War Powers: Declaration of War
Cl. 12. War Powers: Maintenance of Army
Cl. 13. War Powers: Maintenance of Navy
Cl. 14. War Powers: Governance of Armed Forces
Cl. 15. Summoning of Militia
Cl. 16. Governance of Militia
Cl. 17. Seat of Government and Its Jurisdiction
Cl. 18. Making of All Necessary and Proper Laws
Sec. 9. Powers Expressly Denied Congress
Cl. 1. Importation of Slaves
Cl. 2. Suspension of Habeas Corpus
Cl. 3. Bills of Attainder; *Ex Post Facto* Laws
Cl. 4. Capitation Taxes
Cl. 5. Export Duties on Goods From State
Cl. 6. Discrimination Between Ports
Cl. 7. No Expenditure Unless by Appropriation
Cl. 8. No Titles of Nobility
Sec. 10. Powers Expressly Denied the States
Cl. 1. Foreign Relations; Impairment of Contracts
Cl. 2. Export-Import Duties
Cl. 3. Exercise of War Powers

The Preamble

We, the People of the United States, in order to form a more perfect Union, establish Justice, insure domestic Tranquillity, provide for the common Defense, promote the general Welfare, and secure the

Blessings of Liberty to ourselves and our Posterity, do ordain and establish this Constitution for the United States of America.

The Preamble to the Constitution is the best evidence of what the Convention of 1787 conceived as its own objectives—to form a union "more perfect" than the "perpetual union" which had been proclaimed by the Articles of Confederation, thereby tending to "insure domestic Tranquillity" in the face of the progressive balkanization of the states which was taking place under the Articles. To accomplish this purpose the Founding Fathers looked to the creating of a government which had the attributes of sovereignty lacking under the Confederation. Among these attributes were the exclusive authority to "provide for the common Defense" —an inherent responsibility of sovereignty—to establish a uniform system of justice appertaining to issues which transcended the borders and concerns of a single state, and to "promote the general Welfare" where the subject matter concerned more than local interests.

A sovereign power, by ancient and universal understanding in the law of nations, is a state controlling a definite territory, over which its authority entirely extends, and with a body of subjects or citizens deriving rights and responsibilities, claims and liabilities, under this authority.[1] In consequence of its established paramountcy in domestic affairs, other sovereign powers recognize such a government as possessing sole authority to deal in foreign affairs; and upon this balance of prerogatives the status of a national state is defined.[2]

The Preamble is not in itself a source of power for any branch of the Federal government, as Justice John Marshall Harlan observed in 1905.[3] Such powers as the Constitution confers, Harlan declared, are those expressly granted in the main body of the document, or reasonably implied. Implied powers are those "necessary and proper" for the carrying out of the enumerated powers, the powers to be inferred from the subject matter of any other constitutional provision, or those which are inherent in the nature of sovereignty itself. The Constitution has never been treated as a "self-defeating charter," in the phrase of Justice Hugo L. Black; the government created by it always has been conceived to have the power "to accomplish the full purpose of a granted authority," using "all appropriate means plainly adapted to that end, unless inconsistent with other parts of the Constitution."[4] The Constitution, while it protects the people of the United States against invasion of their individual rights, does not in the process "withdraw from the government the power to safeguard its vital interest."[5]

The people of the United States established this Constitution "*for* the United States of America." Its extension to territorial possessions, particularly to possessions not conceived as having the potential of statehood, was said in the Insular Cases in 1901 to be piecemeal and on sufferance of Congress.[6] The constitutional status of particular territorial acquisitions has been determined by the provisions of the treaties attesting the acquisition.[7]

"We, the People of the United States . . . do ordain and establish this Constitution." Men like Patrick Henry, in the debates over ratification of the original Constitution, and like John Calhoun in the nullification controversy of the 1830s, protested vehemently that the document was to be regarded as having been created by the states, or by the people of the states. But Chief Justice John Marshall had the literal meaning of the words, as well as the logic of circumstances, in his favor when he declared that it was in fact the people of the nation, "acting as sovereigns of the whole country," who devised the new frame of government. Their purpose had been to draft an instrument "for their own government, and not for the government of the individual states." While the state governments, under the terms of the Articles of Confederation, authorized the sending of delegates to the Constitutional Convention of 1787, it was the people in local conventions, rather than the states in legislative assemblies, who ratified the work of the Founding Fathers.

Nor, Marshall concluded, was the Constitution itself "necessarily carved out of existing state sovereignties, nor a surrender of powers already existing in state institutions." The powers of the national government were those which the people of the United States conferred on it, and the limitations "are limitations of power granted in the instrument itself; not of distinct governments, framed by different persons and for different purposes."[8]

Marshall's concept of a duality of citizenship in the Federal system had few practical consequences for the individual American in his time. It was not until the Fourteenth Amendment restated, in specific and unequivocal terms, that "All persons born or naturalized in the United States, and subject to the jurisdiction thereof, are citizens of the United States and of the State wherein they reside" that the Constitution itself explicitly expressed this concept.

Thereafter, the respective status of national citizenship and state citizenship was readily discernible, in the view of Justice Samuel F. Miller; one had to reside in a state to be a citizen thereof, but to be a citizen of the nation "it is only necessary that he be born or naturalized in the United States and subject to the jurisdiction thereof. It is quite clear, then," Miller concluded, that the citizenships are distinct from each other and "depend upon different characteristics or circumstances in the individual."[9]

Further discussion of Miller's interpretation of the citizenship clause in the Fourteenth Amendment will be found under that Amendment. It suffices here to observe that Miller's concept of the rights accruing to national citizenship was fairly formal, and in the half century which followed the *Slaughterhouse Cases* his concept attained little more practical meaning than had Marshall's in the fifty years prior to 1873.

Chief Justice Edward D. White contributed to the further advancement of the concept in 1918 when he declared that national citizenship was not "subordinate and derivative" but "paramount and dominant."[10] But it was not until the 1920s, when there began the judicial trend toward incorporation of the Bill of Rights into the Fourteenth Amendment, as restraints upon the states, that the practical importance of the rights of national citizenship began to manifest itself. Ultimately, the judicial conclusion that the "privileges and immunities" of national citizens which were protected from state infringement embraced most if not all of the rights and liberties of the individual which were then or subsequently to be recognized in law, gave final definition to the concept of the "people of the United States."

In the nineteenth-century federalism of Marshall and Miller, the individual still looked to the states for protection of his personal liberties. With the centralizing tendencies of American social and economic institutions in the twentieth century, the individual came to look to the national Constitution to insure uniform and universal protection of these liberties. The "dual federalism" of the earlier era has become a "unitary federalism" today, and the "people of the United States" today are the embodiment of a full, vital and viable concept of national citizenship.[11]

1. "For all purposes of international law, a state . . . may be defined to be a people permanently occupying a fixed territory . . . bound together by common laws, habits and customs into one body politic, exercising, through the medium of an organized government, independent sovereignty and control over all persons and things within its boundaries, capable of making war and peace, and of entering into all international relations with other communities of the globe." Cited in Moore, *Digest of International Law* (Washington, 1906), I, 44–45. *Cf.* also Whiteman, ed., *Digest of International Law* (Washington, 1963), I, 233–83.
2. *Cf. United States v. Curtiss-Wright Export Corp.*, 299 U.S. 304 (1936); *United States v. Pink*, 315 U.S. 203 (1942).
3. *Jacobson v. Massachusetts*, 197 U.S. 22 (1905).
4. *Case v. Bowles*, 327 U.S. 92, 102 (1946).
5. *United States v. Robel*, 389 U.S. 258 (1967).
6. *Cf. Downes v. Bidwell*, 182 U.S. 270 (1901); and *cf. DeLima v. Bidwell*, 182 U.S. 1 (1901); *Dooley v. United States*, 182 U.S. 222 (1901).
7. *Cf. Rasmussen v. United States*, 197 U.S. 522 (1905); *Hawaii v. Mankitchi*, 190 U.S. 211 (1903); *Grafton v. United States*, 206 U.S. 333 (1907).
8. *Cf. Barron v. Baltimore*, 32 U.S. 247 (1833); *McCulloch v. Maryland*, 17 U.S. (4 Wheat.) 403 (1819); *Martin v. Hunter's Lessee*, 14 U.S. (1 Wheat.) 324 (1816).
9. *Slaughterhouse Cases*, 16 Wall. 36 (1873).
10. *Arver v. United States*, 245 U.S. 366 (1918). And *cf. Wilson v. New*, 243 U.S. 332 (1917).
11. *Cf.* Miller, *The Supreme Court and American Capitalism* (New York, 1968), ch. 3; Miller, "Toward a Concept of Constitutional Duty," *1968 Supreme Court Review* (Chicago, 1968), 225.

Article I. The Legislative Power

I. 1. The Nature of Legislative Power

All legislative powers herein granted shall be vested in a Congress of the United States, which shall consist of a Senate and a House of Representatives.

The opening words of the Constitution express both a philosophical and a practical concept of the legislative function, and both are of substantial importance to an understanding of the constitutionalism of the twentieth century. Indeed, the fundamental significance of the great shift in judicial ideology in the New Deal era—the pivotal period in modern American constitutional history—is revealed in the 180-degree turn in the Supreme Court's theory of the legislative function, made at that time. For more than half a century before the depression decade, the judicial concept of legislative power was generally narrow and literalistic, decreeing that broad areas of activity—particularly the areas of private enterprise—were beyond the reach of government. This fundamental proposition of a *laissez-faire* economy collapsed in ultimate bankruptcy in the 1930s, to be replaced by an alternative concept of legislative latitude which has prevailed until the present.[1]

Sources and Varieties of Congressional Authority

The phrase "All legislative powers herein granted . . ." has been taken to affirm that the functions of lawmaking, within the scope of the constitutional provisions, are exclusively vested in Congress. But what are these powers, and are they granted in terms (i.e., enumerated) or do they include, in Chief Justice Marshall's phrase, authority which is "a result of the whole mass of the powers of the National Government, and from the nature of a political society"?[2] In periods of strict or narrow construction the Court has been disinclined to follow Marshall's proposition to its logical extreme, except perhaps in matters of foreign relations.[3] The view of the Court in the second and third quarters of the present century has been more liberal: "The Constitution does not deny to Congress the necessary resources of flexibility and practicality to perform its function," said Chief Justice Stone in 1944.[4] Ten years later Justice Douglas declared that the legislative branch, either Federal or state, was the sole agency to determine "public needs to be served by social legislation."[5]

Specifically enumerated powers of Congress appear in several sections of this Article, but particularly in Section 8, and inferentially in some portion of Section 10, as well as in parts of Articles II through V and in Amendments XIII through XVI, XX, and XXIII through XXV. Specifically denied powers are set out in Section 9 of Article I and Amendments I through VIII. Beyond these passages in the document itself, however, there are a number of other powers to be implied, inferred or derived from certain general clauses, or from the scope of judicial definition of other clauses—e.g., the general welfare and "necessary and proper" clauses of Section 8 of Article I, the commerce or tax clauses of the same section, or the directives set out in the several Amendments cited above. Legislative power may be indirectly broadened, also, by changing judicial construction of previously restrictive clauses—e.g., the contracts clause of Section 9 of Article I.[6]

Finally, there are investigatory and supervisory powers of Congress which are recognized as inherent in the legislative function generally. An elemental power is the power to gather information on which to base legislative action,[7] but it is when this extends, as it rather promptly does, to the seeking of information which may incriminate the individuals from whom the information is sought that constitutional safeguards may operate to circumscribe the Congressional power. While the Court "will not lightly impute to Congress an intent to invade freedoms protected by the Bill of Rights,"[8] and while it has, since 1927, given broad sanction to the investigative power as "an essential and appropriate auxiliary to the legislative function,"[9] the expansion of this activity by Congress in the loyalty-security issues of the 1950s led to a series of "Fifth Amendment" cases which sought to set practical limits to this form of legislative inquisition.

The limits were first suggested in 1953, when the Court ruled that legislation authorizing an investigation of lobbying aimed at promoting or defeating bills could not exceed its own defined scope and demand information beyond the activities of the lobbyists; should the statute be broadened to attempt to reach this matter, said Justices Black and Douglas in concurrence, the First Amendment guarantees would in all likelihood invalidate the inquiry.[10] Two years later it was held that, although Congress in the course of a legitimate exercise of its investigatory power could compel testimony of witnesses, the testimony must be pertinent to the subject under inquiry and must not effect a forfeiture of the witnesses' rights against self-incrimination.[11] In 1957 the due-process clause of the Fifth Amendment was invoked to reverse a conviction for contempt of Congress where a witness declined to answer questions which he considered outside the scope of the proper inquiry. Chief Justice Warren declared that while the investigative function is inherent in the legislative power, it "is not unlimited. There is no general authority to expose the private affairs of individuals without justification in terms of the functions of Congress."[12]

Although there was much Congressional outcry against this holding, Congress did in fact reform its criticized rules of procedure, and in 1959 a divided (5–4) Court sustained a contempt conviction of a witness who had refused to answer questions as to his own activities which were properly under investigation.[13] But the government in such cases must sustain the burden of proving the pertinence of the questions,[14] and grand-jury indictments for Congressional contempt must clearly identify both the subject of investigation and the pertinence of the questions.[15]

Thus the legislative powers of Congress are broad and varied, subject today only to the specific limitations placed on the use of them by specific sections of the Constitution or the counterbalancing constitutional protections of individuals as against the state. After the furore of the 1950s, Congress itself has policed its own exercise of the investigative power.

Delegation of Legislative Power

The common-law maxim *delegata potestas non potest delegari**has frequently been cited in constitutional law as a limitation on the legislature. One of the basic points of attack by the Supreme Court on the early emergency legislation of the New Deal was the unqualified vesting of power in executive departments or administrative agencies to draft and apply regulations which had the force of legislation.[16] The legislature, it was insisted, must set standards and guidelines for executive or administrative action— although this would not of itself validate the delegation of power if the subject of the legislation was constitutionally invalid.[17] Thus, in the age of rigidly circumscribed areas of legislative action, the Court consistently held that the power to act on certain subjects could not be delegated because Congress itself had no power to act on these subjects. When the Court, after 1937, be-

* Essentially meaning that power once delegated and vesting in one agency (e.g., Congress) cannot be delegated further.

gan to define Congressional competence in progressively broader terms, the standards by which legislative power could be delegated progressively broadened.[18]

There must be "an intelligent standard" to which executive and administrative agencies must conform,[19] but the Court in the mid-century has tended to accept any reasonable standard which Congress itself considers adequate. World War II, with its vast extension of administrative responsibility, considerably accelerated this trend of judicial thought.[20] For the most part, a statute will be read in the light of conditions to which it is to be applied, and where the conditions call for flexible and discretionary applications of administrative regulations, the authority delegated by the statute can necessarily have only general guidelines.[21] Congress need not be expected to anticipate every factual circumstance under which the delegated authority may be variously implemented by the agency involved.[22] In 1890, in one of the early Minnesota rate cases, the Court sustained as a general principle the rule that in areas of economic regulation the only practical means of implementing the legislative purpose was through a continuing administrative body periodically adjusting the details of its surveillance to periodically changing practices and needs.[23] The state regulatory commissions validated by cases running from *Munn v. Illinois*[24] through the various rate cases, even though construed with increasing narrowness in the last third of the century,[25] served as models for Federal regulatory bodies beginning with the Interstate Commerce Commission in 1887[26] and growing in number and variety to the present.

Congress's determination of the extent and nature of delegation of power may be of two types: either a general statute directing the executive or administrative agency to "fill up the details,"[27] or a specific command that, on a finding of relevant facts, the executive or administrative officer carry out an action prescribed by statute.[28] Where Congress has authorized certain executive action subject to its review and ratification, this has been held not to be an infringement on the separate power of the executive.[29]

Pre-emption of Legislative Power

A final element in the definition of the power created by this Article is the issue of pre-emption—the exclusive occupation of a field of legislation by Congress. Because most, although not by any means all, of the serious questions of pre-emption arise in matters of interstate commerce, the doctrine will be discussed in more detail at that point in this commentary. But it warrants preliminary mention here because it fundamentally affects the nature and exercise of the "legislative powers herein granted" which are "vested in a Congress of the United States."

In the American Federal system, there is not only a separation of powers as between the legislative, executive and judicial (and, it is occasionally suggested, the separate administrative) branches of government, but there is also a separation of these powers as between the state and national governments. So far as the legislative power is concerned, it is a truism that all statutes validly enacted by Congress are the supreme law of the land (Article VI). But this does not, in the nature of the case, necessarily exclude state legislative power from the subject area of these statutes, unless there is a potential conflict of authorities— or unless Congress by express statement, or circumstances which reasonably permit the inference, has asserted its intention to take over the matter.[30]

A series of general guidelines appeared in Justice Douglas's opinion in the 1947 case of *Rice v. Santa Fe Elevator Corp.*: "The scheme of Federal regulation may be so pervasive," he suggested, as to make state law on the same subject redundant. Or state policy if permitted to be operative might "produce a result inconsistent with the objective of the Federal statute." The Congressional enactment, indeed, may simply "touch a field in which the Federal interest is so dominant that the Federal system will be assumed to preclude enforcement of state laws on the same subject."[31] Six years earlier, in *Hines v. Davidowitz*, Justice Black had reviewed judicial formulae for identifying the fact of pre-emption but confessed that "there can be no one crystal clear distinctly marked formula."[32] As later discussion of the subject indicates, certain leaders in Congress in the 1940s and 1950s undertook to disclaim the pre-emption doctrine except as it might be expressly asserted by Congress itself; but the fact of pre-emption has become so engrained in constitutional interpretation of the twentieth century that it is hardly possible to excise it by legislative fiat.[33]

The other side of the coin is the division of a subject area between Federal and state jurisdiction, or the application of the doctrine of concurrent jurisdiction.[34] There is also the simple fact of dormancy of Federal power which affects the status of state legislation where Congress elects not to assert pre-emption.[35] For more than a century the Court has adhered to the principle that Congress may refrain from legislating on a subject where variable local conditions, adequately covered by local laws, implement the national policy as effectively as, or more effectively than, a general national law.[36] This may either be a case of dormant pre-emption or of concurrent jurisdiction[37]—and either of these may be confused with somewhat related doctrines (e.g., "unbroken package," "direct-indirect burdens," etc.) in contiguous areas of interstate commerce (see Article I, Section 8, Cl. 3). Federal incorporation or adoption of state law, as in the Federal Assimilative Crimes Act of 1948,[38] and the Federal requirement of implementing complementary state legislation, as in the Social Security Act of 1935,[39] add further juridical issues to the general matter of pre-emption which are considered in relation to various sections of the Constitution which follow.

1. *Cf.* the general history of these developments in the two volumes of Swindler, *Court and Constitution in the 20th Century.*
2. Cited in Story, *Commentaries on the Constitution* (Boston, 1833), 1, §1256.
3. *Cf.* Sutherland, J., in *United States v. Curtiss-Wright Export Corp.*, 299 U.S. 304, 317 (1936); *United States v. Belmont*, 301 U.S. 324 (1937).
4. *Yakus v. United States*, 321 U.S. 414 (1944).
5. *Berman v. Parker*, 348 U.S. 26 (1954).
6. *Cf.* Swindler, *The Old Legality*, Chs. 2, 3, 13 and 14; *The New Legality*, Chs. 2, 6 and 7.
7. *Cf.* Act of May 3, 1798, Ch. 36, I Stat. 554, continued in present 2 U.S.C. §191. "The informing function of Congress should be preferred even to its legislative function." Wilson, *Congressional Government* (New York, 1885), p. 303.
8. *Eastern Ry. Pres. Conf. v. Noerr Motor Frt.*, 365 U.S. 127 (1961).
9. *McGrain v. Daugherty*, 273 U.S. 135, 177 (1927); and *cf. Sinclair v. United States*, 279 U.S. 263 (1927), specifically rejecting the narrow view of the Court in 1881 when Justice Miller had warned against Congressional inquiries which

were "judicial" in nature and hence could serve no legislative purpose. *Kilbourn v. Thompson*, 103 U.S. 168.

10. *United States v. Rumeley*, 345 U.S. 41 (1953). The previous year the Court had held, in a 4–2 decision with three Justices not participating, that Congressional powers of investigation included authority to compel testimony of witnesses currently under indictment in a state court, and that the Court would not question Congress's declaration that the testimony served a bonafide legislative purpose and was not in aid of the state prosecution by circumventing the constitutional bar to self-incrimination. *Hutcheson v. United States*, 369 U.S. 599 (1952).

11. *Quinn v. United States*, 349 U.S. 155 (1955), raising both First and Fifth Amendment questions; *cf.* also *Emspak v. United States*, 349 U.S. 190 (1955), and *Bart v. United States*, 349 U.S. 219 (1955).

12. *Watkins v. United States*, 354 U.S. 178, 187 (1957).

13. *Barenblatt v. United States*, 360 U.S. 109 (1959); *cf.* also *Wilkinson v. United States*, 365 U.S. 399 (1961) and *Braden v. United States*, 365 U.S. 431 (1961).

14. *Deutch v. United States*, 367 U.S. 456 (1961); and *cf. Sacher v. United States*, 356 U.S. 576 (1958).

15. *United States v. Russell*, 369 U.S. 749 (1962). *Cf.* also *McPhaull v. United States*, 364 U.S. 372 (1960) (officer of organization under investigation must produce pertinent records properly in his custody).

16. *Schechter Poultry Corp. v. United States*, 295 U.S. 495 (1935); *Opp Cotton Mills v. Administrator*, 312 U.S. 126 (1941).

17. *United States v. Rock Royal Cooperative*, 307 U.S. 533 (1939); *United States v. Butler*, 297 U.S. 1 (1936); and *cf. Kent v. Dulles*, 357 U.S. 116 (1958).

18. *Bowles v. Willingham*, 321 U.S. 503 (1944); *Currin v. Wallace*, 306 U.S. 1 (1939).

19. *Sunshine Coal Co. v. Adkins*, 310 U.S. 503 (1944); *Lichter v. United States*, 334 U.S. 742 (1948); and *cf. Panama Ref. Co. v. Ryan*, 293 U.S. 388 (1935).

20. *Yakus v. United States*, 321 U.S. 414 (1944); and *cf. Hirabayashi v. United States*, 320 U.S. 81 (1943).

21. *Lichter v. United States*, 334 U.S. 742 (1948); *Yakus v. United States*, 321 U.S. 414 (1944).

22. *Id.*, at 424.

23. *Chi., Milw. & St. P. Ry. Co. v. Minnesota*, 134 U.S. 418 (1890).

24. *Munn v. Illinois*, 94 U.S. 113 (1877).

25. *Wabash, St. L. & Pac. Ry. Co. v. Illinois*, 118 U.S. 557 (1886); *Brass v. North Dakota*, 153 U.S. 391 (1894); *Smyth v. Ames*, 169 U.S. 466 (1898).

26. Act of February 4, 1887, Ch. 104, 24 Stat. 379.

27. *Lichter v. United States*, 334 U.S. 742 (1948); *United States ex rel. Knauff v. Shaughnessy*, 338 U.S. 537 (1950).

28. *Bowles v. Willingham*, 321 U.S. 503 (1944).

29. *Humphrey's Exec. v. United States*, 295 U.S. 602 (1935), overruling *Myers v. United States*, 272 U.S. 52 (1926).

30. *Uphaus v. Wyman*, 364 U.S. 388 (1960).

31. *Rice v. Santa Fe El. Corp.*, 331 U.S. 218 (1947).

32. *Hines v. Davidowitz*, 312 U.S. 52 (1941).

33. *Cf.* Hepburn Act of June 29, 1906, ch. 3591, 34 Stat. 584, with Taft-Hartley Act of June 27, 1947, Ch. 120, 61 Stat. 136.

34. *Cf.* the specific provision on concurrent jurisdiction in Amendment XVIII, Sec. 2, and the possible salvaging of the doctrine in Amendment XXI, Sec. 2. *Cf.*

also Chief Justice Taft's effort to distinguish between joint powers and concurrent powers, in *United States v. Lanza*, 260 U.S. 377, 381 (1922).
35. *Seagram & Sons v. Hostetter*, 384, U.S. 35 (1966); *Pennsylvania v. Nelson*, 350
36. *Cf. Cooley v. Board of Wardens*, 12 How. 299 (1851).
    U.S. 497 (1956).
37. *Clark Distilling Co. v. Western Md. Ry. Co.*, 242 U.S. 311 (1917); *Prudential Ins. Co. v. Benjamin*, 328 U.S. 408 (1946).
38. Act of June 25, 1948, Ch. 645, 62 Stat. 686; 18 U.S.C. 13; *United States v. Sharpnak*, 355 U.S. 285 (1958).
39. Act of August 14, 1935, Ch. 531, 49 Stat. 620; 42 U.S.C., Ch. 7; *Carmichael v. So. Coal & Coke Co.*, 301 U.S. 495 (1937).

I. 2. Cl. 1. The House of Representatives: Composition

The House of Representatives shall be composed of Members chosen every second Year by the People of the several States, and the Electors in each State shall have the qualifications requisite for Electors of the most numerous Branch of the State Legislature.

Apportionment

The reapportionment decisions of the 1960s have fundamentally affected the electoral process, with the Court in 1964 declaring that the Founding Fathers intended that, whatever the mechanics of election, whether statewide or by districts, it was population which was to be the basis of membership in the lower house of Congress.[1] The Court then proceeded, on the basis of earlier reapportionment cases, to declare that as nearly as practicable the electoral unit was to be defined in such a way as most likely to carry out the constitutional objective of equal representation for equal numbers of people.[2] This suggests that population variances are continually subject to the requirement that they be justified, and the "as nearly as possible" standard does not excuse variances fixed by numerical limits which actually or potentially tend to effect distinct population differences between purportedly equal electoral units.[3]

While Congressional apportionment is essentially a legislative function, the judicial doctrine on the subject as now developed makes clear that Congressional districts must be as contiguous and symmetrical as possible and must be defined without regard to race, sex, economic status or place of residence within a state.[4] Thus the Court by the end of the 1960s had long since departed from its position in the mid-1940s, when it had affirmed dismissal of a complaint of malapportionment with an opinion that the Constitution had left this question to Congress, and whether Congress "faithfully discharged its duty or not" it was the only branch of the government which could take remedial action.[5] Even when it ruled on the merits, the Court in this period saw no conflict with the equal-protection clause of the Fourteenth Amendment "to deny a State the power to assure a proper diffusion of political initiative as between thinly populated counties and those having concentrated masses."[6] The position of the Warren Court was at the other end of the spectrum; even without reference to equal protection, said the Court in 1964, "the command of Article I, Section 2, that Representatives be chosen 'by the People of the several States,' means that as nearly as practicable one man's vote in a Congressional election is to be worth as much as another's."[7] Lower Federal courts and state courts now follow this basic guideline.[8]

Qualifications of Electors

In 1884 the Court held that although the Constitution stipulated that the same persons qualified under state law to vote for members of "the most numerous Branch of the State Legislature" could also vote for Representatives in Congress, the right to vote for these Representatives did not depend in any sense on state law.[9] If the right is to be protected by legislation, it is Congressional legislation which is required.[10] In 1941 the Court affirmatively extended the general principle of a Federally protected right to state primary elections: If a state undertook to establish the primary as another step in the electoral process, said Chief Justice Stone, the right guaranteed by Article I, Section 2 would be understood to extend to that step.[11]

Finding that the *Classic* doctrine established "the unitary character of the electorial process," the Court in *Smith v. Allwright* held that where primary elections were conducted under laws making the political party the agent of the state in administering the primary as a preliminary to the general election, denial of primary participation by a qualified voter on the basis of race was an impermissible state action.[12] Moreover, an attempt to evade this rule by repealing all primary laws was an obvious subterfuge which was equally invalid under the Fifteenth Amendment.[13] Proceeding from the racial-discrimination cases, a variety of other laws or practices affecting practical implementation of the electoral privilege—registration systems, grandfather clauses, literacy tests, poll taxes—have become the subject of extended adjudication under the Fifteenth and Twenty-fourth Amendments. Discussion of the judicial doctrine on these subjects appears thereunder.

1. *Reynolds v. Sims*, 377 U.S. 533 (1964).
2. *Id.*, at 577; and *cf. Baker v. Carr*, 369 U.S. 186 (1962).
3. *Kirkpatrick v. Preisler*, 394 U.S. 526 (1969).
4. *Wells v. Rockefeller*, 394 U.S. 542 (1969); *Reynolds v. Sims*, 377 U.S. 533 (1964); *WMCA, Inc. v. Lomenzo*, *id.*, at 633; *Maryland Committee for Fair Representation v. Tawes*, *id.*, at 656; *Davis v. Mann*, *id.*, at 678; *Roman v. Sincock*, *id.*, at 695; *Lucas v. Colorado General Assembly*, *id.*, at 713.
5. *Cf. Colgrove v. Green*, 328 U.S. 542 (1946); *Highland Farms Dairy Co. v. Agnew*, 300 U.S. 608 (1937); *Cook v. Fortson*, 329 U.S. 675 (1946).
6. *MacDougall v. Green*, 335 U.S. 283 (1948).
7. *Wesberry v. Sanders*, 376 U.S. 1 (1964); and *cf. Gray v. Sanders*, 372 U.S. 368 (1963).
8. *Cf. Baker v. Clement*, 247 F.S. 886 (1965); *Moore v. Moore*, 246 F.S. 578 (1965); *Norton v. Campbell*, 359 F. 2d 608 (1966); *Dennis v. Volpe*, 264 F.S. 425 (1967); etc.
9. *Ex parte Yarbrough*, 110 U.S. 651 (1884); *Breedlove v. Suttles*, 302 U.S. 277 (1937).
10. *Cf. United States v. Moseley*, 238 U.S. 383 (1915); *United States v. Saylor*, 322 U.S. 385 (1944).
11. *United States v. Classic*, 313 U.S. 299 (1941); and *cf. Logan v. United States*, 144 U.S. 263 (1892).
12. *Smith v. Allwright*, 321 U.S. 649 (1944).
13. *Terry v. Adams*, 345 U.S. 461 (1953).

I. 2. Cl. 2. *Qualifications of Members*

No Person shall be a Representative who shall not have attained to the Age of twenty five Years, and been seven Years a Citizen of the United States, and who shall not, when elected, be an Inhabitant of that State in which he shall be chosen.

Although the courts have generally avoided adjudicating questions arising under this clause, preferring to leave the matter to Congress under the provisions of Section 5 (*q.v.*), jurisdiction of the question was accepted in 1969 in the case of *Powell v. Mc-Cormack*.[1] The Court in that case held, first, that the three provisions of the present section—minimum age, minimum years of citizenship and residency in the state represented—were the sole qualifications which could be demanded of a Congressman; second, that a member thus qualified could not be excluded under Section 2 but only expelled after seating under Section 5.[2] The case thus appears to have disposed of questions left unanswered in the 1906 case of *Burton v. United States*,[3] by establishing that Congress cannot add to the constitutional language of Section 2.

Most of the issues under Sections 2 and 5 have been disposed of by the legislative rather than the judicial branch. As early as 1856 the House of Representatives declared that a state might not add to the qualifications prescribed by the Constitution and reaffirmed its position in 1884;[4] but query whether "disqualifications" enumerated by the House of Representatives amount to added qualifications. In 1880 the House excluded one B.F. Whittemore of South Carolina who had resigned his seat to avoid expulsion and won a special election to be returned to his seat in the same session; the House maintained that exclusion in these circumstances was a means of effectuating the voted expulsion.[5] In the late 1890s a series of polygamy issues resulted in exclusion.[6]

The state courts have consistently held that both the constitutional language and Congressional discretion prevail over state law on the subject in instances of conflict.[7]

1. 395 U.S. 486 (1969); and *cf.* generally *Texas v. White*, 74 U.S. 721 (1869).
2. 395 U.S. at 506.
3. 202 U.S. 344 (1906).
4. 1 Hinds' Precedents, 415, 417.
5. *Id.*, at 464.
6. *Id.*, at 474–80.
7. *Cf. Stockton v. McFarland*, 56 Ariz. 138, 106 P. 2d 328 (1940); *State ex rel. Chavez v. Evans*, 446 P. 2d 445 (1968); *Richardson v. Ware*, 160 N.W. 2d 883 (1968); *Hellman v. Collier*, 217 Md. 93, 141 Atl. 2d 908 (1958).

I. 2. Cl. 3. *Apportionment*

[Representatives and direct Taxes shall be apportioned among the several States which may be included within this Union, according to their respective Numbers, which shall be determined by adding to the whole number of free Persons, including those bound to Service for a Term of Years, and excluding Indians not taxed, three fifths of all other Persons.] The actual Enumeration shall be made within three Years after the first Meeting of the Congress of the United States, and within every subsequent Term of ten Years, in such Manner as they shall by Law direct. The Number of Representatives shall not exceed one for every thirty Thousand, but each State shall have at Least one Representative; [and until such enumeration shall be made, the State of New Hampshire shall be entitled to choose three, Massachusetts eight, Rhode-Island and Providence Planations one, Connecticut five, New-York six, New Jersey four, Pennsylvania eight, Delaware one, Maryland six, Virginia ten, North Carolina five, South Carolina five, and Georgia three.]

This section has either been superseded by Amendment XIV, Section 2, or has been rendered obsolete (see Part I of this volume) as concerns apportionment of Representatives. All that is viable in this section is the provision that "direct Taxes shall be apportioned. . . ."

The two central questions, therefore, are: (1) What is a direct tax, and (2) how is it equitably apportioned? From the first decade of national history, the Court had suggested that direct taxes were either capitation (i.e., per person) taxes, or taxes on real estate[1] and that taxes laid on personal income, including gains and property from any source, were "within the category of an excise or duty" and hence not direct or apportionable.[2] This presumption was refuted by a 5–4 holding in 1895 (*Pollock v. Farmers' Loan and Trust Co.*)[3] in a case which was strongly criticized at the time. In due course, the decision was nullified by the adoption of the Sixteenth Amendment (although, in the intervening years, the Court steadily retreated from its position in *Pollock*).[4] Further discussion of the income tax will be found under that Amendment.

The rejection of the *Pollock* doctrine encouraged the Court to limit direct taxes again to the capitation and real-estate categories, so that in 1929 it was held that "a tax imposed upon a particular use of property, or the exercise of a single power over property incidental to ownership, is an excise which need not be apportioned."[5] Thus Congress has the power to treat estate and succession taxes as death duties rather than taxes on real property even though, in the absence of Congressional action, they would be construed as taxes on property and hence apportionable.[6]

The Supreme Court has not undertaken to define apportionment beyond this. The appellate courts have defined direct taxes as those bearing on possession and enjoyment of rights (presumably in real property) and indirect taxes as levied on exchanges of property.[7] Income and other indirect taxes are subject only to the rule of geographic uniformity; indirect taxes must conform to a proportionate distribution among the states in terms of population.[8]

1. *Hylton v. United States,* 3 Dall. (3 U.S.) 175 (1796).
2. *Springer v. United States,* 102 U.S. 602 (1881); and *cf. Veazie Bank v. Fenno,* 75 U.S. 539 (1869).
3. 158 U.S. 625 (1895).
4. *Knowlton v. Moore,* 178 U.S. 80 (1900); *Flint v. Stone Tracy Co.,* 220 U.S. 107 (1911); *Nicol v. Ames,* 173 U.S. 518 (1899); *Spreckels Sugar Ref. Co. v. McClain,* 192 U.S. 410 (1904).
5. *Bromley v. McCaughn,* 280 U.S. 124 (1929); and *cf. Patton v. Brady,* 184 U.S. 608 (1902).
6. *Tyler v. United States,* 281 U.S. 497 (1930).
7. *Kohl v. United States,* 226 F. 2d 381 (1955); and *cf. Knowlton v. Moore,* 178 U.S. 46 (1900).
8. *Cf. Kingan & Co. v. Smith,* 17 F.S. 217 (1936).

I. 2. Cl. 4. Vacancies

When vacancies happen in the Representation from any State, the Executive Authority thereof shall issue Writs of Election to fill such Vacancies.

I. 2. Cl. 5. Offices; Impeachment

The House of Representatives shall choose their Speaker and other Officers; and shall have the sole Power of Impeachment.

These two sections vest responsibility for certain procedures in specific officers or agencies, and such legislative or judicial interpretation on these subjects as there has been has simply confirmed the exclusive power of each over the respective subject matter. Thus the power of the governor to fix the time and place of elections for filling of vacancies in the House of Representatives has been held, because of the specific charge of responsibility to him, to be a non-delegable power.[1] The impeachment power of the House of Representatives has been confirmed as extending to all officers of the national government.[2]

1. Cf. Bottomly v. Ford, 157 P. 2d 108 (1964).
2. Kilbourn v. Thompson, 103 U.S. 168 (1881).

I. 3. Cl. 1. The Senate: Composition

The Senate of the United States shall be composed of two Senators from each State, [chosen by the Legislature thereof, for six Years;] and each Senator shall have one vote.

I. 3. Cl. 2. Classification of Senators; Vacancies

Immediately after they shall be assembled in Consequence of the first Election, they shall be divided as equally as may be into three Classes. The Seats of the Senators of the first Class shall be vacated at the Expiration of the second Year, of the second Class at the Expiration of the fourth Year, and of the third Class at the Expiration of the sixth Year, so that one third may be chosen every second Year; [and if Vacancies happen by Resignation, or otherwise, during the recess of the Legislature of any State, the Executive thereof may make temporary Appointments until the next Meeting of the Legislature, which shall then fill such Vacancies.]

The first and second clauses of this section have been substantially superseded by the first two sections of the Seventeenth Amendment (q.v.). The theory of the original Constitution was that the Senators should be representatives of the state governments, as the Representatives were representatives of the people of the states.[1] The Populist-Progressive movement of the turn of the century demanded the popular election of Senators as a means of loosening the alleged corporation control of the upper chamber through control of the state legislatures which elected the Senators.[2]

The Senate is a continuing body, one-third of its membership changing every two years but a two-thirds majority always being in office. As the Court observed in 1927, actions of the Senate which have no terminal date are automatically continued without regard to the expiring of one session of Congress and the beginning of the next.[3]

1. *Cf.* James Madison in Federalist LVIII: "There is a peculiarity in the federal constitution . . . that one branch of the legislature is a representation of citizens, the other of the states." *The Federalist* (Cooke ed., 1961), p. 392.
2. *Cf.* Swindler, *The Old Legality*, pp. 167–68.
3. *McGrain v. Daugherty*, 273 U.S. 135, 181–182 (1927).

I. 3. Cl. 3. *Qualifications of Senators*

No Person shall be a Senator who shall not have attained to the Age of thirty Years, and been nine Years a Citizen of the United States, and who shall not, when elected, be an Inhabitant of the State for which he shall be chosen.

The state courts have held, as in the case of the House of Representatives, that the state cannot add to the qualifications of Senators as set out in this section.[1] The fact that candidates for Federal office must comply with state election laws before their names will appear on the ballot does not authorize the states to add to the qualifications for the Federal office; and where the law disqualifies certain candidates for state office this law cannot be constitutionally applied to candidates from the same state for Federal office.[2] Where there is a conflict between state law and the specific provisions of the Constitution in respect of Senatorial candidates, the Constitution prevails.[3]

1. Application of *Ferguson*, 294 N.Y.S. 2d 174 (1968); *cf. Benesch v. Miller*, 446 P. 2d 400 (1968); *State ex rel. Handley v. Superior Court*, 238 Ind. 421, 151 N.E. 2d 508 (1958).
2. *Shub v. Simpson*, 196 Md. 177, 76 Atl. 2d 332 (1950); *State ex rel. Sundford v. Thorson*, 72 N.D. 246, 6 N.W. 2d 89 (1942); and *cf. Lassiter v. Northampton County Board of Elections*, 360 U.S. 45 (1959).
3. *Stockton v. McFarland*, 56 Ariz. 138, 106 P. 2d 328 (1940).

I. 3. Cl. 4. *The President of the Senate*

The Vice President of the United States shall be President of the Senate, but shall have no Vote, unless they be equally divided.

I. 3. Cl. 5. President Pro Tempore; Other Officers

The Senate shall choose their other Officers, and also a President pro tempore, in the Absence of the Vice President, or when he shall exercise the Office of President of the United States.

Presidents pro tempore are elected to serve at the pleasure of the Senate, or until they submit their resignations to the Senate. Since 1890 they have tended to be elected for the duration of one or more sessions of Congress. Unlike the Vice President, they retain their right to vote. The Vice President's so-called "casting vote," in crucial questions which are evenly divided, is obviously a valuable political asset in the circumstances.

The status of the President of the Senate became an acute question in the fall of 1973 with the resignation of Vice President Spiro Agnew. Aside from the political and legal complications which were involved in this particular case, certain anomalies were evident: The occupant of the position is elected as an executive officer (Article II. 1), but his only specified duties are those of a legislative officer. His executive status is analogous to an estate in expectancy, but he has no executive authority at all until he succeeds to the Presidency, either under Article II or as Acting President under Amendment XXV (q.v.). For impeachment purposes, Article II identifies him as an executive officer or "civil officer," but in fact he is only a contingency executive.

I. 3. Cl. 6. Trial of Impeachments

The Senate shall have the sole Power to try all Impeachments. When sitting for that Purpose, they shall be on Oath or Affirmation. When the President of the United States is tried, the Chief Justice shall preside; And no Person shall be convicted without the Concurrence of two thirds of the Members present.

I. 3. Cl. 7. Judgment in Impeachments; Punishment

Judgment in Cases of Impeachment shall not extend further than to removal from Office, and disqualification to hold and enjoy any Office of honor, Trust or Profit under the United States; but the Party convicted shall nevertheless be liable and subject to Indictment. Trial, Judgment and Punishment, according to Law.

Impeachment, in Alexander Hamilton's phrase, is "a method of national inquest into the conduct of public men." It was conceived by the Constitutional Convention as a quasi-judicial proceeding, the House of Representatives acting as the counterpart of a grand jury and its vote on the question of impeachment being analogous to a grand-jury presentment or indictment (*cf.* Art. I. 2. Cl. 5). The persons liable to impeachment are the President, Vice President and other "civil officers of the United States" who may be charged with "treason, felony, or other high crimes and misdemeanors" (Art. II. 4). Judges are further charged with "good behavior" (Art. III. 1). Members of Congress appear not to be holders of "civil office" (Art. I. 6. Cl. 2) and in any event are subject to equivalent penalties in the form of exclusion or expulsion (Art. I. 5).

Although there has been occasional argument in favor of a special court of impeachment to be created by Congress, the "sole Power to try Impeachments" vested by this section in the Senate would cast doubt on the validity of such a measure. In view of the rarity of the exercise of the power, the question is unlikely to become critical; hardly a dozen cases, with four convictions, have been recorded in national history. The two most famous trials—of Supreme Court Justice Samuel Chase and President Andrew Johnson—both failed to muster the necessary two-thirds majority.

The constitutional crisis of the fall of 1973, however, raised the question of whether an impeachable officer was also indictable while still in office. The wording of this section, taken with Article II. 4, is subject to two interpretations:(1) If the theory of separation of powers (itself undeclared in terms in the Constitution) immunized executive officers from process by the judicial branch, they could only become liable if divested of immunity through impeachment. (2) On the other hand, the language of the present section may be treated as preserving the liability to indictment for actions not reached by impeachment; impeachment, a legislative power, does not affect indictment, a judicial power. Under this theory, impeachment either would not affect the judicial process—i.e., the officeholder would be liable to indictment because immunity would amount to an evasion of the uniform processes of justice—or would toll any statute of limitations for the term of office.[1]

As indicated in reference to Article I.6.1 (*infra*), privilege from arrest is provided in the Constitution only with reference to legislative personnel, and there only in a highly limited context. Moreover, such privilege (i.e., immunity) does not prohibit service of process.[2] And it may be worth noting that in the case of *Powell v. McCormack*[3] the Congressman concerned took elaborate precautions not to enter the jurisdiction of the New York courts for a time, where process was waiting to be served.

1. On the general subject, cf. Berger, *Problems of Impeachment* (Cambridge, 1973).
2. *Long v. Ansell*, 69 F. 2d 386 (1934), aff'd. 293 U.S. 76 (1934); and *cf. James v. Powell*, 250 N.Y.S. 2d 635 (1966).
3. 395 U.S. 486 (1969).

I. 4. Cl. 1. Times, Places and Manner of Holding Elections

The Times, Places and Manner of holding Elections for Senators and Representatives, shall be prescribed in each State by the Legislature thereof; but the Congress may at any time by Law make or alter such Regulations, except as to the Places of choosing Senators.

Two questions emerge from this clause—the powers of the states as conferred on them by the Constitution in this regard and the powers of Congress to "make or alter such Regulations."

State Powers and Duties

The powers of the states under this clause are legislative powers, and hence the veto power of the governor, if provided by the state constitution as part of the lawmaking process, is applicable to statutes relating to the time, manner and place of holding such elections.[1] Unless Congress exercises its own constitutional prerogative under this clause, the states have broad discretion as to defining the conditions under which the right to vote may be exercised; but these conditions must not amount to a frustration of the constitutional guarantee of the right to vote itself.[2]

The reapportionment decisions already cited under Art. I. 2. Cl. 1 have substantially circumscribed the states' legislative powers on this subject. In the early Supreme Court cases affecting state elections, the constitutional issue was the equal-protection clause of the Fourteenth Amendment (*q.v.*);[3] but with *Wesberry v. Sanders*[4] the Court turned its attention to the question of Congressional apportionment under Sections 2 and 4 of Article I and ruled that equality of values of individual votes was a general constitutional principle which governed the validity of state laws on the subject. By 1969 the Court was enforcing a standard of equality of electoral strength in all districts within a state "as nearly as practicable." Variations in electoral strength between districts was basically suspect and subject to a judicial requirement of justification.[5] Thus a New York Congressional districting formula designed "to keep regions with distinct interests intact" was set aside; the flaw, said the 6-to-3 majority, was in "subdividing" the state by regions of unequal population, even though the Congressional districts within the "subdivisions" were equal.[6]

Congressional Powers

As early as 1880 the Court held that Congressional power in this subject area might be concurrent rather than exclusive. Both state and Congress might regulate a particular phase of the "time, manner and place" of holding elections; if there was a conflict the Congressional regulation prevailed, but if there was none the two laws might "form a harmonious system."[7] However, Congress has power to abrogate all state laws on the subject, as a Kentucky court recognized in 1944.[8]

In the landmark case of *United States v. Classic,* it was held that a state primary election was an election within the meaning of this Clause, although the primary concept was unknown to the Founding Fathers; it was a necessary step in the selection of candidates for Congress and hence subject to Congressional regulation.[9] The reason for this safeguard was clearly established four years later in *Smith v. Allwright,* when the Court struck down discriminatory provisions of primary laws restricting the right to vote for candidates of a particular political party.[10] As early as 1930 the Court had upheld a Federal statute limiting the right of elected Federal officials to solicit or receive campaign contributions from other Federal officeholders.[11]

The rule was substantially expanded in the Hatch Act of

1939,[12] barring Federal executive employees from participating in political campaigns. The Corrupt Practices Act of 1947 was invalidated under the First Amendment as to the forbidding of campaign contributions by labor unions,[13] although its provision for punishment of bribery was upheld.[14]

In general, the powers of Congress under this clause extend to all steps necessary to protect and promote honest and fair elections.[15] This includes the power to punish a state officer violating a state law relating to Congressional elections.[16]

1. *Smiley v. Holm*, 285 U.S. 355 (1932).
2. *Harman v. Fortenssius*, 380 U.S. 28 (1965); and *cf. Grills v. Branigan*, 284 F.S. 176 (1968) (under state and Federal constitutions, legislatures alone have the right to establish Congressional districts).
3. *Baker v. Carr*, 369 U.S. 186 (1962); *Gray v. Sanders*, 372 U.S. 368 (1963).
4. 376 U.S. 1 (1964).
5. *Kirkpatrick v. Preisler*, 394 U.S. 526 (1969).
6. *Wells v. Rockefeller*, 394 U.S. 542 (1969).
7. *Ex parte Siebold*, 100 U.S. 383 (1880).
8. *Commonwealth ex rel. Dummit v. O'Connell*, 298 Ky. 44, 181 S.W. 2d 691 (1944).
9. *United States v. Classic*, 313 U.S. 299 (1941).
10. 321 U.S. 649 (1944).
11. *United States v. Wurzbach*, 280 U.S. 396 (1930); query whether the 1921 case of *Newberry v. United States*, 256 U.S. 232, denying Congress power to limit campaign expenditures in primary elections, has any current validity.
12. Act of August 2, 1939, Ch. 410, 53 Stat. 1147; upheld inferentially in *United Public Workers v. Mitchell*, 330 U.S. 75 (1947).
13. *United States v. C.I.O.*, 77 F.S. 355 (1948).
14. *United States v. Foote*, 42 F.S. 717 (1942).
15. *In re Coy*, 127 U.S. 752 (1888); *United States v. Kelsey*, 42 F. 882 (1890); *cf.* also *Ex parte Yarbrough*, 110 U.S. 661 (1884).
16. *Ex parte Siebold*, 100 U.S. 373 (1880).

I. 4. Cl. 2. Sessions of Congress

[The Congress shall assemble at least once in every Year, and such meeting shall be on the first Monday in December, unless they shall by Law appoint a different Day.]

The Twentieth Amendment has superseded this provision.

I. 5. Cl. 1. Powers of Each House; Legislative Procedure

Each House shall be the judge of the Elections, Returns and Qualifications of its own Members, and a Majority of each shall constitute a quorum to do business; but a smaller Number may adjourn from day to day, and may be authorized to compel the Attendance of absent Members, in such Manner, and under such Penalties as each House may provide.

The basic questions of construction in this clause concern (1) the procedure for judging elections and returns, (2) the qualifications of members, and (3) the maintenance of a quorum to do business. As to the second of these, the presumption in favor of the validity of the findings of either house is virtually beyond judicial question,[1] although in *Powell v. McCormack* the Court admonished the legislative branch that the Constitution expressly and conclusively defined the qualifications of members as to seating and that Congress's sole function in this instance was to confirm the fact that the member met the qualifications.[2]

Whether the committees examining elections, returns and qualifications have in the past, or may in the future, make the distinctions that *Powell* suggests is conjectural, the findings of the committees on qualifications have often been merged with evidence which presumably went to the question of elections and returns. Among factors cited in contesting the right of a member-elect to his seat have been irregularities in the form of the electoral ballot, inordinate campaign expenditures, fraudulent registration of voters, mental competence, alleged conspiracies on the part of the candidate or his supporters and violation of state laws.[3]

In the matter of judging elections and returns, state and Federal courts alike aver that Congress has exclusive jurisdiction, so that the courts are precluded from adjudicating the validity of such elections.[4] The state courts, of course, have jurisdiction over the question of whether their own election statutes have been complied with.[5] As to the member-elect, however, it is the particular house of Congress which acts as a judicial body,[6] with full power to compel attendance of witnesses and receive testimony at the bar of the house.[7]

As for the question of a quorum, "the general rule of all parliamentary bodies is that, when a quorum is present, the act of the majority of the quorum is the act of the body."[8] Although the continual going and coming of members during a session of either house frequently prompts a member to suggest the absence of a quorum, this is more often than not a maneuver to gain time in debate or in mustering supporters for a coming vote. However, in instances where a witness in testifying before a committee has subsequently been charged with perjury, a reasonable doubt as to whether a quorum had been present at the time of administration of the oath to the witness has been held to be prejudicial error.[9]

1. *Barry v. United States ex rel. Cunningham,* 279 U.S. 547 (1929).
2. 395 U.S. 486 (1969).
3. *Cf.* Cannon's *Precedents of the House of Representatives,* I, § 476, etc.
4. *Reed v. County Commissioners,* 21 F. 2d, 144 (1927); *Koegh v. Horner,* 8 F.S. 933 (1934); *Manion v. Holtzman,* 379 F. 2d 843 (1967); etc.
5. *Odegard v. Olson,* 119 N.W. 2d 717 (1963); *Wickersham v. State Election Board,* 357 P. 2d 421 (1960).
6. *Wettengell v. Zimmerman,* 24 N.W. 2d 504 (1946).
7. *Barry v. United States ex rel. Zimmerman,* 279 U.S. 547 (1929).
8. *United States v. Ballin,* 144 U.S. 1, 7 (1892).
9. *Christoffel v. United States,* 338 U.S. 84 (1949).

I. 5. Cl. 2. Rules; Punishment and Expulsion of Members

Each House may determine the Rules of its Proceedings, punish its Members for disorderly Behavior, and, with the Concurrence of two thirds, expel a Member.

Rules for Each House

The rules adopted by each house, including rules affecting the procedure to be followed by any of its committees, are judicially cognizable,[1] and the courts will strictly construe such rules as they affect the powers of the house or its committees, or the rights of persons summoned before the committees.[2] In rule-making, Congress may not ignore constitutional restraints or violate fundamental rights, and "there should be a reasonable relation between the mode or method of proceeding established by the rule, and the result which is sought to be attained."[3]

The house exercises its rule-making powers within limits which it fixes itself, and in the case of the House of Representatives the rules of a previous session are not in effect until adopted by the sitting house.[4] In construing a rule, the courts are expected to give great weight to the construction of the rule by the house which adopted it, as this construction bears on the facts in controversy.[5] And the rule is not the less a rule because, as occasionally has happened, the house elects to frame it as a statute and thus involve the concurrence of the other branch of Congress.[6]

Punishment and Expulsion

The power of the house to expel a member is unlimited and is a matter purely of discretion to be exercised by a two-thirds majority without a right of appeal.[7] The power is limited in its application to the conduct of a member during his term of office[8] and terminates with the resignation of a member while a question of expulsion is under consideration.[9] In lieu of expulsion, whether or not an attempt to expel has been made, the house may censure a member for his conduct.[10]

Exclusion—a proceeding which Congress itself has never clearly defined but which presumably takes the form of a refusal to seat a member and therefore may depend for its validity upon the *Powell* construction of Article I, Section 2, Clause 2 *(supra)* —is distinguished from expulsion, which must follow the requirements of the present clause and which applies to a sitting member of the house. Expulsion is very rare—only a handful of Representatives and Senators to date have suffered this penalty. Censure has been voted on only half a dozen occasions, the most recent having been the late Senator Joseph McCarthy of Wisconsin in 1957.

1. *Yellin v. United States,* 374 U.S. 109 (1963).
2. *Gojack v. United States,* 384 U.S. 702 (1966).
3. *United States v. Ballin,* 144 U.S. 5 (1892).
4. 8 Cannon's Precedents, §§ 3376ff., 3383.
5. *United States v. Smith,* 286 U.S. 6 (1932).
6. *Chapman v. United States,* 8 App. D.C. 302 (1896), pet. den. U.S. 661 (1896).
7. 6 Cannon's Precedents, § 78.
8. *Id.,* § 56.
9. *Id.,* § 238.
10. *Id.,* § 236.

I. 5. Cl. 3. Journal for Each House

Each House shall keep a Journal of its Proceedings, and from time to time publish the same, excepting such Parts as may in their Judgment require Secrecy; and the Yeas and Nays of the members of either House on any question shall, at the Desire of one fifth of those Present, be entered on the Journal.

The theory behind the journal requirement is that it constitutes a public record of the business of the legislature. In practice, however, the requirement is satisfied by whatever the legislature in its own discretion undertakes to enter into the journal. The Senate, relying on the secrecy provision in this clause, keeps two journals—the executive journal containing votes on nominations, treaties and the like being published only some years after the date of the session.[1] The clause is not judicially enforceable, and the courts rely upon "usage, the orderly conduct of legislative proceedings, and the rules under which the two bodies have acted since the organization of the government."[2] The journal, rather than the *Congressional Record* or its antecedents, is the official record of the proceedings of the House of Representatives[3] as well as of the Senate.[4] Although Congress by statute has provided for certified copies of portions of the journal to be accepted as evidence of Congressional action,[5] the courts are disinclined to accept a journal entry as the best evidence, so far as enacted legislation is concerned. Rather, the enrolled bill, signed by the Speaker of the House and the President of the Senate and thereafter signed by the President of the United States and deposited in the Department of State, is a complete and unimpeachable record of Congressional action.[6]

---

1. *Cf.* Standing Rule IV, Senate Manual.
2. *Field v. Clark,* 143 U.S. 670 (1892).
3. 4 Hinds' Precedents, § 2727.
4. Standing Rule IV, Senate Manual.
5. 62 Stat. 947, 28 U.S.C. 1736.
6. *Field v. Clark,* 143 U.S. 670 (1892); and *cf. Flint v. Stone Tracy Co.,* 220 U.S. 107 (1911).

I. 5. Cl. 4. Adjournment; Consent of Each House

Neither House, during the Session of Congress, shall, without the Consent of the other, adjourn for more than three days, nor to any other Place than that in which the two Houses shall be sitting.

The manifest purpose of this provision is to prevent one of the houses of Congress from bringing legislative business to a standstill by adjourning indefinitely, or moving to some inconvenient site to frustrate the work of the other house.

I. 6. Cl. 1. Privileges and Immunities of Members

The Senators and Representatives shall receive a Compensation for their Services, to be ascertained by Law, and paid out of the Treasury of the United States. They shall in all Cases, except Treason, Felony and Breach of the Peace, be privileged from Arrest during their Attendance at the session of their respective Houses, and in going to and returning from the same; and for any Speech or Debate in either House, they shall not be questioned in any other Place.

The primary principle in this section is that of legislative immunity from prosecution for actions or statements made by members in the course of their official business. The provision has always been broadly construed "to free Congressmen from fear of prosecutions for words spoken, votes cast or actions taken in pursuit of their lawful functions."[1] Manifestly, this privilege can be and has been abused on occasion, with the cloak of privilege being used by members making sweeping and undocumented attacks on individuals and groups.[2] The "claim of unworthy purpose" does not dissipate the privilege, however.[3] The privilege also extends to the testimony of witnesses and to statements by representatives of government agencies responding to official inquiries by Congress.[4]

Immunity from arrest was provided by the Founding Fathers to insure that members of Congress would not be prevented from attending sessions, thus depriving states of their representation.[5] But a service of process, which is not an arrest, may be had on a member,[6] whether the process is civil or criminal. The broad language of the clause—"except treason, felony and breach of the peace"—leaves virtually all criminal acts outside the privilege.[7] But civil process may not be used by a judgment creditor to attempt ouster of the member from his seat.[8]

1. *United States v. Johnson,* 337 F. 2d 180 (1964), aff'd. 383 U.S. 169 (1966).
2. *Cf.* the dissent of Justice Douglas in *Tenney v. Brandhove,* 341 U.S. 367, 382 (1951): "I do not agree that all abuses of legislative committees are solely for the legislative body to police. . . . If a committee departs so far from its domain to deprive a citizen of a right protected by the Constitution, I can think of no reason why it should be immune."
3. *Tenney v. Brandhove,* 341 U.S. 367 (1951) (majority opinion); and *cf. Barsky v. United States,* 167 F. 2d 241 (1948), cert. den., 334 U.S. 843 (1948).
4. *Cf. Pearson v. Wright,* 156 F.S. 136 (1957).
5. *Burton v. United States,* 196 U.S. 295 (1905).
6. *Long v. Ansell,* 69 F. 2d 386 (1934), aff'd. 293 U.S. 76 (1934); and *cf. James v. Powell,* 250 N.Y.S. 2d 635 (1966).
7. *Williamson v. United States,* 207 U.S. 425 (1908).
8. *Application of James,* 241 F.S. 858 (1965).

I. 6. Cl. 2. Incompatible Offices

No Senator or Representative shall, during the Time for which he was elected, be appointed to any civil Office under the Authority of the United States, which shall have been created, or the Emoluments whereof shall have been encreased during such time; and no Person holding any Office under the United States, shall be a member of either House during his Continuance in Office.

This article has been invoked twice in the twentieth century. The first instance required a legislative remedy: When Senator Philander Knox was nominated for Secretary of State in 1909, Congress had already increased the salary for that position, and the increase had been made during Knox's term as Senator. Accordingly, new legislation was passed restoring the prior salary for this office.[1]

In the second instance, the judiciary disposed of the matter: When Senator Hugo L. Black was nominated for a position on the Supreme Court, it was argued that during his term in the Senate the emolument for the Justices had been increased by extending to the Supreme Court the retirement privileges accorded to other judges in the Federal system.[2] In a test case, the Court declared that since the new Justice would not be eligible for the retirement benefits for nineteen years (he then being fifty-one years of age), this was not an increased emolument *"as to him."*[3]

1. 34 Stat. 948 (1907); 35 Stat. 626 (1909).
2. 50 Stat. 24 (1937).
3. *Ex parte Levitt*, 302 U.S. 633 (1937). Query whether the Court should not have dismissed the petition as not being within the original jurisdiction of the Court as defined by Article III, § 2, Cl. 2. *Cf.* the discussion of jurisdiction under that clause. It is worth noting that Justice Black served on the Court for thirty-four years and retired only one week before his death in September 1971.

I. 7. Cl. 1. House Origin of Revenue Bills

All Bills for raising Revenue shall originate in the House of Representatives; but the Senate may propose or concur with Amendments as on other Bills.

While the original theory of this provision was that the more "popular" representation in the lower house would effect a degree of control over public expenditures, in practical effect any revenue measure originating in the House may be substantially altered in the Senate. The courts have rejected arguments that such Senate amendments, substituting new forms of taxation (e.g., a corporation tax for an inheritance tax) are in conflict with this clause; if the subject of the amendment is germane to the subject of the original bill, the Senate's initiative is constitutionally permissible.[1] And where the tax is plainly intended as a regulatory rather than a revenue device (e.g., a tax to drive national bank notes out of circulation and thus pre-empt the field for a government currency),[2] it may validly originate in the Senate.

1. *Flint v. Stone Tracy Co.*, 220 U.S. 107 (1911).
2. *Twin City Bank v. Nebeker*, 167 U.S. 202 (1897).

I. 7. Cl. 2. Procedure for Enacting Legislation

Every bill which shall have passed the House of Representatives and the Senate shall, before it become a law, be presented to the President of the United States; if he approve he shall sign it, but if not he shall return it, with his objections, to that house in which it shall have originated, who shall enter the objections at large on their journal and proceed to reconsider it. If after such reconsideration two-thirds of that house shall agree to pass the bill it shall be sent, together with the objections, to the other house, by which it shall likewise be reconsidered, and if approved by two-thirds of that house it shall become a law. But in all such cases the votes of both houses shall be determined by yeas and nays, and the names of the persons voting for and against the bill shall be entered on the journal of each house respectively. If any bill shall not be returned by the President within ten days (Sundays excepted) after it shall have been presented to him, the same shall be a law, in like manner as if he had signed it, unless the Congress by their adjournment prevent its return, in which case it shall not be a law.

The time in which the President is to consider a bill for approval or veto begins when the bill is actually presented to him by Congress.[1] The method of presentation may be any reasonable one agreed on in the circumstances; by the mid-twentieth century, when the Chief Executive frequently finds it necessary to be away from Washington or even from the country, neither Congress nor the President may frustrate the other's function under this clause by refusing an accommodation in this matter.[2] The contemporary requirements of virtually continuous sessions of Congress have made the "pocket veto"—inaction on a bill after adjournment—less significant than it once was.

1. *Eber Bros. Wine & Liquor Corp. v. United States*, 337 F. 2d 624 (1964), cert. den. 380 U.S. 950 (1965).
2. *Id.*, at 633.

I. 7. Cl. 3. Procedure Concerning Resolutions

Every order, resolution or vote to which the concurrence of the Senate and House of Representatives may be necessary (except on a question of adjournment) shall be presented to the President of the United States; and before the same shall take effect shall be approved by him, or being disapproved by him shall be repassed by two-thirds of the Senate and House of Representatives, according to the rules and limitations prescribed in the case of a bill.

"Resolution" is an ambivalent term in legislation; for many state legislatures it is a synonym for a statutory enactment, while for Congress it is qualified in usage: e.g., a resolution may be a simple expression of the sense of either house, or occasionally it may be a joint expression of both houses. Other joint resolutions, or concurrent resolutions, may for all practical purposes be equivalent to statutory measures, being authorizations of action by some agency of government, and having the force of law when signed by the President or passed over his veto.[1] Beginning with the first Reorganization Act of 1939,[2] the concurrent resolution took on a new function, when the consolidation or reassignment of functions of the executive department was subjected to legislative veto within sixty days of the announcement of the reorganization plan. In several instances, wartime legislation of the 1940s carried similar provisions for Congressional termination of the legislation by concurrent resolution.[3] Whether this practice violates the spirit or the letter of the constitutional formula for lawmaking has not been adjudicated; like the use of the executive order to give the President more maneuverability in areas where Congress has been slow to act, it is an attempt to limit some of the checks and balances which the Founding Fathers believed essential to a government of limited powers.

1. *Cf. United States v. Stockslager,* 129 U.S. 470 (1889).
2. 53 Stat. 561, 3 U.S.C. 106.
3. *Cf.* Emergency Price Control Act of 1942, 56 Stat. 23; Stabilization Act of 1942, 56 Stat. 765.

I. 8. Cl. 1. *Powers of Congress; the Taxing Power*

The Congress shall have power to lay and collect taxes, duties, imposts and excises, to pay the debts and provide for the common defense and general welfare of the United States; but all duties, imposts and excises shall be uniform throughout the United States.

Although strict constructionists have urged that this section represents an express and limited grant of powers to the Federal government, the modern Court has repeatedly pointed out that the grants in most instances, although they may be express, are not limited. This opening clause is a case in point: The grant of tax power is complete and unqualified; moreover, it is reasonably susceptible of the conclusion which the Court, at least since the crisis of the New Deal era, has consistently drawn—that Congress is the sole judge of the purpose for which the tax is authorized.[1] Correlatively, Congress is the sole judge of the proper purposes for which moneys raised by taxes may be spent.[2]

The Power and Purpose of Taxation

Since the taxing power is unlimited, except for the uniformity and apportionment provisions in the Constitution, Congressional enactment within these provisions is free from judicial restraint, whatever the results arising from such enactment.[3] This 1904 opinion reflected a long line of similar holdings; and the 1922 departure from the rule in *Bailey v. Drexel Furn. Co.*[4] was justified by Chief Justice Taft by the contention that the purpose of the tax—regulation or abolition of child labor in interstate commerce—was not a subject constitutionally under Federal jurisdiction. In the same manner, regulatory taxes of the first New Deal period were struck down as attempts to control activities beyond the reach of government.[5] Rather clearly, the valid exercise of the tax power depended on a broader judicial understanding of what *was* within the reach of government. This came in 1937 with the historic shift in the Court's position.

It was foreshadowed in *Sonzinsky v. United States,*[6] when Justice Stone observed that the judiciary would not "ascribe to Congress an attempt, under the guise of taxation, to exercise another power denied by the Federal Constitution." From this rather oblique holding, the Court moved in 1940 to a more affirmative position, that Congress could indeed use its taxing power as a means of implementing any other constitutional power.[7] This ruling, upholding the second Bituminous Coal Conservation (Guffey) Act, specifically rejected the opposing argument used in 1936 to strike down the first Guffey Act.[8] The final affirmation of the scope of the taxing power came in 1956 when the Court declared that the tax might be valid even when "it touches upon activities which Congress might not otherwise regulate."[9] Thus, Congress may even tax activities which are themselves unlawful (e.g., gambling), provided that Fifth Amendment rights against self-incrimination are not infringed,[10] and may fix liability for failing to follow procedures not actually available to the wrongdoer—the rather strained holding being that if self-incrimination turns on the procedure (filling out certain forms) and the procedure is not available, there is no self-incrimination.[11]

The Spending Power and the General Welfare

After the Court had withdrawn from the extremely restrictive position of the early (pre-1937) New Deal cases, it was prepared to treat as plenary the power of Congress to spend such moneys as it raised by taxation for any public purpose it considered appropriate. Thus the *Butler* doctrine of judicial determination of valid purpose was rejected in favor of Congressional determination—e.g., in the second Agricultural Adjustment Act.[12] The Social Security Act was upheld as to the valid purpose of public expenditures both for unemployment relief[13] and old-age retirement benefits.[14] The power of Congress to devote its revenues to public-works projects in competition with private utilities[15] and low-cost housing[16] has consistently been affirmed, as well as, more recently, the conditioning of grants-in-aid to local accommodation of Federal civil-rights programs.[17]

The general-welfare provision (as distinguished from the same phrase appearing in the Preamble) has been restricted to the tax clause, rather than being developed as an unlimited area of public purposes. While some broad constructionists have thus been disappointed, the Court at least has passed beyond the narrow construction of the *laissez-faire* era, in which conservatives had denied that because a problem transcended state or regional areas it became a national problem affecting the general welfare.[18] The prevailing view is expressed in one of the Social Security cases of 1937: Where Congress has a reasonable basis for believing that a problem is so pervasive that it cannot be dealt with effectively by the laws of the individual states, it may determine the particular welfare interest which it intends to accommodate. "Only a power that is national can serve the interests of all."[19]

Uniformity of Taxation

The essential purpose of the uniformity provision is to protect the states and their residents from discriminatory taxation; such taxes as are levied by the Federal government are "to operate generally throughout the United States."[20] Wherever it is appropriate for the tax to apply, it must apply identically.[21] Geographic uniformity is what is required, but not uniform geographic division of the tax itself as in the case of a direct tax (*cf.* Art. I, Sec. 9, Cl. 4, below).[22] Thus the Federal tax may be progressive, or vary according to classes of taxables as Congress may determine;[23] and its uniformity is not affected by the fact that different states may add different amounts of local taxes on the same subject.[24] Nor does the fact that certain tax powers (e.g., import duties) operate to protect certain domestic industries limit the government in applying the tax power in this manner.[25]

1. *Cf. License Tax Cases,* 5 Wall. 462 (1867); *Champion v. Ames,* 188 U.S. 321 (1903); *Sonzinsky v. United States,* 300 U.S. 506 (1937).

2. *Cf. Helvering v. Davis,* 301 U.S. 619 (1937); *Stewart Machine Co. v. Davis,* 301 U.S. 548 (1937).

3. *McCray v. United States,* 195 U.S. 27 (1904).

4. 259 U.S. 20 (1922).

5. *Cf.* references to attempted tax implementation of commerce power in *Schechter Poultry Corp. v. United States,* 215 U.S. 495 (1935); *United States v. Butler,* 297 U.S. 1 (1936); and *cf.* earlier rationale in *Hill v. Wallace,* 259 U.S. 44 (1922) and *Chicago Board of Trade v. Olsen,* 262 U.S. 1 (1922).

6. 300 U.S. 506 (1937).

7. *Sunshine Anthr. Coal Co. v. Adkins,* 301 U.S. 381 (1940).

8. *Carter v. Carter Coal Co.,* 298 U.S. 238 (1936).

9. *United States v. Sanchez,* 340 U.S. 42 (1950).

10. *Cf. United States v. Kahriger,* 345 U.S. 22 (1953), overruled on self-incrimination grounds only in *Marchetti v. United States,* 390 U.S. 39 (1968); *cf.* also *Grosso v. United States,* 390 U.S. 62 (1968), *Haynes v. United States,* 390 U.S. 85 (1968) and *Leary v. United States,* 395 U.S. 6 (1969). When Congress amended the National Firearms Act, Stat. 1227, 26 U.S.C. 5801 *et seq.* to correct the self-incrimination flaw identified by the Haynes case, the regulatory tax was upheld. *United States v. Freed,* 401 U.S. 601 (1971).

11. *Minor v. United States,* 396 U.S. 87 (1969). *Cf.* statement of Federal District Court in 1939: "Congress may tax by one statute that which it prohibits and makes criminal by another." *United States v. U.S. Indus. Alcohol Co.,* 103 F. 2d 97.

12. *Mulford v. Smith,* 307 U.S. 38 (1939); and *cf. Currin v. Wallace,* 306 U.S. 1 (1939).

13. *Stewart Machine Co. v. Davis,* 301 U.S. 548 (1937).

14. *Helvering v. Davis,* 301 U.S. 619 (1937).

15. *Cf.* generally *Ashwander v. T.V.A.,* 297 U.S. 288 (1939); *Tennessee Power Co. v. T.V.A.,* 306 U.S. 118 (1939); *Alabama Power Co. v. Ickes,* 302 U.S. 464 (1938).

16. *Cf.* opinion in early case of *New Brunswick v. United States,* 276 U.S. 547 (1928).

17. *Cf.* Title VI, Civil Rights Act of 1964, 78 Stat., 2, 28 U.S.C. 14.

18. *Cf.* Swindler, *The Old Legality,* Chs. 13, 14.

19. *Helvering v. Davis,* 301 U.S. 619, 644 (1937).

20. *Knowlton v. Moore,* 178 U.S. 41 (1900).

21. *Fernandez v. Wiener,* 326 U.S. 340 (1945).

22. *Id.,* at 359; and *cf. Patton v. Brady,* 184 U.S. 608 (1902).
23. *Brushaber v. Union Pacific,* 240 U.S. 1 (1916); *Knowlton v. Moore,* 178 U.S. 41 (1900).
24. *Florida v. Mellon,* 273 U.S. 12 (1927).
25. *Hampton & Co. v. United States,* 276 U.S. 394 (1928).

I. 8. Cl. 2. The Borrowing Power

[The Congress shall have power] to borrow money on the credit of the United States.

The Founding Fathers, by vesting both taxing and borrowing powers in Congress under the Constitution, remedied two fatal defects in the national government created by the Articles of Confederation. The borrowing power, indeed, is even broader than the tax power, since it has no limitations analogous to the uniformity and apportionment provisions of Article I, Section 8, Clause 1, and Article I, Section 9, Clause 4. The power may be used to meet either present or anticipated expenses of the United States, in furtherance of any general or national interest.[1] The question of whether the evidence of Federal indebtedness (e.g., treasury notes) may be made legal tender was answered negatively at first[2] and then, following an alleged "packing" of the Supreme Court, affirmatively.[3] The further question of whether such government notes could abrogate a clause in an antecedent obligation (e.g., a World War I Liberty Bond) providing for payment of the bond in gold was answered in the negative in the early New Deal era. (However, in this instance Chief Justice Hughes saved the government from the consequences of its own actions in the monetary crisis of 1933 by denying the bondholder a remedy on the ground that he was unable to show actual damage.)[4]

Further evidence of the complete freedom of the borrowing power is the consistent holding of the courts that state taxes may not be laid on Federal obligations. Immunity from such taxes "always has been deemed an attribute of national sovereignty and essential to its maintenance. The power . . . would be burdened and might be destroyed by state taxation of the means employed for that purpose. As the tax-exempt feature tends to increase and is reflected in the market prices of such securities, a state tax burden thereon would adversely affect the terms upon which the money may be borrowed to execute the purpose of the general

government."[5] The related questions of how broad the recipro-
cal immunities of national and state governments may be are
part of the judicial construction both of the preceding (tax) and
succeeding (commerce) clauses of this section of the Constitution.[6]

1. *Legal Tender Cases*, 110 U.S. 444 (1884); and *cf. United States v. Kay*, 89 F. 2d
   19 (1937), vacated on other grounds, 303 U.S. 1 (1937).
2. *Hepburn v. Griswold*, 8 Wall. 603 (1870).
3. *Knox v. Lee*, 12 Wall. 457 (1871). These early Legal Tender Cases, and the
   crisis they presented to the national administration of the day, are discussed in
   Warren, *Supreme Court in United States History* (Boston, 1926), II, 498–527.
4. *Perry v. United States*, 294 U.S. 330 (1935); *cf.* Swindler, *The New Legality*,
   Ch. 2.
5. *State ex rel. Missouri Ins. Co. v. Gehner*, 281 U.S. 313, 321 (1930).
6. Intergovernmental tax immunities have been subjected to vacillating doctrines.
   Chief Justice Marshall in *McCulloch v. Maryland*, 4 Wheat. 316 (1819), and
   Weston v. Charleston, 2 Pet. 449 (1829), unequivocally denied state or local
   power to tax Federal instrumentalities. The Supreme Court in 1842 held that
   Federal immunity included the salaries of Federal officers. *Dobbins v. Erie
   County*, 16 Pet. 435, and in 1871 ascribed similar immunity to salaries of state
   officers. *Collector v. Day*, 11 Wall. 113. In the heyday of *laissez-faire*, immunities
   proliferated, on the theory that even a tax burden on a private individual doing
   business with government could theoretically be a burden on the government itself; *cf. Gillespie v. Oklahoma*, 257 U.S. 501 (1922), and *Burnet v. Coronado Oil & Gas Co.*, 285 U.S. 393 (1932); *cf.* also *Panhandle Oil Co. v. Mississippi*, 277 U.S. 218 (1928), *Indian Motorcycle Co. v. United States*, 283 U.S.
   570 (1931), and *Fox Film Corp. v. Doyal*, 286 U.S. 123 (1932). The trend was
   reversed beginning in 1937 with a 5–4 holding of tax liability in *James v.
   Dravo Contracting Co.*, 302 U.S. 134, followed by the overruling of the Gillespie and Burnet cases in 1938: *Helvering v. Mt. Producers Corp.*, 303 U.S. 376.
   Collector v. Day was essentially nullified by *Helvering v. Gerhardt*, 304 U.S. 405
   (1938), and *Dobbins v. Erie County* by *Graves v. New York ex rel. O'Keefe*,
   306 U.S. 466 (1939). For other aspects of intergovernmental immunities, see some
   of the commentary under the commerce clause and under the supremacy
   clause of Article IV.

I. 8. Cl. 3. The Commerce Power

[Congress shall have power] to regulate commerce with foreign
nations, and among the several states, and with the Indian tribes.

This was the clause on which the Marshall Court, in the
early nineteenth century, firmly established the strength of the
national government. The power over interstate and foreign commerce, declared the great Chief Justice, "is complete in itself, may

be exercised to its utmost extent, and acknowledges no limitations, other than are prescribed in the Constitution."[1] It was a definition, said Justice Robert Jackson a century later, "with a breadth never exceeded."[2] Yet there has been a prolonged and continuing struggle for a definition of the definition, so to speak: Was "commerce" merely a term describing either the act of economic exchange or the process of making the exchange? Did it reach any physical or corporeal things, or function within any definable spacial area? Did it include the means of transporting the goods—as Congress ultimately determined that it did in passing the Interstate Commerce Commission Act of 1887—and did it reach the goods themselves? If it could reach the goods, could the Federal power operate within the geographic and political jurisdiction of the states to the point where the "stream of commerce" began or ended? And could it be used as an implement of the police power to regulate the nature of the goods (e.g., lottery tickets) or the conditions of their manufacture (e.g., child labor)? For all these questions, the conservative or strict constructionist had one answer and the liberal or broad constructionist another—or the conservative of the *laissez-faire* era might have an answer different from the conservative of the Frankfurter–Jackson–Harlan era.[3]

The Definition of Commerce

The original objective of the commerce clause was to free the national economy from local entanglements by vesting its regulation in the national government.[4] It was intended to establish free trade throughout the United States, to the extent that any state burdens placed on this trade were to be treated as burdening the national interest.[5] This much, established by Marshall in 1819, had sufficed to leave private economic activity largely free from both state and Federal surveillance for most of the nineteenth century. But the expanding and complex corporate activities which came to dominate economic life in the generation after the Civil War, epitomized in the growth of interstate railroads and in the consolidation of private economic power through industrial combinations, pools and trusts, led to a demand for both state and Federal initiative in the regulation of these activities.

In 1877, the Court found constitutional a number of state regulatory processes,[6] and ten years later Congress undertook to complement the state efforts by creating the Interstate Commerce Commission.[7] In 1890 another national regulatory process was projected in the Sherman Anti-Trust Act.[8] The new issues thus presented to the Court by the end of the century found few relevant guidelines in the earlier commerce doctrines of Marshall; for these had focussed on a division of authority between state and national governments but had given little attention to the commerce to which that authority applied. In an age when the Jeffersonian-Emersonian ideals of individual initiative and self-reliance found congenial echoes in the doctrines of *laissez-faire*, the courts sought to minimize the power of control even as they confirmed their constitutional validity.

Thus Chief Justice Fuller, in 1890, undertook to insulate interstate shipments from local taxation by enunciating his "unbroken package" doctrine. Although Fuller contended that this rule, denying to states a right to tax incoming goods not yet divided into retail lots, was dictated by the policy against internal tariffs which the Constitution provided, Congress expressly declared that products shipped in interstate commerce might be liable to such taxes.[9] The net effect of this line of development was to establish the fact that some agency of government, either state or Federal, could in fact reach goods in transit as well as the carriers; but in 1895 the Court severely limited this proposition with a holding that a combination to control the marketing of most of the sugar in the nation was not a conspiracy within the definition of the Sherman Act because the commodity itself was not subject to the commerce jurisdiction of Congress.[10] In subsequent cases involving state efforts to regulate goods and services in interstate activity, the Court imposed a similar restraint on state governments.[11]

A retreat from this excessively restrictive judicial position began, however, with a 5–4 holding in 1897 that a rate-fixing combination of carriers fell under the prohibitions of the Sherman Act,[12] and this was followed in 1900 by a similar holding with respect to rate-fixing by shippers as well.[13] The ultimate breadth of Federal rate regulating power was attained in 1914, when the Court held that the power extended to intrastate rates where this was necessary to protect the structure of interstate rates which the Interstate Commerce Commision had devised: "Interstate trade was not left to be destroyed or impeded by the rivalries of local government."[14]

The Regulation of Commerce: Federal Power

The regulation of commerce—both commerce as the process of exchange and as the medium of exchange (carrier)—through the anti-trust laws and the Interstate Commerce Act as amended, thus gradually expanded in the judicial constructions from the late 1890s to the early 1920s. But the related question of the government's power over the subject matter of commerce—the goods and services themselves, and activities which bore a substantial relationship to them, or through them to interstate commerce—was threshed out over a considerably longer period of time. This was because, in the first place, it required a recognition of a police power in the national government analogous to the police power in the state governments, a concept which depended on a broader definition of Federal sovereignty.[15] Related to this, as the first Justice Harlan observed in 1903, was the recognition of the principle that "Congress may . . . exclude from commerce among the states any article, commodity, or thing . . . which it may choose . . . to declare shall not be carried from one state to another."[16] In this case, the interstate transportation of lottery tickets was prohibited. Congress soon thereafter acted on the police-power principle in passing the Pure Food and Drug Act;[17] and other police-power extensions were soon effected in the Hepburn Act and the Employers' Liability Acts.[18]

The use of the commerce power as an instrument of police power thus became the ultimate issue in the jurisprudence of the commerce clause. While the validity of the use in principle had been established,[19] there remained the question of how many subjects lay within the jurisdiction of the national police power. Congress could propose, but the Court would dispose.[20] The firmly negative position of the Court in the matter of child labor[21] and minimum wage controls[22] was to limit severely the development of this power for two decades.[23] It was not until the crisis of the New Deal in 1937 that the Court abandoned the *laissez-faire* concept of narrowly limited Federal police power and left to Congress the primary responsibility for determining its breadth. Since that time, the general tendency of judicial construction has been to uphold the Congressional assumption of authority under this clause to act in progressively wider areas of national interest.

From the original criminal sanctions incorporated into various early statutes on goods and transport in interstate commerce, the commerce clause has evolved into a medium for the enforcement of criminal law in general. After the courts confirmed Federal power over interstate kidnapping,[24] a series of other criminal statutes relying on the commerce clause have been enacted.[25] Even after interstate shipments have been completed and goods repackaged for local retail sale, it has been held, the liability for failure to comply with Federal packaging and labeling regulalations continues to apply.[26] Thus the spread of Federal criminal jurisdiction under the commerce clause has steadily expanded, the only significant qualification of this process being the stipulation that statutory liability must not be unconstitutionally vague.[27] Aside from that fundamental principle, the Court by 1971 could describe the commerce power as extending to "three categories of problems: First, the use of channels of interstate or foreign commerce which Congress deems are being misused, as for example, the shipment of stolen goods. . . . Second, protection of the instrumentalities of interstate commerce. . . . Third, those activities affecting commerce."[28]

The ultimate extreme in the use of the commerce clause to implement national policy has been in the attack on racial discrimination in the past decade. After several basic enactments under the "appropriate legislation" section of the Fourteenth and Fifteenth Amendments, Congress in 1964 enacted the Civil Rights Act[29] on the basis of the commerce power, declaring that any public accommodations (e.g., food services and traveling facilities) affecting interstate commerce were required to be available to all members of the public equally. In generally upholding this statute, the Court observed: "The commerce power invoked here by Congress is a specific and plenary one authorized by the Constitution itself. The only questions are: (1) whether Congress had a rational basis for finding that racial discrimination . . . affected commerce, and (2) if it had such a basis, whether the means it selected to eliminate that evil are reasonable and appropriate."[30]

Job discrimination under the commerce clause has also been held within the reach of Federal prosecutors in matters of race, sex or religion.[31]

Regulation of Commerce: State Power

While state power affecting interstate commerce is substantially circumscribed—it must, as Justice Stone often emphasized, be essential to effecting a local policy or need which overshadows the general national interest and does not unreasonably burden it—the power may be accommodated by the Supreme Court wherever Congress has not pre-empted the field. The primary test of valid state power, in the view of Stone and Brandeis, was the nature of the state policy which was involved: Where public safety was a paramount reason for limiting local issuance of certificates of convenience and necessity for interstate carriers, the limitation was upheld;[32] where it was found to be a limitation on competition, it was struck down.[33] A state load limit on interstate trucks, to preserve the usability of the interstate highway within the state boundaries, was affirmed;[34] but state limits on train lengths[35] and on mud guards for transport trucks[36] were denied.

The division of jurisdiction is an essential responsibility of the courts in a federal system; and the burden is usually on the national government to establish a conflict so fundamental as to compel denial of state power.[37] But once Federal administrative regulations have been validly promulgated with manifest intention to cover the subject completely, state regulation is invalid even in parts of the subject not yet reached by the Federal regulations.[38] It remains for Congress, or its agencies, to declare unequivocally that the Federal intention is to occupy only part of the field of jurisdiction.[39] But even where state authority is exercised in the absence of a Federal enactment, the eventual enactment of a Federal statute, if determined by the Court to pre-empt the field, at that point extinguishes the state authority.[40] While this judicial doctrine has proved unpopular with Congress on occasion,[41] it remains a fundamental limitation on state powers in the area of interstate commerce. While Chief Justice Hughes averred that there was "no constitutional rule which compels Congress to occupy the whole field,"[42] the state regulation of the same subject

matter is most readily acceptable when it can be shown to complement rather than duplicate or overlap the Federal authority.[43] The
latter, indeed, is in many instances the more appropriate medium
for effectuating state policy,[44] while to leave Federal policy to
implementation by state agencies would be to invite a conflict
with rather than an accommodation of national interests.[45]

The fundamental historic concern of the Court has been to
forestall the tendency toward "balkanization" of the national
economy as it had developed under the Articles of Cenfederation.
Thus states' attempts to protect their domestic economy by discriminatory legislation have been consistently struck down,[46] although a local law which protects "the social, as distinguished from
the economic, welfare of the community" may be upheld,[47] and
where the Court is persuaded that the facts "justify the conclusion that the effect of the law on interstate commerce is incidental"
rather than primary,[48] the local law creates no constitutional conflict. The purpose and effect of a state's laws—particularly its tax
laws—compel judicial scrutiny and proliferate the decisions. "The
power of the state to tax and the limitations upon that power
imposed by the commerce clause have necessitated a long, continuous process," Justice Frankfurter observed in 1946.[49] The
doctrine of multiple burdens, and the criteria for sustaining or
denying them, has continued to occupy judicial attention in the
quarter of a century since then.[50]

The basic judicial policy which has emerged from this economic thicket has been the product of Justice Stone's long advocacy of balancing of public interests—sometimes clothed in a distinction between "direct"and "indirect" burdens but ultimately
requiring a value judgment on which to justify or not justify the
concurrent application of state and Federal taxes, or the impact
of state taxation on interstate interests.[51] If "the burden on the
interstate commerce is too remote," or the subject taxed "cannot
again be taxed elsewhere," the state tax may be sustained.[52] If the
state tax burden falls on the consumer, it is by definition not a
tax on interstate commerce,[53] but it may be attacked as a "quasi-
tariff" where it is identified as a "use" tax which aims at equaliz-
ing the taxpayer liabilities established by "sales" taxes on local
goods.[54] Thus the question ultimately comes back to the proper
relationship between the state tax and interstate commerce; where

the state action inhibits the free flow of this commerce,[55] or discriminates against it locally,[56] it is invalid; where it seeks a reasonable, apportioned revenue from the proceeds of such commerce, it will be reviewed on the merits.[57]

1. *Gibbons v. Ogden,* 9 Wheat. 1 (1824).
2. *Wickard v. Filburn,* 317 U.S. 111 (1942).
3. *Cf.* Swindler, *The New Legality,* Chs. 7, 9.
4. *Cf. National Bellas Hess v. Dept. of Revenue,* 386 U.S. 753 (1967).
5. *Cf. McLeod v. Dilworth Co.,* 332 U.S. 324 (1944); *Parker v. Brown,* 317 U.S. 341 (1943).
6. *Munn v. Illinois,* 94 U.S. 113 (1877).
7. 24 Stat. 379; 26 Stat. 209.
8. 28 Stat. 553. The Court subsequently accepted the Congressional declaration of policy. *In re Rahrer,* 140 U.S. 545 (1891). *Cf.* also *Plumley v. Massachusetts,* 155 U.S. 461 (1894).
9. *Leisy v. Hardin,* 135 U.S. 100 (1890).
10. *United States v. E. C. Knight & Co.,* 156 U.S. 1 (1895).
11. *Allgeyer v. Louisiana,* 165 U.S. 578 (1897); *Smyth v. Ames,* 169 U.S. 466 (1898).
12. *Trans-Missouri Frt. Assn. v. United States,* 166 U.S. 290 (1897).
13. *Addyston Pipe & Steel Co. v. United States,* 175 U.S. 211 (1900).
14. *Houston & Texas R. Co. v. United States,* 234 U.S. 342 (1914). *Cf.* also *Swift & Co. v. United States,* 196 U.S. 375 (1905), where Justice Holmes first enunciated his "current of commerce" principle. *Cf. Armour Pkg. Co. v. United States,* 209 U.S. 56 (1908); *Standard Oil Co. v. United States,* 221 U.S. 1 (1910); *United States v. Am. Tobacco Co.,* 221 U.S. 106 (1910), illustrating Justice White's doctrine of the "rule of reason."
15. See the excellent review of this subject in Freund, "Umpiring the Federal System," 54 *Colum. L. Rev.* 561 (1954).
16. *Champion v. Ames,* 188 U.S. 321 (1903); Chief Justice Fuller's reasoned dissent is also notable; *id.,* at 364.
17. 34 Stat. 768.
18. The first Congressional act eliminating the common-law doctrine of contributory negligence in case of employee injuries on interstate railroads was held unconstitutional because the statute applied in some cases to intrastate lines. 207 U.S. 463 (1908). When Congress amended the law to meet this objection, the constitutionality of the basic legislative doctrine was then upheld. *Second Employers' Liability Case,* 223 U.S. 1 (1912).
19. *Cf. Champion v. Ames,* 188 U.S. 321 (1903): *Public Clearing House v. Coyne,* 194 U.S. 497 (1904).
20. *Lochner v. New York,* 198 U.S. 45 (1905), a state police power case invalidated under the contract clause; *Adair v. United States,* 208 U.S. 161 (1907), a Federal police power case seeking to eliminate "yellow dog" labor contracts from interstate commerce, held unconstitutional.
21. *Hammer v. Dagenhart,* 247 U.S. 251 (1918). An alternative Congressional effort to prohibit child labor through the tax clause was struck down in *Bailey v. Drexel Furn. Co.,* 259 U.S. 20 (1922).
22. *Adkins v. Children's Hosp.,* 261 U.S. 525 (1923).

106 · *Court and Constitution in the Twentieth Century*

23. *Cf. West Coast Hotel Co. v. Parrish,* 300 U.S. 379 (1937); *United States v. Darby,* 312 U.S. 100 (1941). *Cf.* also, on power to prohibit or regulate interstate shipment of convict-made goods, *Kentucky Whip & Collar Co. v. Ill. Cent. R. Co.,* 299 U.S. 334 (1937).
24. *Gooch v. United States,* 297 U.S. 124 (1934).
25. Anti-racketeering, civil rights and equal-opportunity legislation all have relied on this means of implementing the national police power. *Cf. Heart of Atlanta Motel Corp. v. United States,* 379 U.S. 241 (1964); 60 Stat. 420, 15 U.S.C. 17; 86 Stat. 382, 42 U.S.C. 2902.
26. *United States v. Sullivan,* 332 U.S. 689 (1948).
27. *United States v. Five Gambling Devices,* 346 U.S. 441 (1953); *cf.* also *Rewis v. United States,* 401 U.S. 808 (1971); *United States v. Bass,* 404 U.S. 336 (1971).
28. *Perez v. United States,* 402 U.S. 146, 150 (1971).
29. 79 Stat. 437.
30. *Heart of Atlanta Motel Corp. v. United States,* 379 U.S. 241 (1964); *Katzenbach v. McClung,* 379 U.S. 294 (1964): *Daniel v. Paul,* 395 U.S. 298 (1969).
31. *Phillips v. Martin Marietta Corp.,* 400 U.S. 542 (1971); *Griggs v. Duke Power Co.,* 401 U.S. 424 (1971); *Dewey v. Reynolds Metals Co.,* 402 U.S. 904 (1971).
32. *Bradley v. Pub Util. Comm.,* 289 U.S. 92 (1933).
33. *Buck v. Kuykendall,* 267 U.S. 307 (1925).
34. *South Carolina Hwy. Dept. v. Barnwell Bros.,* 303 U.S. 177 (1938); and *cf. Huron Portland Cement Co. v. Detroit,* 362 U.S. 440 (1960).
35. *Southern Pac. R. Co. v. Arizona,* 325 U.S. 761 (1945).
36. *Bibb v. Navajo Frt. Lines, Inc.,* 359 U.S. 520 (1959).
37. *Head v. Board of Examiners,* 374 U.S. 424 (1963).
38. *Bethlehem Steel Co. v. New York Board,* 330 U.S. 767 (1947).
39. *United Constr. Workers v. Laburnum Corp.,* 347 U.S. 656 (1954).
40. *Cloverleaf Butter Co. v. Patterson,* 315 U.S. 148 (1942).
41. *Cf. Prudential Ins. Co. v. Benjamin,* 328 U.S. 408 (1946), following Congressional restatement of policy in the McCarran Act, 59 Stat. 33, contradicting the Court's holding in *United States v. Southeastern Underwriters Assn.,* 322 U.S. 533 (1944).
42. *Kelly v. Washington,* 302 U.S. 1 (1937).
43. *Maurer v. Hamilton,* 309 U.S. 598 (1940); *Napier v. Atl. Coast R. Co.,* 272 U.S. 605 (1926); and *cf. Florida Lime & Avocado Growers v. Paul,* 373 U.S. 132 (1963).
44. *Cf. Castle v. Hayes Frt. Lines,* 348 U.S. 61 (1954); *California v. Zook,* 336 U.S. 725 (1949); *Railroad Trans. Service v. Chicago,* 386 U.S. 351 (1967).
45. *Cf. Perez v. Campbell,* 402 U.S. 637 (1971).
46. *Baldwin v. G.A.F. Seelig, Inc.,* 294 U.S. 511 (1935); *Dean Milk Co. v. Madison,* 340 U.S. 349 (1951); *Hood & Sons v. DuMond,* 336 U.S. 525 (1949).
47. *Breard v. Alexandria,* 341 U.S. 622 (1951).
48. *Milk Control Bd. v. Eisenberg,* 306 U.S. 346 (1939).
49. *Freeman v. Hewit,* 329 U.S. 249 (1946).
50. *Capitol Greyhound Lines v. Brice,* 339 U.S. 542 (1950); *Central Greyhound Lines v. Mealey,* 334 U.S. 653 (1948); *Joseph v. Carter & Weeks Stevedoring Co.,* 330 U.S. 442 (1947); *Spector Motor Co. v. O'Connor,* 340 U.S. 602 (1950). *Cf.* also *Norton & Co. v. Dept. of Revenue,* 340 U.S. 534 (1951); *Northwest States Portland Cement Co. v. Minnesota,* 358 U.S. 450 (1959); *General Motors Corp. v. Washington,* 377 U.S. 436 (1964).

51. *Cf. DiSanto v. Pennsylvania,* 273 U.S. 34 (1927); *South Carolina Hwy. Dept. v. Barnwell Bros.,* 303 U.S. 177 (1938); *Southern Pacific Ry. Co. v. Arizona,* 325 U.S. 761 (1945).
52. *Western Livestock v. Bureau of Revenue,* 303 U.S. 250 (1938); *Adams Mfg. Co. v. Storen,* 304 U.S. 307 (1938); *Gwinn, White & Prince v. Henneford,* 305 U.S. 434 (1939).
53. *McGoldrick v. Berwind-White Mining Co.,* 309 U.S. 33 (1940).
54. *Cf. Henneford v. Silas Mason Co.,* 300 U.S. 577 (1937); *Halliburton Oil Well Co. v. Reily,* 373 U.S. 64 (1963); *McLeod v. Dilworth Co.,* 332 U.S. 327 (1944); *National Bellas Hess v. Dept. of Revenue,* 386 U.S. 753 (1967).
55. *Cf. General Motors Corp. v. Washington,* 377 U.S. 436 (1964).
56. *Nat. Bellas Hess v. Dept. of Revenue,* 386 U.S. 735 (1967).
57. *Northwest States Portland Cement Co. v. Washington,* 358 U.S. 450 (1959); and *cf. Heublein, Inc. v. Tax Commission,* 409 U.S. 275 (1972).

I. 8. Cl. 4. Naturalization; Bankruptcy

[The Congress shall have power] to establish an uniform rule of naturalization, and uniform laws on the subject of bankruptcies throughout the United States.

Naturalization

The exclusive right of the Federal government to provide for "adopting a foreigner and clothing him with the privileges of a native citizen"[1] is one of the attributes of sovereignty.[2] The uniform rule required by the Constitution does not deny Congress the power to define by statute the classes of aliens eligible for citizenship and the conditions for qualification.[3] Conversely, certain aliens may be excluded or disqualified by Congress,[4] their terms of entry and residence regulated,[5] and undesired individuals deported.[6]

Expatriation—voluntary renunciation of citizenship on the part of the individual—or loss of citizenship by operation of law are two subjects obviously related to naturalization. Marriage to an alien, until well into the twentieth century, could divest an American woman of her native citizenship.[7] A number of other activities were listed in a series of statutes as effecting loss of citizenship.[8] But it was in the Nationality Act of 1960[9]—itself a post-World War II revision of the Immigration and Nationality Act of 1952 and the Nationality Act of 1940[10]—that various constitutional conflicts presented themselves. In *Perez v. Brownell,*[11] a divided Court upheld a provision of the 1940 law denationalizing one who voted in the elections of a foreign country. *Perez* was overruled in 1967,[12] both on the basis of the statutory revision of 1960 and the prevailing of the prior minority view that where the foreign law permitted voting by non-citizens, the United States had to prove intention in the voter to relinquish citizenship. Three years earlier the Court had narrowly construed the power of Congress to rescind naturalization where the individual had failed to take up residence in American territory within a specified period.[13]

Service in a foreign army, particularly in time of hostilities between the United States and the other military power, effects loss of citizenship if the service is not coerced.[14] Deportation of an alien, the Court held with exceedingly strained reasoning, justifies Congress in expropriating his retirement benefits earned under Social Security.[15] Draft evasion, as a ground for loss of citizenship, was held to be unconstitutional where the statute fails to provide for Fifth and Sixth Amendment safeguards of due process.[16]

Bankruptcy

Bill of Rights safeguards have similarly been applied to the bankruptcy laws, as Congress has undertaken to broaden the law to protect debtors as well as creditors.[17] Part of the crisis of the early New Deal revolved about debtor relief laws attempted by Congress, where the Court narrowly circumscribed the government's power in the matter of easing bankruptcy proceedings for municipal corporations.[18] But even the *laissez-faire* Court found validity in Congressional efforts to help insolvent individuals and corporations seeking to effect composition and extension of their debts in order to avert formal bankruptcy.[19]

Congress exercised its power under this clause only sporadically until the first general statute in 1898. State insolvency statutes, which occupied the field in periods of Federal inactivity, have been held to be suspended whenever Congress elects to move into the field.[20] In certain circumstances, state law may be held to be compatible with and complementary to Federal law.[21]

1. *Boyd v. Thayer*, 143 U.S. 135, 162 (1892).
2. *Mackenzie v. Hare*, 239 U.S. 299 (1915).
3. *Cf. Boyd v. Nebraska*, 143 U.S. 168 (1892).

4. *Cf. Hines v. Davidowitz,* 312 U.S. 52 (1941); *Knauff v. Shaughnessy,* 338 U.S. 537 (1950).
5. *Keller v. United States,* 213 U.S. 138 (1909).
6. *Cf. Carlson v. Landon,* 342 U.S. 524 (1952); *Harisiades v. Shaughnessy,* 342 U.S. 580 (1952); *United States v. Spector,* 343 U.S. 169 (1952).
7. *Cf.* 34 Stat. 1228 (Citizenship Act of 1908).
8. *Cf. Trop v. Dulles,* 356 U.S. 86 (1958); *Kennedy v. Mendoza-Martinez,* 372 U.S. 144 (1963).
9. 74 Stat. 505, 8 U.S.C. 1182.
10. 76 Stat. 123, 1247, 8 U.S.C. 1104, 1154; 54 Stat. 1137, 8 U.S.C. 1101.
11. 356 U.S. 44 (1958).
12. *Afroyim v. Rusk,* 387 U.S. 253 (1967).
13. *Schneider v. Rusk,* 377 U.S. 163 (1964); but *cf. Rogers v. Bellei,* 401 U.S. 815 (1971).
14. *Nishikawa v. Dulles,* 356 U.S. 129 (1958); on desertion and citizenship, *cf. Trop v. Dulles,* 356 U.S. 86 (1958).
15. *Flemming v. Nestor,* 363 U.S. 603 (1960).
16. *Kennedy v. Mendoza-Martinez,* 372 U.S. 144 (1963).
17. *Louisville Bank v. Radford,* 295 U.S. 555 (1935), invalidating a Congressional act which failed to preserve creditors' security under a mortgage moratorium. A revised act was upheld in *Wright v. Vinton Branch,* 300 U.S. 440 (1937).
18. *Ashton v. Cameron County District,* 298 U.S. 513 (1936); *cf. Bekins v. United States,* 304 U.S. 27 (1938).
19. *Cf. Continental Bank v. Rock Island R. Co.,* 294 U.S. 648 (1935); and *Wright v. Union Central Ins. Co.,* 304 U.S. 502 (1938).
20. *Butler v. Goreley,* 146 U.S. 303 (1892); *Int. Shoe Co. v. Pinkus,* 278 U.S. 261 (1929).
21. *Cf. Kalb v. Fauerstein,* 308 U.S. 433 (1940); *Kesler v. Dept. Pub. Safety,* 369 U.S. 153 (1962); *New York v. Irving Trust Co.,* 288 U.S. 329 (1933).

I. 8. Cl. 5. Money

[The Congress shall have power] to coin money, regulate the value thereof, and of foreign coin, and fix the standard of weights and measures.

I. 8. Cl. 6. Counterfeiting

[The Congress shall have power] to provide for the punishment of counterfeiting the securities and current coin of the United States.

The first major crisis of the New Deal developed under the coinage clause, when the 1933 emergency in money and public credit caused the new Roosevelt administration to suspend gold payments. The Court upheld the authority of the government to abrogate gold clauses in private contracts,[1] as well as in Treasury notes,[2] but denied the right of Congress to repudiate a pledge of the United States to pay in gold for Liberty Bonds issued on the national credit.[3] (However, Chief Justice Hughes thereafter denied recovery to the bondholders since the increase in value of money borrowed from the bondholder amounted to unjust enrichment against the national interest.)[4]

Congress's exclusive authority over money enables it to restrain chartered banks from issuing circulating notes in their own names,[5] and it may impose a prohibitive tax to drive such currency out of circulation.[6] Under the companion clause, Congress may punish counterfeiting and forbid the simulation of coins or currency.[7] The Federal authority overrides state authority in matters of rights attaching to Federal bonds—e.g., rights of survivorship in bonds jointly held by husband and wife.[8]

1. *Norman v. B. & O. R. Co.*, 294 U.S. 240 (1935).
2. *Nortz v. United States*, 294 U.S. 317 (1935).
3. *Perry v. United States*, 294 U.S. 330 (1935).
4. *Id.* at 356. The power of Congress to substitute other obligations as legal tender was settled after a "Court packing," in the post-Civil War Legal Tender Cases. *Cf. Hepburn v. Griswold*, 8 Wall. 603 (1870); *Knox v. Lee*, 12 Wall. 457 (1871).
5. *Veazie Bank v. Fenno*, 8 Wall. 533 (1869).
6. *National Bank v. United States*, 101 U.S. 1 (1880).
7. *Baender v. Barnett*, 255 U.S. 224 (1921).
8. *Free v. Bland*, 369 U.S. 663 (1962).

I. 8. Cl. 7. The Postal Power

[The Congress shall have power] to establish post-offices and post-roads.

The right of Congress to control the use of the mails in the public interest was first asserted in 1872 in a statute prohibiting the use of the mails for purposes of fraud or corruption of morals.[1] In an age when the latter phrase, at least, did not appear to require definition, the power was upheld.[2] In the labor struggles of the end of the nineteenth century, interference with the mails was one of the charges used to break strikes in railroad disputes.[3] In 1913 the power was sustained in a postal regulation requiring information on ownership, circulation and advertising data from publications seeking second-class-mail privileges.[4]

Denial of postal privileges to seditious publications, although severely criticized as an easy step to bureaucratic censorship, was sustained after World War I.[5] But in 1946 the Court rejected as too vague a regulation which barred the mails to publications of "poor taste" and "vulgarity."[6] After World War II this same condemnation of vagueness struck down a postal barrier to "foreign Communist propaganda."[7] Aside from the lack of definable standards for terms such as "obscenity," the Court has insisted on due-process safeguards in any general policy of limiting access to the mails.[8] But where an addressee requests that no further material be sent to him unsolicited, because of its "pandering" nature, the Post Office has been held to have the power to prevent the particular mailing.[9]

A general power in Congress to deny mail privileges as a means of enforcing a valid law was upheld in 1938, where a section of the Public Utility Holding Company Act of 1935[10] forbade use of the mails for any purpose by holding companies which failed to comply with the registration provisions of the act.[11]

1. 17 Stat. 300. *Cf.* also *Public Clearing House v. Coyne*, 194 U.S. 497 (1903).
2. *Ex parte Jackson*, 96 U.S. 727 (1878); and *cf. Public Clearing House v. Coyne*, 194 U.S. 497 (1904).
3. *In re Debs*, 158 U.S. 564 (1895).
4. *Lewis Pub. Co. v. Morgan*, 229 U.S. 288 (1913).
5. *Cf. Milwaukee Pub. Co. v. Burleson*, 255 U.S. 407 (1921).
6. *Hannegan v. Esquire*, 327 U.S. 146 (1946).
7. *Lamont v. Postmaster General*, 381 U.S. 301 (1965).
8. *Blount v. Rizzi*, 400 U.S. 410 (1971).
9. *Rowan v. Post Office*, 397 U.S. 728 (1970).
10. 49 Stat. 803.
11. *Electric Bond & Share Co. v. S.E.C.*, 303 U.S. 419 (1938).

I. 8. Cl. 8. *Copyrights and Patents*

[The Congress shall have power] to promote the progress of science and useful arts by securing for limited times to authors and inventors the exclusive right to their respective writings and discoveries.

The chief difference between Anglo-American copyright and patent theory and that of virtually all of the rest of the world is its policy against a monopoly in perpetuity. Even English law, in the early modern period, vested in the Crown, or the Crown in Parliament, a power to create monopolistic privileges for lengthy terms. The "limited times" stipulated by the present clause have been variously defined by statutes, and courts have stressed the related condition that the protection provided by Congress is "to promote the progress of science and useful arts."[1] The same policy against undue exclusion of users of knowledge has been expressed in the general principle that the "discovery" of a law of nature is not patentable, but only the application of the law "to a new and useful end."[2]

The public benefit, rather than the private gain from the monopoly, is the primary justification for the clause;[3] and accordingly Congress may attach various conditions to its grant.[4] By this same reasoning, the scope of copyright protection has been explicitly if not narrowly defined: Such rights as the government elects to enforce are defined by law and subject to Congressional revision.[5] They are for a term of years, renewable for one additional term and thereafter the matter is released into the public domain.

Coypright as a restraint on press freedom was one of the incidental issues in the struggle for the public right of unrestricted communication of ideas in English law; and in American law as well as English the doctrine early developed that news media could not, as such, claim copyright privileges.[6] In a general revision of the copyright statutes in 1909, protection was extended to those parts of periodical publications which were clearly literary creations;[7] and a Federal court subsequently held that where copyright was claimed in an exclusive news story, evidence of copying the facts (presumably non-copyrightable) "in the very garb wherein the author clothed them" was "an unauthorized appropriation" of literary property.[8] In such cases, the public policy of protecting the literary property outweigh any technical delay in securing copyright where evidence reasonably tends to establish an intention to avail the author of the protection.[9]

The commerce clause, and the law of unfair competition based thereon, have afforded news communications certain relief from wrongful appropriation of non-copyrightable matter which nevertheless is marketable in terms of the individual effort made to gather the facts.[10] The same clause has been the vehicle for effecting a degree of trade-mark protection, since the famous *Trade*

Mark Cases of 1879[11] in which the court denied a power to protect such commercial devices under the copyright and patent clause. Since such trade marks have "no necessary relation to invention or discovery," said Justice Miller, and in his view did not depend on "novelty, invention, discovery, or any work of the brain,"[12] this clause in itself could not offer direct protection.

1. *Seymour v. Osborne,* 11 Wall. 516 (1871).
2. *Funk Bros. Seed Co. v. Kalo Co.,* 333 U.S. 127 (1948); *Sinclair Co. v. Inter-Chemical Corp.,* 325 U.S. 327 (1945). The Court has tended to rely on rather subjective criteria in speaking of "inventive" or "intuitive" genius in striving for a test of patentability. *Cf. Mantle Lamp Co. v. Aluminum Co.,* 301 U.S. 544 (1937); *Potts v. Creager,* 155 U.S. 975 (1895).
3. *Cf.,* generally, *Mazer v. Stein,* 347 U.S. 201 (1954).
4. *Mercoid Corp. v. Mid-Continent Inv. Co.,* 320 U.S. 661 (1944); *Special Equipment Co. v. Coe,* 324 U.S. 370 (1945).
5. *Holmes v. Hurst,* 174 U.S. 85 (1899). The public is always one of the parties in interest in a patent or copyright. *Butterworth v. United States,* 112 U.S. 50 (1884).
6. *Cf. Tribune Co. v. Associated Press,* 116 F. 126 (1900); the classic case in American law is *Clayton v. Stone,* 2 Paine 382, Fed. Cas. No. 2872 (1835).
7. 33 Stat. 4.
8. *Chicago Record-Herald Co. v. Tribune Assn.,* 275 F. 797 (1921).
9. *Washingtonian Co. v. Pearson,* 306 U.S. 30 (1939); *cf.* also *Nat. Comics Pubs. v. Fawcett Pubs.,* 191 F. 2d 594 (1951).
10. *Int. News Service v. Associated Press,* 248 U.S. 215 (1918); *cf.* also *Public Ledger v. New York Times,* 275 F. 2d 562 (1922), cert. den. 258 U.S. 627 (1922); *Associated Press v. KVOS, Inc.,* 80 F. 2d 575 (1935).
11. 100 U.S. 82 (1879).
12. *Id.,* at 94.

I. 8. Cl. 9. Establishment of Courts

[The Congress shall have power] to constitute tribunals inferior to the Supreme Court.

I. 8. Cl. 10. International Law

[The Congress shall have power] to define and punish piracies and felonies committed on the high seas and offenses against the law of nations.

These clauses looked respectively to the internal judicial functioning and the international legal responsibilities of the Federal government. Clause 9 logically relates to the provision in

Article III for "such inferior courts as the Congress may from time to time ordain and establish" and is discussed thereunder. As for Clause 10, and particularly its reference to "offenses against the law of nations," the incorporation of international law—at least as a frame of reference and as understood at the time of the adoption of the Constitution—into the rules of decision of the courts was established.[1] The specific authority vested by this clause is limited to international criminal cases, but the treaty power (*cf.* Article IV, Clause 2) and the general attributes of sovereignty complement the authority of the United States to discharge other duties laid on independent nations by international law.

The fundamental power vested in this clause was recognized in 1942 in a judicial denial of *habeas corpus* for accused Nazi saboteurs who had been landed on the Atlantic coast during World War II. Congress, said the Court, having constitutional responsibility for defining and punishing crimes against the law of nations, and particularly the law of war, could limit the trials of persons under this clause to military courts.[2] The responsibility of the United States to punish a crime against another nation with which it is at peace, especially where the act is recognized domestically as a crime (e.g., counterfeiting), has been affirmed.[3]

1. *Cf.* Chancellor James Kent's statement: "When the United States ceased to be a part of the British Empire, and assumed the character of an independent nation, they became subject to that system of rules which reason, morality and custom had established among civilized nations of Europe, as their public law." *Commentaries* (12th ed., 1873), 1, 2. *Cf.* also Moore, *Digest of International Law*, I, 4.
2. *Ex parte Quirin*, 317 U.S. 1, 28 (1942). On the role of the United States in the international war crimes trials after World War II, *cf. In re Yamashita*, 327 U.S. 1, 12, 23 (1946).
3. *United States v. Flores*, 289 U.S. 137 (1933).

I. 8. Cl. 11ff. War Powers Generally

[The Congress shall have power] to declare war, grant letters of marque and reprisal, and make rules concerning captures on land and water; [*Cl. 12*] to raise and support armies, but no appropriation of money to that use shall be for a longer term than two years; [*Cl. 13*] to provide and maintain a navy; [*Cl. 14*] to make rules for the government and regulation of the land and naval forces; [*Cl. 15*] to provide for calling forth the militia to execute the laws of the Union, suppress insurrections, and repel invasions; [*Cl. 16*] to provide for organizing, arming and disciplining the militia, and for governing such part of them as may be employed in the service of the United States, reserving to the states respectively the appointment of the officers, and the authority of training the militia according to the discipline prescribed by Congress.

The war powers of Congress, another attribute of sovereignty and thus definable by international law as well as by the detailed provisions of these clauses, have been broadened, since World War II, by judicial decision. Their general definition in a twentieth-century context dates from World War I, where the Court affirmed the power of military conscription,[1] balanced the national defense interests against Bill of Rights guarantees[2] and concluded that the war powers were as broad as the demands of national security required.[3] In World War II the specific complementary application of the war powers was further delineated to include authority to renegotiate wartime contracts to control profiteering at public expense,[4] to permit rent controls to be continued after cessation of actual hostilities,[5] to uphold price controls under the same reasoning[6] and to enforce housing and rent controls during the war itself.[7]

The most controversial issues concerned a curfew on Japanese-Americans in the West[8] and the relocating of Japanese-Americans from critical defense areas of the West Coast,[9] with the government actions being upheld against charges that they were based on invidious racial discriminations. The power to seize enemy property in the United States has been generally affirmed,[10] as well as the power to requisition property owned by American nationals provided that just compensation, as required by the Fifth Amendment, is assured.[11] In the twentieth century, as suggested in the preceding paragraph, the continuing application of war powers in peacetime has been confirmed (some would say rationalized), particularly where peacetime benefits and the potential need for preparedness in event of war can be discerned. Thus, in *Ashwander v. T.V.A.*,[12] the Court declared the continuing force of the National Defense Act of 1916[13] as a proper basis for government development of the Authority. The Atomic Energy Act of 1946,[14] providing for development of a broad program of nuclear power under stringent controls over dissemination of technical information on the subject, has not been challenged.

1. *Selective Draft Cases* (esp. *Arver v. United States*), 245 U.S. 366 (1918); *Goldman v. United States*, 245 U.S. 474 (1918).
2. *Cf. Schenck v. United States*, 249 U.S. 47 (1919).
3. *Northern Pac. R. Co. v. North Dakota*, 250 U.S. 135 (1919). A general wartime prohibition law was also upheld under this power. *Hamilton v. Kentucky Distillers*, 251 U.S. 146 (1920).
4. *Lichter v. United States*, 334 U.S. 742 (1948).
5. *Woods v. Miller Co.*, 333 U.S. 138 (1948); *cf. Block v. Hirsch*, 256 U.S. 135 (1921).
6. *Yakus v. United States*, 321 U.S. 414 (1944).
7. *Bowles v. Willingham*, 321 U.S. 503 (1944).
8. *Hirabayashi v. United States*, 320 U.S. 81 (1943).
9. *Korematsu v. United States*, 323 U.S. 214 (1944).
10. *Stoehr v. Wallace*, 255 U.S. 239 (1921); *United States v. Chemical Foundation*, 272 U.S. 1 (1926); *Silesian-American Corp. v. Clark*, 332 U.S. 469 (1947).
11. *United States v. Commodities Corp.*, 339 U.S. 131 (1950); *United States v. Cors*, 337 U.S. 325 (1949). But this limitation does not apply to property destroyed to keep it out of enemy hands. *United States v. Caltex, Inc.*, 344 U.S. 149 (1952).
12. 297 U.S. 288 (1936).
13. 39 Stat. 166.
14. 60 Stat. 755.

I. 8. Cl. 17. Federal District

[The Congress shall have power] to exercise exclusive legislation in all cases whatsoever over such district (not exceeding ten miles square) as may, by cession of particular states and the acceptance of Congress, become the seat of the government of the United States, and to exercise like authority over all places purchased by the consent of the legislature of the state in which the same shall be, for the erection of forts, magazines, arsenals, dockyards, and other needful buildings. . . .

The status of the District of Columbia has varied over the years. Land was originally ceded by both Maryland and Virginia, but in 1846 Congress provided for retrocession of Alexandria County to Virginia, and in 1871 the present form of government, with subsequent amendments, was established.[1] The ultimate legislative authority resides in Congress,[2] although Congress is empowered to create a local government equivalent to a municipal corporation,[3] and it may also vest jurisdiction in the United States

District Court in matters of diversity of citizenship, as if District residents were residents of a state.[4] Taxes may be levied by Congress as the local government authority.[5] The long-disputed home-rule issue is constitutionally feasible as for any territory of the United States,[6] but the greatest concession to date is the Twenty-third Amendment, permitting the District three electoral votes in Presidential elections.

Other Federal property has presented problems unanticipated in the early years of the republic, as "enclaves" of Federally controlled land have "impacted" state areas and services, most particularly public schools which have been required to serve children of non-taxpaying Federal employees on Federal property. While Congress has been disposed to grant subventions to the states in such hardship cases, other problems have remained. It was long held that, unless a state retained jurisdiction for specific purposes in ceding certain lands to the United States, its laws were without force in the Federally acquired areas.[7] In the matter of state criminal law, Congress sought to solve the problem by incorporating the law in the Federal Assimilative Crimes Act of 1948.[8] As for state civil law, the courts have tentatively suggested that since a Federal military reservation remains a geographic part of the original area subject to the jurisdiction of local government,[9] laws in effect at the time of Federal acquisition may continue in effect where not in conflict with Federal policy,[10] assuming the now general practice of conditionally retained jurisdiction in such cessions.

---

1. *Cf.* 16 Stat. 419.
2. *Cf. O'Donaghue v. United States*, 289 U.S. 516 (1933).
3. *District of Columbia v. Bailey*, 171 U.S. 161 (1898).
4. *Nat. Ins. Co. v. Tidewater Co.*, 337 U.S. 582 (1949).
5. *Heald v. District of Columbia*, 259 U.S. 114 (1922).
6. *District of Columbia v. Thompson*, 364 U.S. 100 (1953).
7. *Pac. Coast Dairy v. Dept. of Agriculture*, 318 U.S. 285 (1943); *Stewart & Co. v. Sadrakula*, 309 U.S. 94 (1940); *cf.* also *Palmer v. Barrett*, 162 U.S. 399 (1896).
8. 62 Stat. 686, 18 U.S.C. 13; affirmed in *United States v. Sharpnack*, 355 U.S. 286 (1958). For the law prior to this statute, *cf. James v. Dravo Contracting Co.*, 302 U.S. 134 (1937) and *Bowen v. Johnson*, 306 U.S. 19 (1939).
9. *First Hardin Nat. Bank v. Ft. Knox Nat. Bank*, 361 F. 2d 276 (1966), cert. den. 385 U.S. 959 (1966).
10. *Paul v. United States*, 371 U.S. 245 (1963).

I. 8. Cl. 18. "Necessary and Proper" Laws

[The Congress shall have power] to make all laws which shall be necessary and proper for carrying into execution the foregoing powers, and all other powers vested by this Constitution in the government of the United States, or in any department or officer thereof.

This so-called coefficient, or "necessary and proper" clause, has been the subject of continuing debate between strict and broad constructionists ever since Chief Justice Marshall declared: "Let the end be legitimate; let it be within the scope of the Constitution, and all means which are appropriate, which are plainly adapted to that end, which are not prohibited, but consist with the letter and spirit of the Constitution, are constitutional."[1] The philosophical or semantic issue arises from the phrase "all other powers vested by this Constitution"; does this mean specifically or explicitly vested—even though the clause does not contain either qualifying adverb—or does it mean that since, as Marshall said in another context, the powers of a sovereign national government are more than the sum of its parts, the powers normally vested in sovereignty are included in the clause?[2]

The intention of the Founding Fathers to create such a sovereignty is manifest in the structure of the government established by the Constitution in contrast to the government established by the Articles of Confederation. While the Constitutional Convention intended also to create a government of limited powers, the powers which were granted were plenary except where the text provided a limitation on a specific grant. But "all other powers" have been defined by the courts over the ensuing years as including those which are implied or inferred by reason of the Federal government's being sovereign in its sphere. Thus, while not explicitly stated, the government has been found to have the inherent power to create criminal liability by statute.[3] Federal incorporation of banks (and later other agencies) was judicially inferred from "the great powers, to lay and collect taxes; to borrow money;" etc.[4]—and with this went the power to provide for the effective administration of these corporations.[5] The sweeping extension of the charter power was confirmed even by the *laissez-faire* Court as not being necessarily dependent on other powers.[6]

Although there is no specific authorization in the Constitution for Congress to regulate foreign affairs, whatever is necessary for the government's effective participation in the society of nations is to be inferred from the nature of the government created by the Constitution.[7] Whether other responsibilities devolving on the United States as a member of the society of nations may require "necessary and proper" legislation has been periodically debated. Justice Holmes in 1920 read the treaty power in Article VI to distinguish between domestic acts of Congress, which "are the supreme law of the land only when made in pursuance of the Constitution," and international treaty obligations which need only be "made under the authority of the United States."[8]

Concern in some quarters, appearing at times to approach paranoia, that by international agreement the United States might foist on the domestic institutions created by the Constitution some alien ideas or obligations, led to the proposal of an amendment that would have specifically nullified any treaty provision conflicting with the Constitution. This proposal, sponsored by Senator John W. Bricker of Ohio, never mustered a majority in either house of Congress, but it reflected the chronic suspicion that, absent such a provision, the treaty power might prove to be an independent source of national authority of sinister proportions.[9]

1. *McCulloch v. Maryland,* 4 Wheat. 316, 420 (1819).
2. *Cf. Legal Tender Case,* 110 U.S. 440 (1884).
3. *United States v. Worrall,* 2 Dall. 384, 394 (1798); *Greenwood v. United States,* 350 U.S. 366 (1956).
4. *McCulloch v. Maryland,* 4 Wheat. 316, 407 (1819); and *cf. Franklin Nat. Bank v. People,* 347 U.S. 373 (1954).
5. *Pittman v. H.O.L.C.,* 308 U.S. 21 (1939); *First Nat. Bank v. Union Trust Co.,* 244 U.S. 416 (1917).
6. *Luxton v. North River Bridge Co.,* 153 U.S. 525 (1894); *Clallom County v. United States,* 263 U.S. 341 (1923).
7. *Perez v. Brownell,* 356 U.S. 44 (1958); overruled on other grounds in *Afroyim v. Rusk,* 387 U.S. 253 (1967). *Cf.* also *United States v. Curtiss-Wright Export Corp.,* 299 U.S. 304 (1936).
8. *Missouri v. Holland,* 252 U.S. 416, 432 (1920).
9. *Cf.* Sen. Rep. No. 412, 83 Cong., 1st Sess.

I. *9. Powers Expressly Denied Congress*

I. *9. Cl. 1. Slave Trade*

[The migration or importation of such persons as any of the states now existing shall think proper to admit, shall not be prohibited by the Congress prior to the year one thousand eight hundred and eight, but a tax or duty may be imposed on such importation, not exceeding ten dollars for each person.]

I. 9. Cl. 2. Habeas Corpus

The privilege of the writ of habeas corpus shall not be suspended, unless when in cases of rebellion or invasion that public safety may require it.

By the "great writ," at least from as early as the Parliamentary Act of 1679, anyone placed under restraint may secure prompt judicial inquiry into the proper cause of his detention and his release in cases of insufficient cause. Although President Lincoln's notable suspension of the writ in critical areas at the outset of the Civil War was condemned by Chief Justice Taney,[1] on the ground that the suspension proviso fell in the legislative and not in the executive article, Congress subsequently authorized the executive action.[2] The Court then severely limited its effect in principle in *Ex parte Milligan*.[3] Except for the extraordinary circumstances of the Civil War, the *habeas corpus* power has been affirmatively rather than negatively asserted.

Since 1858 the Court has held that a state *habeas corpus* writ cannot run in a Federal jurisdiction.[4] The opposite has not been true, particularly since the 1963 case of *Fay v. Noia*,[5] which marked the climax in a steady judicial campaign against state procedural rules which allegedly compromised certain rights of defendants to post-conviction review.[6] Even before the emergence of this issue, a Federal right of intervention or removal was applied to state courts where Federal questions were being adjudicated. While the *habeas corpus* issue is more properly discussed under Article III, it warrants noting here at least briefly because of its inherent character as a Federal power; even though referred to in a negative section, the ultimate thrust of the words is that it is one of the attributes of sovereignty taken for granted by the drafters of the Constitution.

1. *Ex parte Merryman*, 17 Fed. Cas. 144 (1861).
2. 12 Stat. 755.
3. 4 Wall. 2 (1866).

4. *Ableman v. Booth*, 21 How. 306 (1868); *cf. Cleflin v. Houseman*, 93 U.S. 130 (1876).
5. 372 U.S. 391 (1963).
6. *Cf.* research report published as "State Post-Conviction Remedies and Federal Habeas Corpus," 12 *Wm. & M. L. Rev.* 147 (1970).

9. Cl. 3. Bills of Attainder; Ex Post Facto Laws

No bill of attainder or ex post facto law shall be passed.

Bills of Attainder

The ancient common-law process of legislative proscription, prohibited by this clause, has had renewed potential in recent years.[1] A post-Civil War statute disbarring attorneys who had aided the Confederacy was invalidated under this clause in 1867,[2] and an appropriation bill denying compensation to government employees charged with subversive activity was similarly invalidated in 1946.[3] Where individuals or groups are singled out for legislative accusation, without due-process safeguards, the prohibition of this clause applies; if there is a provision for exculpation, the clause does not apply.[4] On this balancing test, the Court undertook to define the constitutional limits and guidelines for the loyalty-security issues of the 1950s.[5]

Ex Post Facto Laws

An *ex post facto law* is one which imposes a punishment for an act which was not punishable at the time it was committed, or enlarges on the punishment after the act was committed, said the Court in 1878.[6] Statutes which are retroactive in this sense are invalid under this clause,[7] for defendants must have means of knowing (whether they actually know or not, as a practical matter) the standard of criminal liability prior to their action.[8] Although the clause was cited in a challenge of the validity of war-crimes liability after World War II, the argument was rejected.[9] While the Court has consistently limited the clause to criminal cases, it has applied rather strained reasoning to sustain deportation proceedings for acts made criminal after the fact, on the ground that deportation is not a punishment.[10]

1. *Cf. United States v. Brown,* 381 U.S. 437 (1965).
2. *Ex parte Garland,* 4 Wall. 333 (1867).
3. *United States v. Lovett,* 328 U.S. 303 (1946).
4. *Cf. Communist Party v. Subversive Activities Control Board,* 367 U.S. 1 (1961).
5. *United States v. Brown,* 381 U.S. 437 (1965).
6. *Burgess v. Salmon,* 97 U.S. 381 (1878); *cf. Thompson v. Utah,* 170 U.S. 343 (1898).
7. *Watkins v. United States,* 354 U.S. 178 (1957). Where a law defining liability, which would have expired on a certain date, is continued without interruption, the clause does not apply. *United States v. Powers,* 307 U.S. 214 (1939).
8. *Watkins v. United States,* 354 U.S. 178 (1957).
9. *In re Yamashita,* 327 U.S. 1, 26 (1946).
10. *Cf. Hines v. Davidowitz,* 312 U.S. 52 (1941); and *cf. Flemming v. Nestor,* 363 U.S. 603 (1960), excusing the denial of earned Social Security benefits to deported alien on the ground that it is administratively inconvenient to dispense payments to beneficiaries living abroad.

I. 9. Cl. 4. Direct Taxes

No capitation, or other direct, tax shall be laid, unless in proportion to the census of enumeration herein before directed to be taken.

The definition of direct taxes was first given in 1796, when it was limited to taxes on land, or any tax which could conveniently be apportioned.[1] Capitation taxes (i.e., per head) and any "other direct tax" were thus limited to a small number of revenue measures, which limited correspondingly the qualifications which this clause put on the tax clause in Section 8. Attempts made during the Civil War to challenge various new taxes under this clause—including a tax on incomes—were unsuccessful.[2] It was thus a reversal of a century of construction when the Court in 1895, in a 5–4 holding, declared that a Federal income tax was a direct tax and thus unconstitutional where not apportioned.[3] The decision, coming as part of a sequence of cases drastically limiting the powers of government in areas of free private enterprise, provoked a public outcry at the Court's role as apologist for *laissez-faire.*[4]

As in the case of its extremely narrow construction of the commerce clause in this period, the Court soon began a retreat from the income-tax case. In 1899 it was prepared to distinguish taxes laid on income from business sales as a form of "excise" rather than a direct tax.[5] In similar fashion it distinguished a succession tax,[6] a tax on processed tobacco after a manufacturer's excise tax had been paid,[7] and similar levies which might well have fallen into the *Pollock* definition of direct taxes.[8] The trend suggested to some leaders of the bar that the Court might ultimately overrule *Pollock,* but the submission of the Sixteenth Amendment to the people, and its subsequent ratification, settled the matter.[9] Adoption of the Amendment, in fact, encouraged the Court to abandon some of the fine distinctions it had made in the course of its retreat from *Pollock* and gradually restored the pre-*Pollock* concept of direct taxes as taxes on land.[10]

1. *Hylton v. United States,* 3 Dall. 171 (1796).
2. *Pacific Ins. Co. v. Soule,* 7 Wall. 433 (1869), tax on insurance premiums and assessments; *Veazie Bank v. Fenno,* 8 Wall. 533 (1869), tax on state bank notes; *Scholey v. Rew,* 23 Wall. 331 (1874), inheritance tax on land; *Springer v. United States,* 102 U.S. 586 (1881), income tax.
3. *Pollock v. Farmers' Loan & Trust Co.,* 157 U.S. 429; 158 U.S. 601 (1895).
4. *Cf.* Swindler, *The Old Legality,* Ch. 1.
5. *Nicol v. Ames,* 173 U.S. 507 (1899).
6. *Knowlton v. Moore,* 178 U.S. 41 (1900).
7. *Patton v. Brady,* 184 U.S. 608 (1902).
8. *Cf. Thomas v. United States,* 192 U.S. 363 (1904); *Spreckels Sugar Ref. Co. v. McClain,* 192 U.S. 397 (1904); *Flint v. Stone Tracy Co.,* 220 U.S. 107 (1911).
9. *Cf.* Swindler, *The Old Legality,* Ch. 8.
10. *Cf. New York Trust Co. v. Eisner,* 256 U.S. 345 (1921); *Chase Nat. Bank v. United States,* 278 U.S. 327 (1929); *Phillips v. Dime Trust Co.,* 284 U.S. 160 (1931); *Tyler v. United States,* 281 U.S. 497 (1930).

I. 9. Cl. 5. Export Taxes

No tax or duty shall be laid on articles exported from any state.

This clause has been construed to deny Congress the power to lay taxes on goods shipped abroad from any state.[1] Its purpose was to restrain Congress from favoring one port over another.[2] The correct construction of the clause, said the Court in 1904, is that no burden may be put on the exportation process but not that exported articles are immune from taxes laid equally on all similar articles while similarly situated within the state.[3] Goods do not cease to be part of the taxable property within the state until actually in readiness for shipment,[4] and a tax on the income from export sales is valid under this clause.[5]

1. *Turpin v. Buress,* 117 U.S. 504 (1886); *Dooley v. United States,* 183 U.S. 151 (1901).
2. *Williams v. Fears,* 179 U.S. 270 (1900).

3. *Cornell v. Coyne,* 192 U.S. 419 (1904). *Cf.* also *Liggett & Myers Tob. Co. v. United States,* 77 P. 2d 65 (1935), cert. den. 296 U.S. 580 (1936).
4. *Empresa Sig. S.A. v. Merced Co.,* 337 U.S. 154 (1949); *cf.* also *Spaulding v. Edwards,* 262 U.S. 66 (1923).
5. *Peck v. Lowe,* 247 U.S. 165 (1918).

I. 9. Cl. 6. Port Discrimination

No preference shall be given by any regulation of commerce or revenue to the ports of one state over those of another; nor shall vessels bound to, or from, one state, be obliged to enter, clear or pay duties in another.

This clause obviously complements the preceding clause and further emphasizes the concern of the Constitutional Convention that some of the problems of "balkanization" under the Articles of Confederation be solved by this declaration against discrimination. However, the clause is not to be narrowly construed as preventing Congress from developing the natural advantages of one port to the incidental disadvantage of another.[1] Rate differentials fixed by the Interstate Commerce Commission and based on "merely geographical" differences in ports have been upheld.[2] And Congress may leave to the several states the responsibility for regulating pilotage within ports under their jurisdiction, without being held to discriminate against other ports.[3]

1. *Commission v. Texas & New Orleans R. Co.,* 284 U.S. 125 (1931).
2. *Alabama Great Southern R. Co. v. United States,* 340 U.S. 216 (1951); *cf. Armour Pkg. Co. v. United States,* 153 F. 1 (1907), aff'd. 209 U.S. 56 (1907).
3. *Cooley v. Board of Wardens,* 53 U.S. 299 (1851); *cf. Thompson v. Darden,* 198 U.S. 315 (1905).

I. 9. Cl. 7. Public Appropriations

No money shall be drawn from the Treasury, but in consequence of appropriations made by law; and a regular statement and account of the receipts and expenditures of all public money shall be published from time to time.

Although this clause is in the legislative article, it has been declared to be a limitation on executive agencies; no money in the Treasury (an executive agency) may be paid out unless Congress has appropriated it.[1] More recently, the courts have said that the limitation in this clause applies to tax funds and customs duties.[2] Sales of public land, resulting in proceeds being paid into a reclamation fund as provided by statute, may be used by administrative agencies for any purpose to which the statute directs the fund, without further appropriation.[3]

1. *Cincinnati Soap Co. v. United States,* 301 U.S. 308 (1937); *cf.* also *United States v. Realty Co.,* 163 U.S. 427 (1896).
2. *Varney v. Warehime,* 147 F. 2d 238 (1945), cert. den. 325 U.S. 882 (1945).
3. *United States v. Hanson,* 167 F. 881 (1909).

I. 9. Cl. 8. Titles of Nobility

No title of nobility shall be granted by the United States; and no person holding any office of profit or trust under them shall, without the consent of Congress, accept any present, emolument, office, or title, of any kind whatever, from any king, prince or foreign state.

No judicial opinions on this clause have been given by the Supreme Court. Administrative opinions have occasionally been written on the specific application of the clause: Thus, in 1964, the Comptroller General ruled that a member of an American military agency, on retainer for recall to active duty, could not at the same time accept employment in a foreign government without consent of Congress.[1] In 1902 the Attorney General ruled that the prohibition against accepting a gift under the terms of the clause applied to a gift from a non-reigning sovereign.[2] Approval by an administrative officer under a statute providing for certain services to foreign powers by retired officers of the United States is held to be sufficient evidence of Congressional consent.[3]

1. 44 Compt. Gen. Op. 227 (1964).
2. 24 Ops. Atty. Gen. 117 (1902).
3. 41 Compt. Gen. Ops. 715 (1962).

I. 10. Powers Denied to the States

I. 10. Cl. 1. General Prohibitions; Contract Clause

No state shall enter into any treaty, alliance, or confederation; grant letters of marque and reprisal; coin money; emit bills of credit;

make any thing but gold and silver coin a tender in payment of debts; pass any bill of attainder, *ex post facto* law, or law impairing the obligation of contracts, or grant any title of nobility.

This general section denies to the states certain powers because they are reserved to the Federal government, others because they are prohibited to all government. Thus the prohibitions of state treaty and monetary authority recognize the exclusive authority over these subjects in the Federal government; bills of attainder, *ex post facto* laws and titles of nobility are denied to all governments within the Union. The specific injunction directed at the states concerning impairment of contract obligations has proved historically to be the most litigated clause in this section.

Miscellaneous Prohibitions

The treaty prohibition was cited by the Court to invalidate Confederate obligations after the Civil War,[1] and more recently was cited as vesting in the national government exclusive jurisdiction over a three-mile coastal zone containing oil resources which might be the subject of international dispute.[2] The coinage clause was adjudicated, at the state-court level, in the question of state issuance of sales-tax tokens, which were held valid because they were not intended to be circulating currency.[3] Bills of credit, said the Court in 1900, were prohibited by the Constitutional Convention in 1787 to cut off the outpouring of unsecured paper money from the original states, and therefore is to be understood today as being limited to that specific matter.[4] States may thus issue coupons or warrants receivable for taxes,[5] and state banks were permitted to issue various types of paper without reference to this clause.[6] Bonds issued for redemption of indebtedness are valid even if the evidence of indebtedness, standing alone, might be condemned as a bill of credit.[7]

The *ex post facto* clause, as is the case with the analogous clause in Section 9, is held to relate only to criminal law[8] and is further construed to relate only to legislative enactments and not to retroactive judicial decisions.[9] Laws changing the method of punishment without increasing its severity do not violate this clause,[10] but any increase in penalty is *ex post facto* as concerning crimes committed before the change in the law.[11] Statutory revisions reducing penalities are not treated as *ex post facto*.[12]

Impairment of Contracts

The contract clause, after the commerce clause, was the most fertile seedbed of older constitutional litigation. It was the first line of defense against state regulation for the *laissez-faire* entrepreneur, as the commerce clause was the first line of defense against Federal regulation—the latter being bolstered by the due-process clause of the Fifth Amendment and the former by the due-process clause of the Fourteenth.[13] This economic freedom from public restraint had its origins in the *Dartmouth College Case* in 1819,[14] in which the Marshall Court laid down the rule that all grants, charters or undertakings between parties were in the nature of contracts, which could not be altered by one party without the consent of the other, and particularly where the alteration was attempted by the state as a party.[15]

While states thereafter made a point of asserting, in subsequent grants or contracts, a reserved right of alteration, amendment or rescission,[16] the basic rule was construed as restraining states from enacting legislation interfering with contractual relations between private parties and particularly with the freedom of individuals to contract generally.[17] The clause, in conjunction with the anti-trust litigation under the commerce clause, served in the first quarter of the twentieth century to hamper labor efforts to organize and bargain collectively.[18] The depression of the 1930s raised new questions of impairment of obligations of contract in the state laws setting moratoria on foreclosure of mortgages, the courts holding that the emergency police power of the states could validly be used in the case of such laws where mortgagees' rights were not extinguished but merely held in abeyance.[19]

A long line of cases have affirmed that Congress is not bound by the contracts clause,[20] but the same effect was achieved, in the *laissez-faire* era, by emphasis on the due-process clause of the Fifth Amendment.[21] The ultimate extreme in *laissez-faire* jurisprudence on the contract clause was reached in a 1936 New York minimum-wage case,[22] which was vigorously criticized. Within a year, the Court reversed itself on this principle,[23] and thereafter there began a steady abandonment of the ultra-restrictive rules derived from the clause.[24] The concept of a labor contract based on collective rather than individual negotiation, as affecting the welfare of interstate commerce and thus as a Federal interest overriding prior rules of the contract clause,[25] signaled the beginning of a new regime of rights under both clauses.[26] The later New Deal statutes on labor law, running from certain World War II emergency laws to the post-war Taft-Hartley Act,[27] have provided the statutory base for construction, for the most part affirmative, of government powers in this subject area.[28]

1. *Williams v. Bruffy*, 96 U.S. 176 (1878).
2. *United States v. California*, 332 U.S. 19 (1947). On the tidelands titles, and the eventual Congressional waiver of sovereignty, see 67 Stat. 29, 10 U.S.C. 7421 *et seq.*
3. *Morrow v. Henneford*, 47 P. 2d 1016 (1935).
4. *Houston R. Co. v. Texas*, 177 U.S. 87 (1900).
5. *Poindexter v. Greenhow* (Virginia Coupon Cases), 114 U.S. 270 (1885).
6. *Woodruff v. Trapnall*, 10 How. 190 (1851).
7. *Walker v. State*, 12 S. Ct. 184 (1879). But treasury warrants are bills of credit and void. *Bragg v. Tuffts*, 6 S.W. 158 (1887).
8. *Rochin v. California*, 342 U.S. 165 (1952); *Kentucky Union Co. v. Kentucky*, 219 U.S. 140 (1911).
9. *Frank v. Mangum*, 237 U.S. 309 (1915). Cf. generally *Garner v. Board of Public Works*, 341 U.S. 716 (1951); *DeVeau v. Braisted*, 363 U.S. 164 (1960); *Bouie v. Columbia*, 378 U.S. 347 (1964).
10. *Malloy v. South Carolina*, 237 U.S. 180 (1915); *Chicago R. Co. v. Trauborger*, 238 U.S. 67 (1915).
11. *Lindsy v. Washington*, 301 U.S. 397 (1937). *Cf.* also *McDonald v. Massachusetts*, 180 U.S. 311 (1901).
12. *Rooney v. North Dakota*, 196 U.S. 324 (1905).
13. *Cf.* Swindler, *The Old Legality*, Ch. 14.
14. *Dartmouth College v. Woodward*, 4 Wheat. 518 (1819).
15. *Id.*, at 712.
16. *Cf. Looker v. Maynard*, 179 U.S. 46 (1900).
17. *Cf. Allgeyer v. Louisiana*, 165 U.S. 578 (1897); *Holden v. Hardy*, 169 U.S. 366 (1898); *Lochner v. New York*, 198 U.S. 45 (1905).
18. *Duplex Prtg. Press Co. v. Deering*, 154 U.S. 443 (1921); *Adkins v. Children's Hosp.*, 261 U.S. 525 (1922); *Bedford Stone Co. v. Journeymen Stonecutters*, 274 U.S. 37 (1927).
19. *Home B. & L. Assn. v. Blaisdell*, 290 U.S. 398 (1934); *cf. Worthen Co. v. Thomas*, 292 U.S. 426 (1934), and *Worthen Co. v. Kavanaugh*, 295 U.S. 56 (1935).
20. *Cf. Sinking Fund Cases*, 9 Otto 718 (1878); *Mitchell v. Clark*, 110 U.S. 643 (1884); *Hepburn v. Griswold*, 8 Wall. 603 (1889); *New York v. United States*, 257 U.S. 591 (1922); *Cont. Ill. Nat. Bank v. Chi., R. I. & P. R. Co.*, 294 U.S. 648 (1935).
21. *Cf. inter alia, Louisville Bank v. Radford*, 295 U.S. 555 (1935).

22. *Morehead v. New York ex rel. Tipaldo,* 298 U.S. 587 (1936).
23. *West Coast Hotel Co. v. Parrish,* 300 U.S. 379 (1937).
24. *Cf.* Swindler, *The New Legality,* Ch. 5.
25. *Cf. N.L.R.B. v. Jones & Laughlin Steel Corp.,* 301 U.S. 1 (1937).
26. *Cf. Dodge v. Board of Education,* 302 U.S. 74 (1937); *Indiana ex rel. Anderson v. Brand,* 303 U.S. 95 (1938); *United States v. Darby,* 312 U.S. 100 (1941).
27. 61 Stat. 136.
28. *Cf. Helvering v. N. W. Mills,* 311 U.S. 46 (1940); *East New York Sav. Bank v. Hahn,* 326 U.S. 230 (1942); *Faitoute I. & S. Co. v. Asbury Park,* 316 U.S. 502 (1942); *El Paso v. Simmons,* 379 U.S. 497 (1965).

I. 10. Cl. 2. State Export-Import Duties

No state shall, without the consent of the Congress, lay any imposts or duties on imports or exports, except what may be absolutely necessary for executing its inspection laws; and the net produce of all duties and imposts, laid by any state on imports or exports, shall be for the use of the Treasury of the United States; and all such laws shall be subject to the revision and control of the Congress.

The constitutional policy against state tax barriers or burdens affecting interstate commerce has been qualified in the twentieth century by commerce-clause cases recognizing the reasonable needs of the states to raise revenues from economic activities within their respective jurisdictions, necessitating in turn a balancing of the impact of state taxes on interstate commerce against the public policy of reasonable claim to revenue in the individual case. The limitations of the commerce clause are not coterminous with this clause, however,[1] and the effect of the tax clause in Section 8 is to vest exclusive authority in the Federal government to tax importation of foreign goods.[2] More recently the Court has narrowly construed the circumstances under which goods retain their import character, declaring state tax jurisdiction validly to apply whenever importers "have so acted upon the materials . . . as to cause them to lose their distinctive character."[3] Conversely, goods do not leave the tax jurisdiction of the state until they have assumed this "distinctive character."[4]

While the "original package" or "unbroken package" concept of Chief Justice Fuller in 1890[5] was qualified by Congress as to interstate commerce, its viability has never been questioned with respect to imports from abroad.[6] Breaking of the original package depends not on literal fact but on the goods' being applied to their intended use within the jurisdiction.[7] And the packaging of goods for export is still subject to state levies until they have entered the "current of commerce."[8] Even after clearly entering this "current," long periods of storage within one jurisdiction may interrupt the continuity of the interstate shipment and render the goods liable to local tax.[9]

1. *Richfield Oil Corp. v. Board of Equalization,* 329 U.S. 69 (1946).
2. *Hooven & Allison Co. v. Evatt,* 324 U.S. 652 (1945). *Cf.* also *Canton R. Co. v. Rogan,* 340 U.S. 511 (1951).
3. *U.S. Plywood Corp. v. Algoma,* 358 U.S. 534 (1959).
4. *Empresa Sid. S.A. v. Merced County,* 337 U.S. 154 (1949).
5. *Leisy v. Hardin,* 135 U.S. 100 (1890).
6. *Department of Revenue v. Beam Dist. Co.,* 377 U.S. 341 (1964).
7. *Youngstown Sheet & Tube Co. v. Bowers,* 358 U.S. 534 (1959).
8. *Cf. Joy Oil Co. v. Tax Commission,* 337 U.S. 286 (1949).
9. *Id.,* at 289. *Cf.* also *Minnesota v. Blasius,* 290 U.S. 1 (1933); *Northwestern Airlines v. Minnesota,* 322 U.S. 292 (1944); *Standard Oil Co. v. Peck,* 342 U.S. 382 (1952). License fees on export-import businesses, based on annual rates plus a percentage of gross sales, have been held invalid under this clause. *Crew Levick Co. v. Pennsylvania,* 245 U.S. 292 (1917).

I. 10. Cl. 3. State Foreign Relations

No state shall, without the consent of Congress, lay any duty of tonnage, keep troops, or ships of war in time of peace, enter into any agreement or compact with another state, or with a foreign power, or engage in war, unless actually invaded, or in such imminent danger as will not admit of delay.

This clause complements the preceding clause under the constitutional policy of vesting all foreign affairs in the Federal government. The tonnage prohibition was intended to prevent states from burdening the access of foreign vessels to their ports.[1] This does not bar states from making reasonable charges for pilotage and wharfage services, but does bar any duty which is a condition for entering or leaving a harbor.[2]

The making of interstate compacts, an act of sovereignty, is continued in the states subject to the consent of Congress.[3] While the settlement of boundary disputes was the most common subject of such compacts in the nineteenth and early twentieth centuries, Congress itself encouraged a broader function with the passage of the Crime Compact Act of 1934,[4] followed by statutes authorizing joint state actions on conservation, flood control and like matters.[5] The consent of Congress, under certain circumstances, is to be implied rather than to require formal expression.[6] In any case, the consent may be conditioned.[7] The execution of a valid interstate compact, finally, places the subject matter under Federal jurisdiction and makes it subject to Federal enforcement.[8]

1. *Mallory Lines v. Alabama Docks Commission*, 296 U.S. 261 (1935). *Cf.* also *Huse v. Glovey*, 119 U.S. 549 (1886).
2. *Mallory Lines v. Alabama Docks Commission*, 296 U.S. 261, 266 (1935).
3. *Hinderliter v. LaPlata Co.*, 304 U.S. 92 (1938).
4. 48 Stat. 909.
5. *Cf.* 49 Stat. 1570.
6. *Virginia v. West Virginia*, 11 Wall. 39 (1871); *Wharton v. Wise*, 153 U.S. 155 (1894).
7. *James v. Dravo Contracting Co.*, 302 U.S. 134 (1937); *Arizona v. California*, 292 U.S. 341 (1934); *cf.* also *DeVeau v. Braisted*, 363 U.S. 144 (1960).
8. *Olin v. Kitzmiller*, 259 U.S. 260 (1922); *Virginia v. West Virginia*, 246 U.S. 565 (1918); *Dyer v. Sims*, 341 U.S. 22 (1951); *Petty v. Tennessee-Missouri Commission*, 359 U.S. 275 (1959).

Article II. The Executive Power

II. *1. The Nature of Executive Power; Election*

The executive power shall be vested in a President of the United States of America. He shall hold office during the term of four years, and, together with the Vice President, chosen for the same term, be elected as follows:

[Each state shall appoint, in such manner as the legislature thereof may direct, a number of electors, equal to the whole number of Senators and Representatives to which the state may be entitled in the Congress: but no Senator or Representative, or person holding an office of trust or profit under the United States, shall be appointed an elector. The electors shall meet in their respective states, and vote by ballot for two persons, of whom one at least shall not be an inhabitant of the same state with themselves. And they shall make a list of all the persons voted for, and of the number of votes for each; which list they shall sign and certify, and transmit sealed to the seat of the government of the United States, directed to the president of the Senate. The president of the Senate shall, in the presence of the Senate and House of Representatives, open all the certificates, and the votes shall then be counted. The person having the greatest number of votes shall be the President, if such number be a majority of the whole number of electors appointed; and if there be more than one who have such majority, and have an equal number of votes, then the House of Representatives shall immediately choose by ballot one of them for President; and if no person have a majority, then from the five highest on the list the said House shall in like manner choose the President. But in choosing the President, the votes shall be taken by states, the representation from each state having one vote; a quorum for this purpose shall consist of a member or members from two thirds of the states, and a majority of all the states shall be necessary to a choice. In every case, after the choice of the President, the person having the greatest number of votes of the electors shall be the Vice President. But if there should remain two or more who have equal votes, the Senate shall choose from them by ballot the Vice President.]

The Congress may determine the time of choosing the electors, and the day on which they shall give their votes; which day shall be the same throughout the United States.

No person except a natural born citizen, or a citizen of the United States, at the time of the adoption of this Constitution, shall be eligible to that office who shall not have attained to the age of thirty five years, and been fourteen years a resident within the United States.

[In case of the removal of the President from office, or of his death, resignation, or inability to discharge the powers and duties of the said office, the same shall devolve on the Vice President, and the Congress may by law provide for the case of removal, death, resignation or inability, both of the President and Vice President, declaring what officer shall then act as President, and such officer shall act accordingly, until the disability be removed, or a President shall be elected.]

The President shall, at stated times, receive for his services, a compensation, which shall neither be encreased nor diminished during the period for which he shall have been elected, and he shall not receive within that period any other emolument from the United States, or any of them.

Before he enter on the execution of his office, he shall take the following oath or affirmation:"I do solemnly swear (or affirm) that I will faithfully execute the office of President of the United States, and will to the best of my ability, preserve, protect and defend the Constitution of the United States."

Although Theodore Roosevelt insisted, as a personal conviction, that the President had both the right and the duty to do anything which the needs of the nation might require, unless expressly forbidden by the Constitution,[1] the Supreme Court took great pains specifically to refute this theory of executive power in Harry Truman's seizure of the steel companies in 1952.[2] To the same effect, the Taft Court in 1926 affirmed a broad power of removal of executive officers by the President,[3] but less than a decade later the Hughes Court rejected the proposition.[4] The Twenty-second Amendment, limiting an incumbent to two terms in office, was another step in circumscribing the general power or influence of the Chief Executive. Despite these various boundary lines supposedly drawn about the office, however, the power of the Presidency in the twentieth century has steadily enlarged.[5]

The judicial effort at circumscribing the executive power has been based, at least in part, on the fact that Sections 2 and 3 of this Article are explicit grants of power without a "necessary and proper" clause or any other phrases which admit of general definition. But the demands of the twentieth century made a strong executive essential: the administrative regulatory process beginning with the Interstate Commerce Commission Act of 1887 and the Sherman Anti-Trust Act of 1890, followed by the decade of trust-busting, the reform legislation of the New Freedom, the crisis of the New Deal and the emergency powers necessitated by both World Wars.[6]

The electoral process was revised in 1804 by the Twelfth Amendment, rendering obsolete the third paragraph in this section. The sixth paragraph was revised in 1967 by the Twenty-fifth Amendment.

Executive Privilege and Prerogative

The constitutional crisis of 1973 represented in the case of *Nixon v. Sirica*[7] emphasized the imperfect definition of general executive power as expressed in this section. If there is an executive privilege (i.e., exemption from judicial process) to be inferred from the nature of the separation of powers, is it greater than, or different from, the legislative privilege set out in Article I.6.1? If there is an executive prerogative (i.e., an inherent and exclusive right to initiate or abstain from accommodation of legislative or judicial requests), how is it to be defined?

The only mention of privilege in the Constitution is in the legislative article, since historically the infringement upon legislative powers came from the Crown or the Crown courts.[8] The privilege, as already suggested (*supra*, Article I.6.1), is limited practically to certain misdemeanors since "treason, felony and breach of the peace" are excepted. This, in turn, is consonant with the common-law maxim that no man is above the law,[9] and all men are answerable at law except for any actions ("speech or debate") associated with the legislative or other governmental function. Privilege, as a constitutional concept and in the context of the American Constitution, is thus essentially a legislative attribute; although, in the struggle between the Senate Select Committee on Presidential Campaign Activities and the White House, the term "executive privilege" was commonly used, it related to a concept more accurately to be described as executive prerogative.

The executive prerogative derives in part from the theory of the separation of powers—a theory implicit but not express in the language of the Constitution—and in part from British constitutional history. The royal prerogative is, of course, feudal in origin, and the history of the development of Parliamentary supremacy in England is essentially a history of the systematic reduction of the scope of the prerogative. It is today a description of "those powers which may be exercised by the Crown without the authority of Parliament,"[10] consisting on the one hand of ceremonial functions of the monarch and on the other of executive power exercised by the government of the day (e.g., the prime minister and the other Crown ministers). Since ministerial accountability to Parliament is an essential part of the British constitution, the control of the executive prerogative is a reserved legislative power.[11] The British constitutional principle is thus not apposite, but merely something of an analogy. The American constitutional position was suggested in a concurring opinion of Justice Jackson in 1952, in the leading American case on the limits to the powers of the executive: the American Constitution, said Jackson, "enjoins upon its branches [of government] separateness but interdependence, autonomy but reciprocity," and executive powers, he concluded, "are not fixed but fluctuate, depending on their disjunction or conjunction with those of Congress."[12]

Nixon v. Sirica,[13] of course, was a separate executive initiative on matters growing out of the Senate "Watergate" hearings—a court action by a special prosecutor appointed by the Department of Justice to compel release of documents in the possession of the Chief Executive, for possible consideration by a Federal grand jury. The Senate committee in its own right was seeking a court order to compel release to it of substantially the same material. The fundamental issue in both instances, however, was whether executive prerogative immunized all materials in the custody of the Chief Executive, or whether it extended only to those documents relating to the business of government and not to those of non-governmental political activity which might be the subject of criminal process.

1. Roosevelt, *Autobiography* (New York, 1925), p. 357.
2. *Youngstown Sheet & Tube Co. v. Sawyer,* 345 U.S. 579 (1952).
3. *Myers v. United States,* 272 U.S. 52 (1926).
4. *Humphrey's Exec. v. United States,* 295 U.S. 602 (1935).
5. The classic and definitive study of the executive is Corwin, *The Presidency: Office and Powers* (1957).
6. *Cf.* Neustadt, *Presidential Power* (1960); and Sorensen, *Decision Making in the White House* (1963), among representative books on the office. For the current debate over the need to restore an equilibrium between the executive and legislative branches of government, *cf.* Berger, *Impeachment: The Constitutional Problems* (Cambridge, Mass., 1973).
7. *Cf.* 42 *U.S. Law Week* 1033 (September 11, 1973).
8. Among current British references, *cf.* Wade and G. Phillips, *Constitutional Law* (London, 8th ed., 1970), Ch. 10; Hood Phillips, *Constitutional and Administrative Law* (London, 5th ed., 1973), Chs. 12–15.
9. *Cf.* Lord Coke's aphorism, *Rex non sub homine sed sub Deo et lege* (the King is under no man but under God and the law). *Cf.* also Dicey, *Introduction to the Study of the Law of the Constitution* (London, 10th ed., 1959), pp. 202–03.
10. Wade and Phillips, *op. cit.,* p. 181.
11. *Id.,* pp. 184–90.
12. *Youngstown Sheet & Tube Co. v. Sawyer,* 343 U.S. 579, at 667 (1952). Oblique allusion to executive prerogative or privilege was made in *Environmental Protection Agency v. Mink,* 410 U.S. 73 (1973), in which Justice White for the majority called attention to Chief Justice Marshall's holding in *United States v. Burr,* 25 Fed. Cas. 30 (1807)—a case in which a Vice President, without impeachment was subject to arrest for treason. *Cf.* also the observation of the

Court of Appeals for the District of Columbia in 1971, that no executive officer can be the sole judge of his own claim of executive privilege (prerogative). *Committee for Nuclear Responsibility v. Seaborg,* 463 F. 2d 788 (1971).
13. *Cf. in re Grand Jury Subpoena to Richard M. Nixon,* 360 F.S. 1 (1973); *Nixon v. Sirica,* No. 73—1962, U.S. App. D.C. (1973).

II. 2. Powers as Commander-in-Chief and Head of State

Section 2. The President shall be commander in chief of the Army and Navy of the United States, and of the militia of the several states, when called into the actual service of the United States; he may require the opinion, in writing, of the principal officer in each of the executive departments, upon any subject relating to the duties of their respective offices, and he shall have power to grant reprieves and pardons for offenses against the United States, except in cases of impeachment.

He shall have power, by and with the advice and consent of the Senate, to make treaties, provided two thirds of the Senators present concur; and he shall nominate, and by and with the advice and consent of the Senate, shall appoint ambassadors, other public ministers and consuls, judges of the Supreme Court, and all other officers of the United States, whose appointments are not herein otherwise provided for, and which shall be established by law: but the Congress may by law vest the appointment of such inferior officers, as they think proper, in the President alone, in the courts of law, or in the heads of departments.

The President shall have power to fill up all vacancies that may happen during the recess of the Senate, by granting commissions which shall expire at the end of their next session.

It is through the delegation of power to the President in wartime—particularly in the First and Second World Wars—that the overall power of the executive department has steadily enlarged in the twentieth century. By this delegation, the President is vested with large segments of authority previously vested in Congress, and adds these delegated powers to his own as commander-in-chief and head of state.[1] It is a truism of modern political process that powers once delegated tend to become more or less permanently vested. This is due in part to the fact that the flow of power may be initiated by the right of the executive to proclaim national emergencies, as well as the power to terminate the state of emergency.[2] Formal activation of war powers depends on a declaration by Congress;[3] but both the Korean and Vietnam experiences demonstrated how broad was the independent power of the President in emergency situations which never reached the stage of formal declaration of war. The right of a citizen to test the constitutionality of Presidential action in such instances has been denied,[4] and the same fate has met state attempts to challenge the White House.[5]

Treaties and Executive Agreements

The treaty-making power of the executive department, like the war power, has become substantially greater in the course of national history than the check-and-balance theory of the Founding Fathers anticipated. The initiative for negotiating a treaty is exclusively in the President, without any power of participation on the part of the Senate,[6] and while the Senate may subsequently attach conditions to a treaty to be accepted by the negotiating parties before being confirmed, the Senate may not prevent the President from abandoning the negotiations altogether if he finds the conditions unacceptable.[7] Congress has power to abrogate a treaty[8] and may modify it as to its domestic operation by subsequent legislation,[9] but treaties which are self-executing may go into effect without further Congressional implementation.[10] The power of the President to affect foreign relations by recognizing or withholding recognition from a foreign power, it has been held, is independent of Congress.[11]

Executive agreements derive from the general executive responsibility for implementing certain Congressional programs—e.g., in postal services, patent and copyright, and foreign commerce, as well as from authority as head of state to implement certain multinational conventions (e.g., the International Telecommunications Convention) to which the United States is a party. Such unilateral commitments of the United States began to be commonplace with the emergence of the nation as a world power after the Spanish-American War: the Peking Protocol of 1901, settling the indemnities due the United States from the Boxer rebellion; the "gentlemen's agreement" of 1907 limiting Japanese emigration to the United States; the Litvinoff Agreement of 1933, effecting American diplomatic recognition of the Union of Socialist Soviet Republics—these are among the most conspicuous of a steadily proliferating series of executive instruments fundamentally affecting the nation in international society.[12] The binding legal effect of such agreements has consistently been affirmed by the courts.[13]

Appointments and Removals

The second clause of Section 2 defines two types of appointing power—one, relating to major public offices, requiring formal Senate confirmation; the other, relating to minor offices, not requiring such action if the Senate so declares. The manifest intent of the clause was to retain a strict legislative control over executive appointments; but in practice this check and balance also has diminished in effectiveness. Statutory definitions of the qualifications and rights of appointees have been expressed in the Civil Service Act of 1883[14] and the Hatch Act of 1940.[15] Essentially, the appointing process still requires, within these statutory limits, the three steps of nomination by the President, confirmation by the Senate and commissioning by the executive department.[16]

The removal power, on which the Constitution is silent, has provoked constitutional litigation out of proportion to the ultimate significance of the facts of the cases. The Taft Court held, in a 6–3 opinion, that a Congressional attempt to make removal subject to its approval was an invalid intrusion into executive prerogatives.[17] In 1935 the Court reversed this position, the unanimous opinion then declaring that, at least in cases where the appointee holds an office in an agency created by Congress to carry out its legislative policies, the President may not remove the appointee at will.[18] The general principle of limited removal power in the executive was reasserted by the Court in 1958.[19] On the other hand, where a removal is necessary to insure the efficient administration of the agency, the power of the President is sustained without reference to Congressional participation.[20]

1. *Chi. & South. Airlines v. Waterman SS. Corp.,* 333 U.S. 103 (1948).
2. *Cf. Werner v. United States,* 119 F. S. 894 (1954), aff'd 233 F. 2d 52 (1956), cert. den. 352 U.S. 842 (1956).
3. *Ex parte Quirin,* 317 U.S. 1 (1942).
4. *Velvel v. Johnson,* 287 F.S. 846 (1968), aff'd. 415 F. 2d 236 (1969), cert. den. sub. nom. *Velvel v. Nixon,* 396 U.S. 1042 (1970); *cf.* also *Mora v. McNamara,* 389 U.S. 934 (1967); *McArthur v. Clifford,* 393 U.S. 1002 (1968).

5. *Massachusetts v. Laird,* 400 U.S. 886 (1970).
6. *United States v. Curtiss-Wright Export Corp.,* 299 U.S. 304 (1936).
7. *Cf. Fourteen Rings v. United States,* 183 U.S. 176 (1901).
8. *Chung Yim v. United States,* 78 F. 2d 43 (1935), cert. den. 296 U.S. 627 (1935); *La Abra Min. Co. v. United States,* 175 U.S. 423 (1899).
9. *Moser v. United States,* 341 U.S. 41 (1961).
10. *Valentine v. United States ex rel. Neidecher,* 299 U.S. 5 (1936).
11. *Cf. United States v. Pink,* 315 U.S. 203 (1942).
12. *Cf.* Mathews, "The Constitutional Power of the President to Conclude International Agreements," 64 *Yale L.J.* 345 (1955).
13. *Cf. United States v. Belmont,* 301 U.S. 324 (1937); *United States v. Pink,* 315 U.S. 203 (1942); and *cf.* also *Guaranty Trust Co. v. United States,* 304 U.S. 126 (1938).
14. 22 Stat. 403.
15. 54 Stat. 767; *cf. United Pub. Workers v. Mitchell,* 330 U.S. 75 (1947). At this writing, another test of the constitutionality of the restrictions in the Hatch Act is in prospect.
16. *Cf. Nishimura Ekiu v. United States,* 142 U.S. 651 (1892); *Shoemaker v. United States,* 147 U.S. 282 (1893).
17. *Myers v. United States,* 272 U.S. 52 (1926); *cf. Parsons v. United States,* 167 U.S. 327 (1897).
18. *Humphrey's Exec. v. United States,* 295 U.S. 602 (1935).
19. *Wiener v. United States,* 357 U.S. 349 (1958).
20. *Morgan v. T.V.A.,* 28 F.S. 732 (1939), cert. den. 312 U.S. 701 (1941).

II. 3. Other Executive Duties

He shall from time to time give to the Congress information of the state of the union, and recommend to their consideration such measures as he shall judge necessary and expedient; he may, on extraordinary occasions, convene both Houses, or either of them, and in case of disagreement between them, with respect to the time of adjournment, he may adjourn them to such time as he shall think proper; he shall receive ambassadors and other public ministers; he shall take care that the laws be faithfully executed, and shall commission all the officers of the United States.

II. 4. Impeachable Officers

The President, Vice President and all civil officers of the United States, shall be removed from office on impeachment for, and conviction of, treason, bribery, or other high crimes and misdemeanors.

Section 3 is a general summary of executive functions—reporting to the legislative branch on the state of national affairs, convening Congress in special sessions, recognizing the representatives of foreign powers and discharging the responsibility for the effective carrying out of the laws of the United States. Section 4 is the ultimate check of the legislative on the executive branch, but rarely used.

The "faithful execution of the laws," a provision common to state constitutions as well, is perhaps only a general hortatory statement, but in the clash between the President and Congress in 1973 over the impounding by the executive branch of funds appropriated by the legislative branch, a new constitutional issue was generated. Was the President required by this clause to carry out a statute enacted by Congress—indeed, was this of the essence of the executive function? Or was it of the essence of executive responsibility to determine whether the public interest was to be best served by controlling the effects of government spending upon an inflationary economy? This was another area in which both constitutional law and constitutional theory was underdeveloped.[1] In the Steel Seizure Case of 1952,[2] Chief Justice Vinson quoted at length from a brief of the Solicitor General which argued that "there are fields which are peculiar to Congress and fields which are peculiar to the Executive," as well as "fields which are peculiar to both." In this third category, the brief concluded, "Congress might elect to act, but the President was not thereby made the agent of Congress."[3]

1. *Cf.* Note, "Presidential Impoundment: Constitutional Theories and Political Realities," 61 *Geo. L. J.* 1295 (1973).
2. *Youngstown Sheet & Tube Co. v. Sawyer,* 343 U.S. 575 (1952).
3. *Id.,* 689–91. In *Mississippi v. Johnson,* 4 Wall. 475 (1867) the Court declared that the Chief Executive could not be compelled by judicial process to exercise his powers, either statutory or constitutional.

Article III. The Judicial Power

III. 1. The Federal Judiciary

The judicial power of the United States shall be vested in one Supreme Court, and in such inferior courts as the Congress may from time to time ordain and establish. The judges, both of the supreme and inferior courts, shall hold their offices during good behavior, and shall, at stated times, receive for their services a compensation which shall not be diminished during their continuance in office.

The third branch of the Federal government—established in all of the state constitutions but, like the separate executive branch, omitted from the Articles of Confederation—was left by the Constitution to the initiative of Congress to organize and has been defined and redefined by statutes throughout the national history.[1] The only tribunal expressly required under the Constitution is "one Supreme Court," all other parts of the Federal judicial structure depending on Congress. Even the size of the Supreme Court—ranging from six to ten and settling at nine in the act of April 10, 1869[2]—changes at the legislative pleasure, as the Roosevelt court-reorganization bill of 1937 proposed. Although the original jurisdiction of the Supreme Court is specifically limited by the second paragraph of Section 2,[3] the appellate jurisdiction has been periodically redefined.[4] Thus dependent on Congressional authorization and lacking, as expressed in a familiar phrase, both the power of purse and sword, the judiciary has depended for its equal (or superior) position in the constitutional structure on the logic of events in national history.[5]

Organization of the Courts

From the original Judiciary Act of 1789,[6] which organized the Supreme Court and established a two-level system of trial courts, the structure of the Federal judiciary varied until the Act of 1911[7] created what is essentially the national court structure of today: a number of United States District Courts within eleven circuits (ten plus the District of Columbia), each circuit under a Court of Appeals having final appellate jurisdiction over a substantial proportion of Federal law. From these so-called intermediate courts, as well as from special three-judge trial courts and certain others in certain circumstances, review may lie to the Supreme Court by right (appeal) or discretion (certiorari).[8] A number of special courts—e.g., Court of Claims, Tax Court, Court of Customs and Patent Appeals—have also been created.[9]

Until the Judicial Conference Act of 1922,[10] the Chief Justice in the Supreme Court was only nominally or honorarily the head of the judicial system of the United States. With this statute—part of a threefold plan of modernization developed under Chief Justice Taft[11]—the Chief Justice of the United States became the leader of the whole system in fact. Through the Conference of Senior Circuit Judges (later the Judicial Conference of the United States) the business of each court in each circuit was annually summarized and reported to the Chief Justice, who was empowered under the statute to transfer District Court judges within the circuit as case loads warranted. The second part of Taft's program was enacted in 1925,[12] redistributing appellate jurisdiction between the intermediate courts and the Supreme Court and limiting the types of cases appealable as of right to the latter. The final phase of Taft's program—the authority to promulgate uniform rules of procedure—was not won from Congress until Hughes's Chief Justiceship.[13]

Under Chief Justice Warren, the Judicial Conference of the United States addressed itself to a continuing series of procedural reforms and in-depth studies.[14] Following and enlarging on this example, Chief Justice Burger found himself in the role of leader of law reform for both Federal and state court systems, demanded by the rapidly approaching crisis of the 1970s in terms of staggering case loads, steadily increasing statutory programs with their attendant reliance on the courts, and the crying need for new thinking in the philosophy underlying much substantive law.[15] Thus the administration of the Federal judicial system under the Chief Justice has climaxed a half-century of growth, from the initial program of Taft to a complex and demanding independent area of national government.

The provision against discrimination through diminution of salaries was intended to preserve judicial independence. In 1920 this was held to exempt the salaries of judges from the new income tax authorized by the Sixteenth Amendment.[16] But this rule was overturned in 1939 by the Hughes Court, on the ground that an equitable income tax in no way jeopardized the independence of the judiciary.[17]

The Nature of Judicial Power

The "judicial power of the United States" has been defined as "the right to determine actual controversies arising between adverse litigants, duly instituted in courts of proper jurisdiction."[18] The central question of Federal judicial power, however, has always had to do with the scope and nature of judicial review; its unique development in American constitutional law has been treated in many volumes and continuing public debate. The principle was adroitly confirmed by Chief Justice Marshall in 1803,[19] and when, in the twentieth century, the use of judicial review to overturn Congressional and state legislative enactments began to proliferate, the general criticism was focussed less on the issue of the legitimacy of review than on the "economic predilections" of the Court which did the reviewing.[20]

There is substantial evidence to indicate that the Constitutional Convention assumed that a primary function of the Federal Supreme Court would be to resolve issues between states and between the states and the national government; the specific details in Section 2 make this much clear. It remained for the Marshall Court to set broad limits to the reviewing power—with reference to Federal legislation in *Marbury,* to state civil[21] and criminal[22] cases and to cases arising under the commerce,[23] tax[24] and contract[25] clauses. Congress contributed to the statutory provisions which added to the Court's business throughout the nineteenth and twentieth centuries;[26] and the Court itself, in the mid-twentieth century, vastly increased its own jurisdiction through sweeping adjudications in areas of the Bill of Rights and the Fourteenth Amendment (*q.v.*).

Thus judicial power has been defined and developed through legislation and adjudication: Statutes expand and contract the judicial function in terms of rights and remedies, outside the constitutional area;[27] jurisdiction may be limited or denied to certain courts or certain cases;[28] and the Court in defining its own inherent powers has, from earliest times, set limits on its own proper activities—e.g., in declining to give advisory opinions[29] and in carefully qualifying its functions under the Declaratory Judgments Act of 1934.[30] Other inherent powers, which all courts by definition are recognized to have, have been exercised by the Federal judiciary: contempt power,[31] injunctive powers except as these have been modified by statute,[32] *habeas corpus* powers under the common law[33] and the power to issue default judgments.[34] Other criteria, peculiar to the American Federal judiciary under Section 2, are discussed thereunder, below.

1. The classic study of the Federal judiciary is Frankfurter and Landis, *The Business of the Supreme Court* (1927), fortuitously supplemented by Hart and Wechsler, *The Federal Courts and the Federal Systems* (1953). The annual review of Supreme Court activity in the *Harvard Law Review* and the annual *Supreme Court Review* of the University of Chicago are other important references on the judicial branch. Most recently *cf*. Federal Judicial Center Report of the Study Group [Freund Committee] on the Caseload of the Supreme Court (Washington, 1972).
2. 16 Stat. 44.
3. *Marbury v. Madison*, 1 Cranch 137 (1803).
4. *Cf*. Frankfurter and Landis, *op. cit*., Chs. 1–3.
5. Among representative works, *cf*. Boudin, *Government by the Judiciary* (1932); Jackson, *The Struggle for Judicial Supremacy* (1941); Bickel, *The Least Dangerous Branch* (1962).
6. 1 Stat. 73.
7. 36 Stat. 1087.
8. *Cf*. generally Wright, *Federal Courts* (1970). As of this writing, a committee under the chairmanship of Professor Paul Freund has prepared a report recommending a special judicial panel to review cases seeking to be heard in the Supreme Court, to reduce the demands of paperwork on the Justices themselves and expedite the disposition of these cases.
9. Formerly the "constitutional courts"—those making up the direct line of trial and appeal provided by this section—were distinguished from "legislative courts"—those created by Congress for specialized purposes. This distinction was generally rejected in *Glidden Co. v. Zdanok*, 370 U.S. 530 (1962).
10. 42 Stat. 837.
11. *Cf*. Taft, "Three Needed Steps to Progress," 7 *A.B.A.J*. 453 (1921).
12. 43 Stat. 936.
13. 47 Stat. 904; 48 Stat. 1064; 54 Stat. 688. For the further modernization of the system *cf*. the creating of the Administrative Office of the United States Courts in 1939, 53 Stat. 1223.
14. *Cf*. Swindler, "The Chief Justice and Law Reform, 1921–1971," *1971 Sup. Ct. Rev*. 241.
15. *Cf*. Swindler, "Fifty-One Chief Justices," 60 *Ky. L.J*. 851 (1971–72).
16. *Evans v. Gore*, 253 U.S. 245 (1920); and *cf. Miles v. Graham*, 268 U.S. 501 (1925).
17. *O'Malley v. Woodrough*, 307 U.S. 277 (1939); *cf*. also *Williams v. United States*, 289 U.S. 516 (1933).
18. *Muskrat v. United States*, 219 U.S. 346 (1911).
19. *Marbury v. Madison*, 1 Cranch 137 (1803). *Cf*. the classic paper by Thayer, "The Origin and Scope of the American Doctrine of Constitutional Law," 7 *Harv. L. Rev*. 129 (1893); and *cf*. Cappellitti and Adams, "Judicial Review: European Antecedents and Adaptations," 79 *Harv. L. Rev*. 1207 (1966). For Congressional reaction to pivotal decisions, *cf*. Swindler, "Reviewing Judicial Review: A Note in Constitutional History," 6 *St. L.U.L.J*. (1959).
20. *Cf*. Swindler, *The Old Legality*, Ch. 6.
21. *Martin v. Hunter's Lessee*, 1 Wheat. 304 (1816).
22. *Cohens v. Virginia*, 6 Wheat. 264 (1821).
23. *Gibbons v. Ogden*, 9 Wheat. 1 (1824).
24. *McCulloch v. Maryland*, 4 Wheat. 316 (1819).
25. *Dartmouth College v. Woodward*, 4 Wheat. 518 (1819).

26. *Cf.* Appendix C in Swindler, *The Old Legality.*
27. *Switchmen's Union v. Mediation Board,* 320 U.S. 297 (1943); *Lockerty v. Phillips,* 319 U.S. 182 (1943).
28. *Bruner v. United States,* 343 U.S. 112 (1952); *Glidden Co. v. Zdanok,* 370 U.S. 530 (1962).
29. *Hayburn's Case,* 2 Dall. 409 (1790); *Muskrat v. United States,* 219 U.S. 346 (1911); *Bell v. Maryland,* 378 U.S. 226 (1964).
30. *Cf. Willing v. Chicago Auditorium Assn.,* 277 U.S. 274 (1928); *Aetna Life Ins. Co. v. Haworth,* 300 U.S. 227 (1937); *Sibron v. New York,* 392 U.S. 40 (1968).
31. *In re Debs,* 158 U.S. 594 (1895); But *cf. Nye v. United States,* 313 U.S. 33 (1941).
32. *Cf.* Norris-LaGuardia Act, 47 Stat. 70.
33. *Price v. Johnston,* 334 U.S. 266 (1948); *United States v. Smith,* 331 U.S. 469 (1947); *Gusik v. Schilder,* 339 U.S. 977 (1950).
34. *Pope v. United States,* 323 U.S. 1 (1944).

III. 2. Cl. 1. Cases and Controversies

Section 2. The judicial power shall extend to all cases, in law and equity, arising under this Constitution, the laws of the United States, and treaties made, or which shall be made, under their authority;—to all cases affecting ambassadors, other public ministers and consuls;— to all cases of admiralty and maritime jurisdiction;—to controversies to which the United States shall be a party;—to controversies between two or more states;—between a state and citizens of another state;— between citizens of different states;—between citizens of the same state claiming lands under grants of different states, and between a state, or the citizens thereof, and foreign states, citizens or subjects.

The "cases and controversies" in which this clause vests jurisdiction in the Federal courts were divided into two categories by Chief Justice Marshall: "In the first, their jurisdiction depends on the character of the cause, whoever may be the parties. This class comprehends 'all cases in law and equity arising under this Constitution, the laws of the United States, and treaties made, or which shall be made, under their authority.' This clause extends the jurisdiction of the Court to all the cases described. . . . In the second class, the jurisdiction depends entirely on the character of the parties."[1] Thus all constitutional questions, questions of Federal statutory construction or application, and questions growing out of international agreements to which the United States is a party, vest jurisdiction primarily (but not necessarily exclusively) in the Federal courts; while other cases described in this clause vest jurisdiction in the Federal courts when the parties in the case come under the categories described in the section. While the Constitutional Convention assumed that the settling of disputes between states would be an essential function of the Federal judiciary, the readiness of the courts to take jurisdiction over cases arising within the states—protested in the famed Kentucky and Virginia Resolutions of 1798[2]—aroused the vigorous antagonism of the states' sovereignty advocates, the Supreme Court itself undertook to devise criteria for assertion of or abstention from jurisdiction.

Thus, while a Federal question adjudicated by a state court may be subject to review in the Federal courts, and under well-recognized circumstances may warrant removal into the Federal courts at the trial stage, the Supreme Court may decline to review cases in which there are "adequate state grounds on which the state court decision may rest.[3] As for the other branches of national government, the Court has often declined to take jurisdiction by relying on Chief Justice Taney's definition of "political" questions which ought to be left to the legislative or executive branches to resolve.[4] In still other cases, the Court may abstain from taking jurisdiction at its discretion—e.g., on the ground that the issues are not "ripe" for the disposition,[5] that the particular parties lack standing to sue,[6] that under the facts of the particular case the Federal judiciary lacks jurisdiction,[7] or that the question of jurisdiction is in doubt.[8]

Essentially, the Court has defined "cases and controversies" as suits "involving litigants of adverse interests," as distinguished from collusive suits or suits involving moot questions.[9] This definition almost as a matter of course raises the question of "ripeness"—whether there is in fact a direct threat to a specific interest[10]—as well as the question of standing—whether the specific interest is vested in the particular litigant.[11] The abstract principle is that a general interest—e.g., as a member of a class generally affected by a law—did not affect an individual's exclusive personal interests sufficiently to permit him to test the constitutionality of the law as to him.[12] However, the Court qualified this principle in 1925, permitting a parochial school to assert the interests of the parents of its pupils in challenging a state law compelling all children to attend public schools.[13] In the evolving jurisprudence of racial equality, the question of standing has been further qualified; a member of a racial group suffering unconstitutional discrimination, for example, may readily be accorded standing.[14] In 1962 the Court accorded standing to one who was a victim of malapportionment in electoral districting,[15] holding that the principle itself is essentially intended to establish "such a personal stake in the outcome of a controversy" as to make possible a definitive disposition of the issue.[16] In 1968 the Court elaborated on this comment by observing that a litigant must establish a logical link between his status and the constitutional issue, and thus a "nexus" between his status and the injury.[17]

With the centripetal tendencies of public affairs in the mid-twentieth century, other abstract principles of limited jurisdiction have been qualified by realities. The "political question" was thus more narrowly construed by the Warren Court in the malapportionment cases; the eschewing of jurisdiction in such cases, said the Chief Justice, had been based on the practical question of justiciability, and "the mere fact that the suit seeks protection of a political right does not mean it presents a political question" in Taney's (or Frankfurter's) concept of such questions.[18] The doctrine of abstention, largely a matter of discretion and policy, had been elaborately described by Justice Brandeis in *Ashwander v. T.V.A.*,[19] and a decade later Justice Rutledge sought to restate the Brandeis criteria—in itself an indication of the continuing pressure of changing facts on the abstract principle.[20] In part, it became evident that in some instances the Court was using the abstention principle to avoid facing up to issues at all;[21] in part, it was a recognition of the harsh fact that the judiciary ultimately had to test the good faith of the states themselves, as in instances of allegedly discriminatory administration of the states' own laws.[22]

The "adequate state ground" limitation on Federal appellate review also brought the Court to an ultimate confrontation with other charges of unconstitutional criminal procedure in state courts. As a general proposition, it was declared in 1935, "where the judgment of a state court rests upon two grounds, one of which is Federal and the other non-Federal in character, our jurisdiction fails if the non-Federal ground is independent of the Federal ground and adequate to support the judgment."[23] This opinion, however, added the factor of "independence" of the state ground —a condition which was not readily to be established in many instances.[24] Particularly has this been demonstrated in the area of state procedure, a subject in which Federal courts customarily deferred to the state's construction of its own rules.[25] Justice Clark pointed out that state procedure might be challenged in Federal courts where there was reason to suspect that the state was seeking to frustrate a Federal right, or even if not so intending had actually frustrated the right by insisting on a procedural rule which had that effect.[26] A familiar example was a state procedural rule which made impossible the raising of a Federal question at the trial level, or preserving it at the appellate level, so that it could subsequently be declared lost.[27]

The climax in this trend of judicial qualifications of abstention came with the so-called "trilogy" of 1963 cases in which the Warren Court laid down a series of rules under which persons convicted under state law could seek collateral review in Federal courts by petitioning for *habeas corpus:* Where the issue involves the guarantees of the Fourteenth Amendment, the question of due process becomes a Federal question.[28] And even if the state court is shown to have ruled on the Federal constitutional right, that fact itself is reviewable in the Federal court.[29]

Specific Subjects of Jurisdiction

Admiralty—the law governing acts committed on the high seas as well as maritime commercial transactions—was placed under the Federal courts by the Constitutional Convention as a means of removing obstacles to commerce created by disparate state admiralty laws. An early series of decisions placed American admiralty law in the context of international law rather than the English common law (thus loosening the authority of state precedents, such as they might be, which had rested substantially on common law).[30] Like international law itself, admiralty is thus subject to statutory revision by Congress.[31] The Jones Act of 1920, creating causes of action for seamen injured at sea was such an instance, sustained by the Court.[32] Federal admiralty jurisdiction has also been construed to extend to all navigable waters of the United States itself.[33]

The right of the United States to sue in its courts was assumed from the outset to be an attribute of sovereignty without the necessity of statutory implementation.[34] Suits may be directed against states as well.[35] Sovereign immunity from suits is generally enjoyed by the Federal government, except as it may be specifically waived by Congress, as in the Federal Tort Claims Act.[36] Suits between states—originally confined to boundary disputes but now embracing a variety of issues[37]—may be brought as original actions in the Supreme Court (see Clause 2), although the Court reserves to itself the decision whether to take jurisdiction of such cases.[38] The same original jurisdiction may apply to suits by states against individuals.[39]

Controversies between citizens of different states may come into the Federal courts under the so-called "diversity jurisdiction" concept of this clause, as implemented by the Judiciary Act of 1789.[40] This means of access to the Federal courts made this forum, very early in the national history, an attractive alternate or optional route for litigants, at the same time that it contributed to the steady growth of caseloads in the Federal courts.[41] Where such cases may invoke no significant Federal question, and thus come accidentally, as it were, into the Federal courts, the added burden on these courts has become a matter of criticism and concern.[42] In any event, the judicial construction of this concept has contributed broadly to the American doctrine of conflict of laws[43] and has evolved through judicial definitions of citizenship (both for natural persons and, more negatively, for corporations) which had become well settled by the time the citizenship concept in the Fourteenth Amendment required definition.[44] In 1922 the Supreme Court unequivocally asserted the right of foreign corporations, under the "diversity jurisdiction" concept, to resort to Federal courts.[45] The holding was widely criticized as creating an easy escape route for corporations wishing to avoid trial of essentially local issues in local courts.[46]

1. *Cohens v. Virginia,* 6 Wheat. 264 (1821).
2. *Cf.* Warfield, *The Kentucky Resolutions of 1798* (New York, 1930).
3. *Cf.* the first extended discussion of this concept in *Murdock v. Memphis,* 20 Wall. 590 (1875); *cf.* also *Minnesota v. Nat. Tea Co.,* 309 U.S. 551 (1940).
4. *Luther v. Borden,* 7 How. 1 (1849).
5. *Cf. Abbott Laboratories v. Gardner,* 387 U.S. 136 (1967); *United Public Workers v. Mitchell,* 330 U.S. (1947).
6. *Cf. Frothingham v. Mellon,* 262 U.S. 447 (1921); but *cf.* also *Flast v. Cohen,* 392 U.S. 83 (1968), and *Sierra Club v. Morton,* 405 U.S. 727 (1972).
7. *Cf. Dahnke-Walker Milling Co. v. Bondurant,* 257 U.S. 282 (1921).

150 · *Court and Constitution in the Twentieth Century*

8. *Cf. Fox Film Corp. v. Muller,* 296 U.S. 207 (1935); *Herb v. Pitcairn,* 324 U.S. 117 (1945).
9. *Cf. St. Pierre v. United States,* 319 U.S. 41 (1943); *Muskrat v. United States,* 219 U.S. 346 (1911); *Fleming v. Rhodes,* 331 U.S. 100 (1947); *Ashwander v. T.V.A.,* 297 U.S. 288 (1936).
10. *Hill v. Florida,* 325 U.S. 538 (1945); *Watson v. Buck,* 313 U.S. 387 (1941).
11. *Doremus v. Board of Education,* 342 U.S. 429 (1952); *Adler v. Board of Education,* 342 U.S. 485 (1952).
12. *Cf. Massachusetts v. Mellon,* 262 U.S. 447 (1923); *Williams v. Riley,* 280 U.S. 78 (1929).
13. *Pierce v. Society of Sisters,* 268 U.S. 510 (1925).
14. *Cf. Barrows v. Jackson,* 346 U.S. 249 (1953); *N.A.A.C.P. v. Alabama ex rel. Patterson,* 375 U.S. 449 (1958).
15. *Baker v. Carr,* 369 U.S. 186 (1962).
16. *Id.,* at 204.
17. *Flast v. Cohen,* 392 U.S. 83 (1968). Injuries to private enterprise arising from public competition do not give standing to the private corporations. *Tennessee El. Power Co. v. T.V.A.,* 306 U.S. 118 (1939).
18. *Baker v. Carr,* 369 U.S. 186, 208 (1962); *Colegrove v. Green,* 328 U.S. 549 (1946); *McDougall v. Green,* 335 U.S. 281 (1948); *South v. Peters,* 339 U.S. 276 (1950).
19. 297 U.S. at 347; the Court will not anticipate a question of constitutional law not directly raised in litigation, nor construe the Constitution if there are other grounds for disposing of the case. *Cf.* Gunther, "The Subtle Vices of the 'Passive Virtues'—A Comment on Principle and Expediency in Judicial Review," 64 *Colum. L. Rev.* 1 (1964).
20. *Rescue Army v. Mun. Court,* 331 U.S. 549 (1947).
21. *Cf.* dissenting views of Justices Douglas and Harlan in *Poe v. Ullman,* 367 U.S. 497, 509, 522 (1961); and *cf.* Vinson, C. J., in *Shapiro v. United States,* 335 U.S. 1, 31 (1948).
22. *Dombrowski v. Pfister,* 386 U.S. 479 (1965); *Wise v. Constantineau,* 400 U.S. 433 (1971); *Younger v. Harris,* 401 U.S. 37 (1971).
23. *Fox Film Corp. v. Muller,* 296 U.S. 207 (1935).
24. *Cf. Herb v. Pitcairn,* 324 U.S. 117 (1945); *Dept. of Mental Hygiene v. Kirschner,* 379 U.S. 985 (1965).
25. *Cf. Williams v. Georgia,* 349 U.S. 375 (1955).
26. *Id.,* at 399 (dissenting opinion); *cf. Reece v. Georgia,* 350 U.S. 85 (1955).
27. *Henry v. Mississippi,* 379 U.S. 443 (1965); *Herndon v. Georgia,* 295 U.S. 441 (1935); *Michel v. Louisiana,* 350 U.S. 91 (1955); *Dorrance v. Pennsylvania,* 287 U.S. 660 (1932).
28. *Fay v. Noia,* 372 U.S. 391 (1963).
29. *Townsend v. Sain,* 372 U.S. 293 (1963). The third of the "trilogy" with *Fay v. Noia,* above, was *Sanders v. United States,* 373 U.S. 1 (1963), extending the principle of post-conviction remedy to Federal prisoners.
30. *Cf. The Vengeance,* 3 Dall. 297 (1796); *The Schooner Becky,* 4 Cranch 443 (1808); *New Jersey Steam Nav. Co. v. Merchants Bank,* 6 How. 344 (1848).
31. *The Lottawanna,* 21 Wall. 558 (1875); *In re Garnett,* 141 U.S. 1 (1891).
32. 41 Stat. 988. *Panama R. Co. v. Johnson,* 264 U.S. 375 (1924); *Romero v. Internat. Term. Co.,* 358 U.S. 354 (1959).
33. *Cf. The Genesee Chief v. Fitzhugh,* 12 How. 443 (1852); *Ex parte Boyer,* 109 U.S. 629 (1884); *United States v Appalachian Power Co.,* 311 U.S. 377 (1940).

Cf. denial of state jurisdiction in *South. Pac. R. Co. v. Jensen,* 244 U.S. 205 (1917) and the ambivalent concession of the Court in *Davis v. Department of Labor,* 317 U.S. 249 (1942).

34. *Dugan v. United States,* 3 Wheat. 172 (1818); *United States v. Bell Tel. Co.,* 128 U.S. 315 (1888).

35. *United States v. North Carolina,* 136 U.S. 211 (1890); *United States v. Minnesota,* 270 U.S. 181 (1926).

36. *Lonergan v. United States,* 303 U.S. 33 (1938); *United States v. Rayon Co.,* 329 U.S. 654 (1947). Actions against agents of government are distinguished from actions against government. *United States v. Lee,* 106 U.S. 196 (1882); *Larson v. Domestic & Foreign Corp.,* 337 U.S. 682 (1949).

37. *Cf. Missouri v. Illinois & Chicago District,* 180 U.S. 208 (1901); *Kansas v. Colorado,* 206 U.S. 46 (1907); *New Jersey v. New York,* 283 U.S. 336 (1931), all on water rights; *South Dakota v. North Carolina,* 192 U.S. 286 (1904), and *Virginia v. West Virginia,* 220 U.S. 1 (1911), on debts; and miscellaneous issues in *Arkansas v. Texas,* 346 U.S. 368 (1953); *Kentucky v. Indiana,* 281 U.S. 163 (1930); *Texas v. Florida,* 306 U.S. 388 (1939); *Pennsylvania v. West Virginia,* 262 U.S. 533 (1923).

38. *Cf. Alabama v. Arizona,* 291 U.S. 286 (1934); *Massachusetts v. Missouri,* 308 U.S. 1 (1934); *Texas v. Florida,* 306 U.S. 398 (1939); and *cf.* the long litigation between Virginia and West Virginia over the division of state debt liability incurred prior to separation of the states, extending from 1907 in 206 U.S. 290 to 1918 in 246 U.S. 565.

39. *Florida v. Mellon,* 273 U.S. 12 (1927); *New Jersey v. Sergeant,* 269 U.S. 328 (1926); *Minnesota v. Northern Securities Co.,* 184 U.S. 199 (1902).

40. 1 Stat. 92. *Cf.* the effort to delineate a reasonable division of jurisdiction under this clause in the American Law Institute's *Study of Division of Jurisdiction Between State and Federal Courts* (Philadelphia, 1968).

41. *Cf.* Frankfurter and Landis, *op. cit.,* 8, 89. In 1941 Congress included the District of Columbia in the "diversity jurisdiction" concept. 54 Stat. 143; *cf. Nat. Ins. Co. v. Tidewater Co.,* 337 U.S. 582 (1949).

42. *Cf.* the American Law Institute study cited in note 40 *supra;* and *cf.* also Wright, *Federal Courts.*

43. *Cf.* Story, *Commentaries on the Conflict of Laws* (Boston, 1834), 451; *Swift v. Tyson,* 16 Pet. 1 (1842); *Erie R. Co. v. Tompkins,* 304 U.S. 64 (1938).

44. *Bank of United States v. Deveaux,* 5 Cranch 61 (1809); *Comm. & R. Bank v. Slocomb,* 14 Pet. 60 (1840); *Louisville R. Co. v. Letson,* 2 How. 497 (1844); *Marshall v. B. & O. R. Co.,* 16 How. 314 (1854).

45. *Terral v. Burke Constr. Co.,* 257 U.S. 529 (1922).

46. *Cf. Black & White Taxi Co. v. B. & Y. Taxi Co.,* 276 U.S. 518 (1928). *Cf.* also *Guaranty Trust Co. v. New York,* 326 U.S. 99 (1945); *Klaxton v. Stentor Co.,* 313 U.S. 487 (1941); *United States v. Standard Oil Co.,* 332 U.S. 301 (1947).

III. 2. Cl. 2. Original and Appellate Jurisdiction

In all cases affecting ambassadors, other public ministers and consuls, and those in which a state shall be a party, the Supreme Court shall have original jurisdiction. In all the other cases before mentioned, the Supreme Court shall have appellate jurisdiction, both as to law and fact, with such exceptions, and under such regulations, as the Congress shall make.

The Court has always insisted that the first sentence in this clause is self-executing and beyond the power of Congress to enlarge.[1] Original jurisdiction is limited to specific cases; appellate jurisdiction is subject to "such exceptions and . . . regulations as the Congress shall make." The original jurisdiction provision is, conversely, self-limiting and "must be construed negatively" as to any cases not enumerated by the Constitution itself.[2] Congress may, however, vest concurrent jurisdiction over such cases in the District Courts.[3] The Court reserves the right to determine whether a case involving a state falls under the definition of this clause; the mere fact that the state is a party to an action does not automatically invoke the clause.[4] Nor does the clause cover cases where a citizen is suing his own state.[5] While a state may sue on behalf of its citizens, the suit must involve the state as *parens patriae* (i.e., the state's direct interest must be involved)[6] rather than being for the convenience of the private parties.[7]

Chief Justice Taft was an ardent advocate of limiting the appellate jurisdiction of the Supreme Court in the interest of broadening the Court's ultimate function as an arbiter of fundamental questions of law, and in the Judiciary Act of 1925[8] he succeeded in prevailing on Congress to narrow the range of cases appealable as of right, making the majority of cases from the intermediate courts reviewable at the *certiorari* discretion of the Supreme Court. By its own rules of practice the Court has further circumscribed its appellate functions, particularly with its so-called "rule of four," which Justice Brennan thus described: "Even though this action is taken on the votes of only a minority of four of the Justices, the Court then approaches plenary consideration of the case anew as a Court . . . and every member of the Court brings to the ultimate discussion of the case his judgment based on the full briefs and the oral arguments."[9]

The Court has also limited the cases coming before it by its various holdings on ripeness, standing, justiciability and related standards, discussed under Section 1 of this Article; and by disposing of a sizable proportion of cases on the merits by means of memorandum decisions of a sentence or two, or a simple notation of denial of *certiorari* or dismissal of appeal.[10] An objective of the Court in jurisdictional questions being to accommodate the balance of state and Federal interests, appeals from state courts are limited to important Federal questions, or cases in which a state court has construed a Federal law as being in conflict with the Federal Constitution, or cases in which a state law has been upheld in the face of contrary Federal decisions.[11] The obligation of state courts to enforce Federal law, affirmed in 1947[12] has been a constitutional principle long recognized by both Congress and the Court.

1. *Marbury v. Madison,* 1 Cranch 137 (1803).
2. *Ex parte Vallandigham,* 1 Wall. 243 (1864); *Texas v. Florida,* 306 U.S. 398 (1939).
3. *Case v. Bowles,* 327 U.S. 92 (1946); *Wisconsin v. Pelican Ins. Co.,* 127 U.S. 265 (1888).
4. *Oklahoma ex rel. Johnson v. Cook,* 304 U.S. 387 (1938). *Cf.* also *United States v. West Virginia,* 295 U.S. 463 (1935); *Minnesota v. Hitchcock,* 185 U.S. 388 (1902).
5. *Duhne v. United States,* 251 U.S. 311 (1920).
6. *Nebraska v. Wyoming,* 325 U.S. 589 (1945). *Cf. Massachusetts v. Missouri,* 308 U.S. 1 (1838); *Arizona v. California,* 373 U.S. 546 (1963).
7. *Georgia v. Pennsylvania R. Co.,* 324 U.S. 439 (1945).
8. 43 Stat. 936; *cf.* Swindler, *The Old Legality,* Ch. 16.
9. *Ohio ex rel. Eaton v. Price,* 360 U.S. 246, 247 (1939).
10. Occasionally, although such memorandum opinions are expected to be unanimous, dissents will be filed; *cf. Jacobs v. New York,* 288 U.S. 431 (1933).
11. *Cf. Ex parte Young,* 209 U.S. 123 (1908); *Home Tel. & Tel. Co. v. Los Angeles,* 227 U.S. 278 (1913); *Railroad Comm. v. Pullman Co.,* 312 U.S. 496 (1941).
12. *Testa v. Katt,* 330 U.S. 386 (1947).

III. 2. Cl. 3. Jury Trial of Crimes

The trial of all crimes, except in cases of impeachment, shall be by jury; and such trial shall be held in the state where the said crimes shall have been committed; but when not committed within any state, the trial shall be at such place or places as the Congress may by law have directed.

The recent doctrines of the Supreme Court with reference to jury trials for such cases under state jurisdiction (discussed under the Sixth Amendment) has brought the matter of jury trial in the Federal courts back into heated discussion. While the common-law definition of a jury of twelve men who reach a unanimous verdict has been defined as a procedural rather than a jurisdictional rule,[1] the recent disposition of Federal circuits to alter this provision with respect to civil cases has been decried.[2] The preservation of the right knowingly to waive a jury trial would seem to be an adequate safeguard to the essential constitutional provision, however.

1. *Hibdon v. United States,* 204 F. 2d 834 (1953). *Cf. Patton v. United States,* 281 U.S. 276 (1930).
2. *Cf.* Gibbons, "New Minijuries: Panacea or Pandora's Box?" 58 *A.B.A.J.* 594 (June 1972).

III. 3. Cl. 1. Treason

Treason against the United States shall consist only in levying war against them, or in adhering to their enemies, giving them aid and comfort. No person shall be convicted of treason unless on the testimony of two witnesses to the same overt act, or on confession in open court.

Twentieth-century treason trials have been rare, even in the context of two world wars. While World War I produced the Trading with the Enemy Act[1] and the so-called Espionage and Sedition Acts,[2] revived in essence in World War II,[3] the Court was reluctant to apply the common-law concept of treason as redefined by acts of Parliament.[4] Thus, in *Cramer v. United States,*[5] the narrow majority insisted on the rule that everything charged as treason must be supported by the testimony of two witnesses. Two years later, however, the two-witness requirement was qualified and the prevailing rule was proof of an overt act which moved the defendant's conduct "from the realm of thought into the realm of action."[6] Never having recognized the Confederate government as a *de facto* political entity, the United States was denied a constitutional power to charge its adherents with treason;[7] and in the "cold war" of the 1940s and 1950s a similar bar to treason trials was asserted.[8]

1. 40 Stat. 411.
2. 40 Stat. 217, 553.
3. 54 Stat. 670.
4. *Cf.* 7 Will. III, c. 3 (1697), and 25 Edw. III, Stat. 5., Ch. 2 (1350).

5. 325 U.S. 1 (1945).
6. *Haupt v. United States,* 330 U.S. 631 (1947); *Kawakita v. United States,* 343 U.S. 717 (1952).
7. *Thorington v. Smith,* 75 U.S. 1 (1869).
8. *United States v. Rosenberg,* 195 F. 2d 583 (1952), cert. den. 344 U.S. 889 (1952).

III. 3. Cl. 2. Punishment of Treason

The Congress shall have power to declare the punishment of treason, but no attainder of treason shall work corruption of blood, or forfeiture except during the life of the person attainted.

Corruption of blood was a feudal penalty extinguishing estates in land, and frequently life as well, for engaging in action inimical to the Crown. In various cases the courts have denied that certain penalties enacted by Congress amounted to attainder.[1] With reference to bills of attainder, or legislative conviction of defendants in treason and other crimes, see *United States v. Lovett.*[2]

1. *Cf.* Confiscation Act of 1862, 12 Stat. 589; Captured and Abandoned Property Act of 1863, 12 Stat. 820. *Walleck v. Van Renswick,* 92 U.S. 202 (1876); Subversive Activities Control Act of 1950, 64 Stat. 987; *Communist Party v. Subversive Activities Control Board,* 367 U.S. 1 (1961).
2. 328 U.S. 303 (1946).

Article IV. Federal-State Relationships

IV. 1. Full Faith and Credit

Full faith and credit shall be given in each state to the public acts, records and judicial proceedings of every other state. And the Congress may, by general laws, prescribe the manner in which such acts, records and proceedings shall be proved, and the effect thereof.

Conflict of Laws in the Federal System

With this section, the Constitutional Convention undertook to dispose of some of the conflicting state laws and policies which had nullified effective interstate relations under the Confederation. Having clarified the powers and functions of Federal government in the first three Articles, the Convention recognized that it was equally essential to insure that "the public acts of every state shall be given the same effect by the courts of another state that they have by law and usage at home."[1] In the process, the independent sovereignty of each state was necessarily circumscribed[2] and subordinated to the fundamental principle that "litigation once pursued to judgment shall be conclusive of the rights of the parties in every other court" and thus should preclude relitigation in successive states.[3] A judgment in State A would presumably be enforced in State B, provided that State B had acquired jurisdiction over the parties or the subject matter and there was no strong conflicting public policy in State B.[4]

This apparently simple principle, however, has been clouded by ambivalence throughout constitutional history. Congress in 1790 undertook to implement this section by a statute declaring that the legislative and judicial records of every state should be given "the same full faith and credit" in the courts of other states with reference to causes of action adjudicated in the original state.[5] The Marshall Court treated the statute as conclusive of the merits of any state judgment in all other states;[6] but the Taney Court, with its zeal for state sovereignty, seriously qualified the statute and thus the effectiveness of the section by stipulating that enforcement of State A's judgment was not "materially to interfere with the essential attributes" of the law of State B, the new forum.[7] This was taken to mean that when the judgment of State A was introduced as evidence of entitlement to remedy in State B, the remedy itself could be determined by the laws of State B.[8] Further, it has been held that where the statutory policies of two states are in conflict, the forum state is not automatically compelled to submit to the public act of the foreign state where the cause of action arose;[9] and since 1877 it has been established that where there was lack of due process in the state of the original action, the judgment is not entitled to full faith and credit in another state.[10]

Divorce Law and Full Faith and Credit

An elaborate, and unique, system of conflict of laws has thus developed in American jurisprudence as a result of the differing interpretations of this section by the Marshall and Taney Courts, the varying doctrines emerging from adjudication of the due-process clause of the Fourteenth Amendment and the differing public policies of the several states. The most critical area in which "full faith and credit" has been tested has been the area of divorce law; the disparity between states with strict divorce laws (e.g., New York) and those with highly flexible divorce laws (e.g., Nevada) raised many disputes—at least in the days before social and statutory postures on the subject of divorce itself had relaxed. While Nevada divorces were generally, even though reluctantly, recognized by other states under this clause, judicial efforts to define limits and conditions of the controlling force of this section have only added to the confusion. It was long contended that a divorce action was an action against the marriage contract (*in rem*) rather than against one of the parties to the marriage (*in personam*).[11] Under this rationale, either party to the marriage could bring a divorce action in a state in which he was domiciled.[12] But when it was held, in 1906, that a divorce action was an action *in personam*,[13] the party against whom the suit was brought was required to be within the jurisdiction of the court.

When the Supreme Court in 1942 held that any state might grant a divorce to any person who was a *bona fide* domiciliary (i.e., tacitly restoring the status of divorce proceedings as *in rem* actions),[14] it invited attacks on the *bona fides* of the domicile. The Court's answer, in 1945, was that "domiciliary intent" was material to the determination of whether another state should give full faith and credit to the foreign divorce decree.[15] To avert criminal liability which could arise from cases where the state granting the divorce treated the domicile as *bona fide* and the other state did not, the Court three years later held that a valid decree should be effective in all states as to marital status of the individuals but not as to disposition of marital interests such as alimony, property distribution and the like.[16]

Other Issues of Full Faith and Credit

The fundamental requirement under this section is that the courts have jurisdiction over the individual in actions affecting personal liability (*in personam*) or over the property in actions affecting property (*in rem*).[17] A state's power to define and limit jurisdiction in its own courts must comply with constitutional standards of due process and equal protection,[18] but the burden of proof of lack of jurisdiction is on the individual.[19] For a person to be liable to a judgment he must have been subject to it or privy to it—either within the jurisdiction of the court pronouncing the judgment or having a mutual interest with another who was within the jurisdiction.[20] Once the fact of jurisdiction is settled, the judgment in the litigated issue is settled as to the issue itself (*res judicata*) and must be so treated by the courts of other states.[21]

An underlying question in the matter of full faith and credit is whether an action is "local" or "transitory"—the former being a cause which is only triable in a particular place, the other being triable wherever the individual or subject may be found.[22] This has led to a substantial body of adjudication itself: whether a contract is to be governed by the law of the place where it was made,[23] whether a stockholder's liability is defined by the law of the incorporating state,[24] whether insurance contracts and business come under the law of the forum state (because the nature of the business requires compliance with local laws in order to do business locally)[25] and a confused rationale as to the applicable law on workmen's compensation where the employer is liable under his home state's laws but his employee may recover under the laws of another state where he was injured in the course of his employment.[26] The details of American conflict-of-laws doctrine need not be considered here beyond the fact that the doctrine itself has been influenced by the basic principle that the full-faith-and-credit clause injects an ultimate constitutional test into all questions of state sovereignty which are ingredients of either private or public law.

1. *Chicago & Alton R. Co. v. Wiggins Ferry Co.*, 119 U.S. (1887). *Cf.* also *Smithsonian Institution v. St. John*, 214 U.S. 19 (1909).
2. *Cf. Estin v. Estin*, 334 U.S. 541 (1948); *Magnolia Petr. Co. v. Hunt*, 320 U.S. 430 (1943).
3. 320 U.S. at 438. And *cf. Sutton v. Leib*, 342 U.S. 402 (1952); *Johnson v. Muelburger*, 340 U.S. 581 (1951).
4. *Cf. Sistare v. Sistare*, 218 U.S. 1 (1910). And *cf. Titus v. Wallick*, 306 U.S. 282 (1939); *Morris v. Jones*, 329 U.S. 545 (1947); *Durfee v. Duke*, 375 U.S. 106 (1963).
5. 1 Stat., 122, now 28 U.S.C. 1738, 1739.
6. *Cf. Mills v. Duryee*, 7 Cranch 481 (1813); *Hampton v. McConnell*, 3 Wheat. 234 (1818).

7. *McElmoyne v. Cohen*, 13 Pet. 312 (1839).
8. *Cf. Cole v. Cunningham*, 133 U.S. 107 (1890).
9. *Hughes v. Fetter*, 341 U.S. 609 (1951); *Pink v. Hwy. Express*, 314 U.S. 201 (1941).
10. *Pennoyer v. Neff*, 95 U.S. 714 (1877); *cf. Griffin v. Griffin*, 327 U.S. 220 (1946).
11. *Cheever v. Wilson*, 9 Wall. 108 (1870).
12. *Atherton v. Atherton*, 181 U.S. 155 (1901); *Andrews v. Andrews*, 188 U.S. 14 (1903). *Cf.* also, on Nevada divorces under this clause, *Temple v. Liebmann*, 186 N.Y.S. 2d 533 (1959), aff'd. 192 N.Y.S. 2d 484 (1959).
13. *Haddock v. Haddock*, 201 U.S. 562 (1906); overruled in *Williams v. North Carolina*, 317 U.S. 287 (1942).
14. *Williams v. North Carolina* (I), 317 U.S. 287 (1942).
15. *Williams v. North Carolina* (II), 325 U.S. 226 (1945).
16. *Estin v. Estin*, 334 U.S. 541 (1948). *Cf. Vanderbilt v. Vanderbilt*, 354 U.S. 416 (1957).
17. *Cf. Western Union v. Pennsylvania*, 368 U.S. 71 (1961); *McDonald v. Mabee*, 243 U.S. 90 (1917); *Thompson v. Whitman*, 18 Wall. 457 (1874).
18. *Thompson v. Thompson*, 226 U.S. 551 (1913); *Broderick v. Rosner*, 294 U.S. 629 (1935); and *cf. Morris v. Jones*, 329 U.S. 545 (1947); *Milliken v. Meyer*, 311 U.S. 457 (1940).
19. *Rice v. Rice*, 336 U.S. 674 (1949); *Esenwein v. Pennsylvania*, 325 U.S. 279 (1945). *Cf.* also *Simmons v. Saul*, 138 U.S. 448 (1891).
20. *Estin v. Estin*, 334 U.S. 541 (1948); *Hansbury v. Lee*, 311 U.S. 32 (1940); *Bagley v. Gen. Fire Exting. Co.*, 212 U.S. 477 (1909); *Harris v. Balk*, 198 U.S. 222 (1905).
21. *Riley v. New York Trust Co.*, 315 U.S. 343 (1942); and *cf. Durfee v. Duke*, 375 U.S. 106 (1963).
22. *Cf.* generally, *Alaska Packers Assn. v. Commission*, 294 U.S. 532 (1955); *Hughes v. Fetter*, 341 U.S. 609 (1951).
23. *Chicago & Alton R. Co. v. Wiggins Ferry Co.*, 119 U.S. 615 (1887); but *cf. Klaxton Co. v. Stentor Co.*, 313 U.S. 487 (1941).
24. *Converse v. Hamilton*, 224 U.S. 243 (1912); *Broderick v. Rosner*, 294 U.S. 629 (1935).
25. *Nat. Mut. B. & L. Assn. v. Brahan*, 193 U.S. 635 (1904); *cf. Watson v. Employers Liab. Corp.*, 348 U.S. 66 (1954).
26. *Bradford El. Co. v. Clapper*, 286 U.S. 145 (1932); *Pac. Ins. Co. v. Commission*, 306 U.S. 493 (1939); *Magnolia Petr. Co. v. Hunt*, 320 U.S. 430 (1943); *Carroll v. Lanza*, 349 U.S. 408 (1955).

IV. 2. Cl. 1. Privileges and Immunities

The citizens of each state shall be entitled to all privileges and immunities of citizens in the several states.

This section was intended to complement the full-faith-and-credit clause; but its resulting adjudication meant that when the Fourteenth Amendment was adopted, the definition of "privileges and immunities" of citizens of the United States in that Amendment had been circumscribed to a degree by the judicial definition of the phrase in this section concerning privileges and immunities of citizens of the several states.[1] The classical definition of privileges and immunities under this section was given on circuit by Justice Bushrod Washington in 1825: "Protection by the government; the enjoyment of life and liberty, with the right to acquire and possess property of every kind, and to pursue and obtain happiness and safety; subject nevertheless to such restraints as the government may justly prescribe for the general good of the whole. The right of a citizen of one state to pass through, or to reside in any other state, for purposes of trade, agriculture, professional pursuits, or otherwise; to claim the benefit of the writ of *habeas corpus;* to institute and maintain actions of any kind in the courts of the state; to take, hold and dispose of property, either real or personal; and an exemption from higher taxes or impositions than are paid by the other citizens of the state."[2]

A substantial reiteration of the Washington doctrine was given by the Supreme Court in 1920;[3] and in 1947 it was declared that the clause, taken with Section 1, prevented any state from denying access to its courts to citizens of another state.[4] The purpose of the clause, the Court added the following year, is to prevent unreasonable discrimination, but not to bar the states from withholding services where there may be valid reason other than the fact that the parties are residents of another state.[5] The privileges and immunities of this clause, it has been further declared, are to be guaranteed to individuals, not to corporations.[6]

States are enjoined under this clause not to discriminate between residents and non-residents in the matter of taxation.[7] While the terms "resident" and "citizen" are not necessarily synonymous, said Justice Pitney in 1920, a taxing scheme which discriminates against all non-residents automatically discriminates against those who are citizens of other states.[8] But occasional inequalities in the operation of a tax system which is generally equitable will not violate the constitutional provision.[9] The basic rule of construction of this clause is that no state may favor its own citizens over citizens of other states in matters which have been recognized as fundamental rights.[10]

1. *Slaughterhouse Cases,* 16 Wall. 36 (1873).
2. *Corfield v. Coryell,* 6 Fed. Cas. 546, 552 (1825).
3. *United States v. Wheeler,* 254 U.S. 281 (1920).

4. *Angel v. Bullington,* 330 U.S. 183 (1947); *cf. Cole v. Cunningham,* 133 U.S. 114
    (1890). But the doctrine of *forum non conveniens* may be constitutionally ap-
    plied if it treats residents and non-residents alike. *Whitney v. Madde,* 79 N.E.
    2d 593 (1948), cert. den. 335 U.S. 828 (1948).
5. *Toomer v. Witsell,* 334 U.S. 385 (1948).
6. *Hemphill v. Orloff,* 277 U.S. 537 (1966).
7. *Ward v. Maryland,* 12 Wall. 418 (1871).
8. *Shaffer v. Carter,* 252 U.S. 37 (1920).
9. *Maxwell v. Bugbee,* 250 U.S. 525 (1919).
10. *Chambers v. B. & O. R. Co.,* 207 U.S. 142 (1907).

IV. 2. Cl. 2. Extradition

A person charged in any state with treason, felony, or other crime,
who shall flee from justice, and be found in another state, shall, on
demand of the executive authority of the state from which he fled, be
delivered up, to be removed to the state having jurisdiction of the
crime.

IV. 2. Cl. 3. Fugitive Slaves

[No person held to service or labor in one state, under the laws
thereof, escaping into another, shall, in consequence of any law or
regulation therein, be discharged from such service or labor, but shall
be delivered up on claim to the party to whom such service or labor
may be due.]

The second and third clauses of this section (the third being
now obsolete) related to interstate comity, particularly with reference to the criminal law.[1] Like other portions of this article, this
clause subjects interstate responsibilities to Federal surveillance.[2]
There is theoretically no right of asylum in a state to which a
fugitive flees, and when an accused person has been charged in
one state and fled to another, the second state is expected under
this clause to deliver up the fugitive.[3] Highly publicized cases in
which extradition has been refused because of public revulsion in
the state of refuge at the criminal process in the claiming state, in
most instances, have been political rather than judicial matters.
The rule of law itself tends to be stated in absolute terms; thus, it
is not necessary to prove that the individual sought for extradition
intended to flee from justice, since it is not the motive of the person wanted, but the proof of his liability to criminal process in the
extraditing state which supports the demand.[4]

1. *Innes v. Tobin,* 240 U.S. 127 (1916).
2. *Smith v. Idaho,* 373 F. 2d 149 (1967), cert. den. 388 U.S. 919 (1967); *cf. Lascelles v. Georgia,* 148 U.S. 541 (1893).
3. *Pierce v. Creecy,* 210 U.S. 387 (1908).
4. *Drew v. Thaw,* 235 U.S. 432 (1914); *Appleyard v. Massachusetts,* 203 U.S. 222 (1906).

IV. 3. Cl. 1. Admission of New States

New states shall be admitted by the Congress into this Union; but no new state shall be formed or erected within the jurisdiction of any other state; nor any state be formed by the junction of two or more states or parts of states, without the consent of the legislatures of the states concerned as well as of the Congress.

The effect of this clause is to provide that new states on admission shall have the same standing in the Federal union as states already in the union.[1] The newly admitted state, the Court has said, may not be bound by a condition that it renounce any sovereign rights enjoyed by other states,[2] and although Congress may postpone admission—as when President Taft vetoed a bill admitting Arizona until it had amended its constitution to delete a provision for popular recall of judges—the right of the state to restore the provision after admission cannot be denied.[3] By the same token, Federal jurisdiction over navigable waters comes into effect automatically with admission,[4] and the same is true of the power to establish reservations on Federal lands within the new state.[5]

1. *United States v. Texas,* 339 U.S. 707 (1950); *Skiriotes v. Florida,* 313 U.S. 69 (1941).
2. *Coyle v. Smith,* 225 U.S. 559 (1911).
3. *Cf.* Swindler, ed., I *Sources and Documents of United States Constitutions* (Dobbs Ferry, N.Y., 1972), Ariz. p. 301.
4. *Arizona v. California,* 373 U.S. 546 (1963); *United States v. Texas,* 339 U.S. 707 (1950).
5. *United States v. Wyoming,* 331 U.S. 440 (1947); *cf.* also *Larsen v. Arizona,* 385 U.S. 458 (1967).

IV. 3. Cl. 2. Public Lands

The Congress shall have power to dispose of and make all needful rules and regulations respecting the territory or other property belonging to the United States; and nothing in this Constitution shall be so construed as to prejudice any claims of the United States or of any particular state.

This clause was cited in 1936 to uphold the authority of the Federal government to dispose of property (electric power generated by the Tennessee Valley Authority) by constructing power lines and bringing the electricity to market.[1] While land in the public domain may be sold only by authority of Congress,[2] the President by executive order may withdraw land from the public domain for other government purposes.[3] No state may tax Federal public lands within its borders or otherwise limit the power of Congress over these lands,[4] although Congress may delegate to a state certain authority to make supplemental laws governing property disposition, as in the case of mining claims which it is considered necessary to make uniform in both state and Federal jurisdictions.[5] Congress has exclusive power, it has been declared, to develop reclamation projects on its public lands[6] and may regulate private developments on private lands which jeopardize the government interest on public lands.[7] In the case of territories of the United States, Congress has complete legislative power, although it may delegate all or part of this power to a territorial legislature.[8]

1. *Ashwander v. T.V.A.*, 297 U.S. 288 (1937); *Alabama Power Co. v. Ickes*, 302 U.S. 464 (1938).
2. *Utah P. & L. Co. v. United States*, 243 U.S. 389 (1917). *Cf.* also *United States v. San Francisco*, 310 U.S. 16 (1940).
3. *Sioux Tribe v. United States*, 316 U.S. 317 (1942).
4. *Wilson v. Cook*, 327 U.S. 474 (1946); *Emblem v. Lincoln Land Co.*, 184 U.S. 660 (1902); and *cf. Williams v. Lee*, 358 U.S. 217 (1959).
5. *Butte City Water Co. v. Baker*, 196 U.S. 126 (1905).
6. *Ivanhoe Irr. Dist. v. McCracken*, 357 U.S. 275 (1959).
7. *United States v. Alford*, 274 U.S. 264 (1927).
8. *Simms v. Simms*, 175 U.S. 162 (1899); *Binns v. United States*, 194 U.S. 486 (1904).

IV. 4. Republican Form of Government

The United States shall guarantee to every state in this Union a republican form of government, and shall protect each of them against invasion, and on application of the legislature, or of the executive (when the legislature cannot be convened), against domestic violence.

The so-called guarantee clause was declared by Chief Justice
Taney to be a political provision which was not justiciable in the
courts,[1] a generalization which has long (but so far unsuccessfully)
invited a qualification.[2] The guarantee is essentially defined in
negative terms: it does not require the United States to do "police
duty" in the states,[3] while on other occasions the intervention with
Federal troops has been on the initiative of executive officers, as
in the case of the Pullman strike in Chicago in 1894.[4] What the
states choose to do in matters of local government is not the concern of Congress, it has been said.[5] And even if Congress should
violate the guarantee, the courts have declared, a judicial remedy
would not necessarily be available.[6] The steadfast policy of avoid-
ing jurisdiction over questions potentially resting on this clause
has led the Court in such momentous constitutional issues as
electoral malapportionment to base adjudication on the due-
process clause of the Fourteenth Amendment rather than on the
guarantee of a "republican" form of government.[7]

1. *Luther v. Borden,* 7 How. 1 (1849).
2. *Texas v. White,* 7 Wall. 700 (1869); *Pac. T.&T. Co. v. Oregon,* 223 U.S. 118
   (1912); *Highland Farms Dairy Co. v. Agnew,* 300 U.S. 608 (1937).
3. *United States v. Cruikshank,* 92 U.S. 542 (1876); and *cf. Cochran v. Board of
   Education,* 281 U.S. 370 (1930).
4. Swindler, *The Old Legality,* Ch. 3.
5. *South Carolina v. United States,* 199 U.S. 454 (1905); *Michigan v. Lowery,* 199
   U.S. 233 (1905); *Forsyth v. Hammond,* 166 U.S. 519 (1897). *Cf.* also *O'Neill v.
   Leamer,* 239 U.S. 244 (1915).
6. *Bauers v. Heisel,* 361 F. 2d 581 (1966), cert. den. 386 U.S. 1021 (1966).
7. *Cf. Baker v. Carr,* 369 U.S. 186 (1962); *Reynolds v. Sims,* 377 U.S. 533 (1964).

Article V. The Amending Process

The Congress, whenever two-thirds of both Houses shall deem it
necessary, shall propose amendments to this Constitution, or, on the
application of the legislatures of two-thirds of the several states, shall
call a convention for proposing amendments, which in either case shall
be valid to all intents and purposes as part of this Constitution, when
ratified by the legislatures of three-fourths of the several states, or by

conventions in three-fourths thereof, as the one or the other mode of ratification may be proposed by the Congress; provided, [that no amendment which may be made prior to the year one thousand eight hundred and eight shall in any manner affect the first and fourth clauses of the Ninth Section of the First Article; and] that no state, without its consent, shall be deprived of its equal suffrage in the Senate.

In the Progressive era there was much academic discussion concerning the subjects which properly could be treated in constitutional amendments, from the income tax to prohibition.[1] There has also been, from time to time, a desultory consideration of how long a proposed amendment could be entitled to consideration, the only judicial suggestion being that if a proposal was clearly obsolete it could be treated as having been rejected.[2] Nor is there any practical distinction between ratification by legislatures or by conventions; Congress may elect the method to be used, as well as stipulate the time period in which the proposed amendment may lie before the states.[3]

The convention method of proposing amendments has sporadically been urged, and an effort to petition Congress to call a new constitutional convention was surreptitiously advanced in the 1960s.[4] Since the purpose of this clandestine effort was to seek means of overriding the Supreme Court holdings in the malapportionment issue, there was manifest doubt as to the validity of many petitions presented by malapportioned legislatures. The alternative, a convention free to draft proposed amendments on any and all subjects, was an even more mischievous idea. Fortunately, the effort fell short of its goal.

1. Swindler, *The Old Legality,* Chs. 8, 10. *Cf.* also *Fairchild v. Hughes,* 258 U.S. 126 (1922).
2. *Dillon v. Gloss,* 256 U.S. 368 (1921); but *cf. Coleman v. Miller,* 307 U.S. 433 (1939).
3. *United States v. Sprague,* 282 U.S. 716 (1931); *Hawke v. Smith,* 253 U.S. 221 (1920); *Leser v. Garnett,* 258 U.S. 130 (1922). *Cf.* also *Chandler v. Wise,* 307 U.S. 474 (1939).
4. *Cf.* Swindler, *The New Legality,* Ch. 16.

Article VI. The Supremacy Principle

VI. 1. Assumption of Confederation Debts

All debts contracted and engagements entered into, before the adoption of this Constitution, shall be valid against the United States under this Constitution as under the Confederation.

VI. 2. Supreme Law of the Land

This Constitution, and the laws of the United States which shall be made in pursuance thereof; and all treaties made, or which shall be made, under the authority of the United States, shall be the supreme law of the land; and the judges in every state shall be bound thereby, anything in the Constitution or laws of any state to the contrary notwithstanding.

It was on this clause that Chief Justice Marshall built his constitutional jurisprudence, based on the fundamental declaration that "the states have no power, by taxation or otherwise, to retard, impede, burden or in any manner control the operation of the constitutional laws enacted by Congress to carry into execution the powers vested in the general government."[1] The Court has relied on this principle ever since; in 1958 it was heard to declare that the supremacy clause entitled the Federal government "to remove all obstacles to its action within its own sphere" and to assert an immunity from regulatory acts of the states in carrying out its own constitutional powers.[2] All conflicting state laws and policies must yield,[3] and where the Federal authority leaves no room for concurrent state action, the Federal power pre-empts the field.[4] Federal claims and interests generally override state claims;[5] Federal immunity statutes protect witnesses from having their testimony used against them in any state court.[6]

It has long been recognized, also, that state courts are bound to enforce Federal law and may not refuse to take jurisdiction in cases properly coming before them on questions of Federal law.[7] And where a Federal criminal statute conflicts with a state law on the same subject, the Federal law precludes state prosecution under its own law even in cases of violation of the state law prior to enactment of the Federal law.[8] The Federal Reserve Act controls specific actions of national banks in the face of contrary rules of state banking law,[9] Treasury Department regulations on Federal bonds override state laws on survivors' interests[10] and Patent Office licensing practice is exempt from state licensing regulations.[11] While the police power of a state is accorded every reasonable respect by the Federal courts, the courts will yet reserve the power ultimately to determine whether there is a conflict with Federal authority which will invoke the supremacy clause.[12] Where there is doubt as to Congressional intent to pre-empt a subject area, however, the courts seek to construe the law so as to accommodate both state and national power.[13]

The punctuation of the opening part of this clause has raised a point of construction: Is the first semicolon merely a peculiarity of eighteenth-century grammar, or does it in fact distinguish between two sources of supreme national power—first, the Constitution and laws made in pursuance thereof; and, second, treaties made under the sovereign authority of the United States?[14] The Court has striven to avoid having to answer this question in most instances. It has, however, conceded that a treaty "is primarily a compact between independent nations" which is governed by international law. "But a treaty may also contain provisions which confer certain rights . . . capable of enforcement as between private parties in the courts of the country."[15]

The closest to an unequivocal answer to the question was given by Justice Holmes: "Acts of Congress are the supreme law of the land only when made in pursuance of the Constitution, while treaties are declared to be so when made under the authority of the United States."[16] In this instance, an act of Congress seeking to regulate the killing of migratory birds had been struck down as interfering with state property rights in the birds;[17] thereupon the United States executed a treaty with Canada in which it undertook to protect such birds as a matter of protecting Canada's interest under the treaty.[18] By a 7–2 division the Court then upheld the treaty and its implementing statute, Holmes observing: "It is obvious that there may be matters of the sharpest exigency for the national well-being that an act of Congress could not deal with but that a treaty followed by such an act could, and it is not lightly to be assumed that, in matters requiring national action, 'a power which must belong to, and somewhere reside in, every civilized government' is not to be found."[19]

While the rule in *Missouri v. Holland* has been gingerly treated by the Court ever since, Congress has periodically been assailed with a xenophobic fear that the treaty power may in fact turn out to be a source of national authority independent of the Constitution. The United Nations treaty in particular was viewed by many persons as a potential infringement on the sovereignty of the United States, and the efforts of Senator John W. Bricker of Ohio to place a qualifying amendment before the people has been discussed elsewhere.[20] The Bricker amendment never got out of Congress; but the Court in 1957, in a divided opinion, [21] held that no treaty may be free from the restraints of the Constitution.[22] Related to this rationale is the consistent judicial rule that treaty obligations at least as they affect internal or municipal law may be modified or abrogated by subsequent acts of Congress.[23]

1. *McCulloch v. Maryland*, 4 Wheat. 316 (1819); *Gibbons v. Ogden*, 9 Wheat. (1824). *Cf.* also *Nash v. Commission*, 389 U.S. 235 (1967).
2. *Public Utility Commission v. United States*, 355 U.S. 534 (1958); *Garner v. Local Union*, 346 U.S. 485 (1953); *Smith v. O'Grady*, 312 U.S. 329 (1941).
3. *Hill v. Florida*, 325 U.S. 538 (1945); and *cf. Testa v. Katt*, 330 U.S. 386 (1947).
4. *Pennsylvania v. Nelson*, 350 U.S. 497 (1956).
5. *United States v. Oregon*, 366 U.S. 643 (1961); and *cf. Brownell v. Singer*, 347 U.S. 403 (1954).
6. *Adams v. Maryland*, 347 U.S. 179 (1954); *Ullmann v. United States*, 350 U.S. 422 (1956); and *cf. Hutcheson v. United States*, 369 U.S. 599 (1962).
7. *Testa v. Katt*, 330 U.S. 386 (1947).
8. *Georgia v. Rachel*, 384 U.S. 780 (1966); and *cf. United Mine Workers v. Gibbs*, 383 U.S. 715 (1966).
9. *Franklin Nat. Bank v. New York*, 347 U.S. 273 (1954).
10. *Free v. Bland*, 369 U.S. 663 (1962).
11. *Sperry v. Florida*, 373 U.S. 379 (1963).
12. *Colorado Commission v. Continental Air Lines*, 372 U.S. 714 (1963); *Kesler v. Dept. of Pub. Safety*, 369 U.S. 153. (1962).
13. *Florida Lime & Avocado Growers v. Paul*, 373 U.S. 132 (1963).
14. *Cf. Maximov v. United States*, 373 U.S. 49 (1963); *Reid v. Covert*, 354 U.S. 1 (1957).
15. *Head Money Cases*, 112 U.S. 580 (1884).
16. *Missouri v. Holland*, 252 U.S. 416 (1920).
17. *United States v. Sheever*, 214 U.S. 514 (1908).
18. 39 Stat. 1702.
19. 252 U.S. at 433.
20. *Cf.* Sen. Rep. No. 412, 83rd Cong., 1st Sess. (1953).

21. The case had first been decided in 1956. *Reid v. Covert,* 351 U.S. 470. It then came on for reargument, with four Justices joining in the majority opinion, two concurring, two dissenting and one abstaining. 354 U.S. 1 (1957).
22. *Cf.* also *Kinsella v. United States,* 361 U.S. 234 (1960).
23. *Cf. Fong Yue Ting v. United States,* 149 U.S. 720 (1893); *Johnson v. Browne,* 205 U.S. 309 (1907).

VI. 3. *Oath of Office*

The Senators and Representatives before mentioned, and the members of the several state legislatures, and all executive and judicial officers both of the United States and of the several states, shall be bound by oath or affirmation to support this Constitution; but no religious test shall ever be required as a qualification to any office or public trust under the United States.

This clause, corroborating the supremacy clause, has been cited in the school desegregation cases as compelling obedience to the Federal law by state agencies.[1] The oath is commonly provided by state law as well and has been upheld in this context.[2] Justice Bradley's 1880 observation has become the general rule: "The Constitution and laws of the United States are the supreme law of the land, and to these every citizen of every state owes obedience, whether in his individual or official capacity."[3] In this same period the Court also declared what has become an axiom of American federalism: The laws of the United States are in full force in every state as the laws of that state, and unless Congress has vested exclusive jurisdiction of some laws in the Federal courts, the state courts are required to take jurisdiction of Federal as well as state cases.[4]

1. *Bush v. Orleans Parish School Dist.,* 190 F.S. 861 (1960), aff'd. 365 U.S. 569 (1961). *Cf.* also *Bond v. Floyd,* 385 U.S. 116 (1966); *Henderson v. United States,* 237 F. 2d 169 (1956).
2. *Connell v. Higginbotham,* 403 U.S. 207 (1971).
3. *Ex parte Siebold,* 100 U.S. 371, 392 (1880).
4. *Claflin v. Houseman,* 93 U.S. 130 (1877); and *cf. Second Employers' Liability Cases,* 223 U.S. 1 (1912); *Keegan v. New Jersey,* 42 F.S. 922 (1941).

Article VII. The Implementing Procedure

The ratification of the conventions of nine states shall be sufficient for the establishment of this Constitution between the states so ratifying the same.

For the historical note on the ratification of the Constitution by the original thirteen states, see page 3 above.

Amendments to the Constitution

The Bill of Rights
    Amendment I—Freedom of Expression and Association
    Amendment II—The Right to Bear Arms
    Amendment III—Prohibition of Quartering of Troops
    Amendment IV—Unreasonable Searches and Seizures
    Amendment V—Due Process of Law
    Amendment VI—Jury Trial and Rights of the Accused
    Amendment VII—Jury Trial in Civil Cases
    Amendment VIII—Excessive Bail or Punishment
    Amendment IX—Preservation of Unenumerated Rights
    Amendment X—Reserved Powers of States or People
Amendments Revising the Original Process
    Amendment XI—Immunity of States
    Amendment XII—The Electoral Process
Reconstruction Era Amendments
    Amendment XIII—Abolition of Slavery
    Amendment XIV—National Citizenship; Protection from
      State Infringement
    Amendment XV—Universal Manhood Suffrage
Progressive Era Amendments
    Amendment XVI—The Income Tax Power
    Amendment XVII—Popular Election of Senators
    Amendment XVIII—Prohibition of Intoxicating Liquor
    Amendment XIX—Woman Suffrage
New Deal Era Amendments
    Amendment XX—The "Lame Duck" Amendment
    Amendment XXI—Repeal of Amendment XVIII
    Amendment XXII—Limitation of Presidential Terms
Amendments Broadening National Citizenship
    Amendment XXIII—District of Columbia Franchise
    Amendment XXIV—Abolition of Poll Taxes
    Amendment XXV—Presidential Disability
    Amendment XXVI—Minimum Voting Age

Amendment I
Freedom of Expression and Association

Congress shall make no law respecting an establishment of religion, or prohibiting the free exercise thereof; or abridging the freedom of speech, or of the press; or the right of the people peaceably to assemble, and to petition the government for a redress of grievances.

The opening Amendment of the Bill of Rights is also one of the most exhaustively adjudicated. This is because, in the first place, the Amendment itself contains such a range of related yet separate subjects, both in terms of written text and in terms of judicial extension.[1] In the second place, the conscious incorporation of many elements of the Bill of Rights into the Fourteenth Amendment[2] began with the freedom-of-expression clause of the First[3]—a peculiar irony, since its Federal reference (*"Congress shall make no law . . ."*) is unequivocal. Justice Black, in his doctrine of constitutional absolutes,[4] and Justice Stone, in his doctrine of "preferred freedoms,"[5] made the major contributions to the rationale of incorporation, which by now seems virtually complete.[6]

The provisions of this Amendment as developed by the Court over the years may be outlined as follows: (1) freedom of religion, which consists of (a) non-establishment and (b) free exercise; (2) freedom of expression, as broken down under headings of (a) tendentious advocacy and the legitimate limits which public security may require, (b) the time and place of permissible freedom of expression, (c) the limitations of the law of libel and the definition of obscenity, and (d) the right to remain silent or not to listen; and, finally, (3) freedom of assembly, which has been expanded by definition to include freedom of association.[7]

Freedom of Religion: Non-Establishment

The opening clause, in Thomas Jefferson's phrase, was intended to erect "a wall of separation between church and state."[8] Justice Joseph Story construed the principle somewhat differently, as a doctrine of "no preference,"[9] which by definition would mean that Congress would not discriminate against religion generally as well as meaning that Congress would not discriminate in favor of or against particular religious beliefs or activities.[10] In the twentieth century this clause has precipitated a succession of issues in both state and Federal jurisdictions over (1) the matter of state aid to religious educational institutions and (2) the role of religious education in the public-school curricula. The propriety of state laws providing free transportation to all children attending both public and parochial schools was affirmed in 1947.[11] But the following year the Court struck down an Illinois school board's provision for "released time" for religious instruction on public premises.[12] Four years later the Court upheld a New York "released time" program where students were permitted to leave school for religious instruction at their respective denominational institutions,[13] a doctrine closer to Story than to Jefferson. And in 1962 the Court held unconstitutional under the "establishment" clause a non-denominational prayer approved by the New York state regents.[14] The "flag salute" cases of the 1940s first upheld, and then overturned, a requirement for saluting the flag in public schools as against the plea that this conflicted with certain sectarian beliefs concerning secular symbols.[15]

In 1925 the Story position was followed by the Court in invalidating an Oregon statute requiring all students to attend public schools and thus in effect abolishing parochial schools,[16] although the case actually turned on the due-process clause of the Fourteenth Amendment. The Story position was also relied on in upholding Sunday closing laws,[17] and the common practice of granting tax immunity to all church properties was upheld in 1970.[18] Exemption of religious groups from paying license taxes for the distribution of their literature had been established in 1944.[19] A state law prohibiting the teaching of evolution theory in public schools has been held to violate the "establishment" clause as recognizing a particular sectarian viewpoint.[20] In the same vein, the Court has avoided taking jurisdiction of disputes over questions of internal denominational policy.[21] As for financial aid to nonpublic church schools, it has been held that this is a valid public expenditure in support of the secular phases of the educational services performed by these schools.[22]

Free Exercise of Religion

The companion provision in the Amendment relating to "free exercise" was intended, said the Court in 1890, to leave exclusively to the individual the choice of "such forms of worship as he may think proper not injurious to the equal rights of others."[23] The best-known instance in which public policy was held to limit the practice of certain religious tenets (e.g., polygamy) was in the anti-Mormon cases preceding Utah's admission to statehood.[24] The use of public streets and parks for preaching has been denied, and the denial upheld, where the habit of the sect was to attack other religious beliefs;[25] and where a license was issued to all, without leaving any discretion to the issuing officer as to when a license was to be granted, the licensing principle has been sustained.[26] Sunday closing laws have been held not to violate the "free exercise" clause,[27] unless the effect is to discriminate against certain sects (e.g., Orthodox Jews).[28] And even where the observance of a day of rest other than Sunday (e.g., Seventh-Day Adventists) affected the individual's economic well-being rather than his religious freedom, a requirement that he accept Saturday employment or be denied unemployment relief was held to be an unconstitutional infringement on the "free exercise" guarantee.[29]

A state law requiring officeholders to affirm a belief in God has been invalidated as a religious qualification under both the "establishment" and "free exercise" clauses.[30] But certain religious beliefs other than polygamy have been held in conflict with public policy—e.g., resistance to compulsory vaccination[31] and drug control laws.[32] The obligations of citizenship have raised First Amendment conflicts in cases of compulsory military service: Exemptions for conscientious objectors whose beliefs condemned all wars have been upheld as "free exercise" rights,[33] and in 1965 this exemption was extended to such beliefs even though not based on a religious creed.[34] But "selective" objectors—claiming the right to comply with the draft law only when personally convinced that the war was justified—have been denied exemption.[35]

Freedom of Expression: Tendentious Speech

Federal and state constitutional provisions fall into two classes: those which, like the First Amendment, make a generalization (*cf.* Virginia's "the freedom of the press is one of the great bulwarks of liberty, and can never be restrained but by despotic governments")[36] and those of a number of states which incorporate the so-called Blackstone dictum, that freedom of expression is subject to the reasonable limits of the law of defamation.[37] As for the guarantee in either case, it is a personal right of citizens of the United States—not a property right of the communications media, even though, as a practical matter, the media are the primary instrumentalities for exercising the right.[38] Finally, there is the argument advanced by Justice Black that the guarantee is an absolute ("Congress shall make no law . . .");[39] or, as Justice Stone put it in an oft-quoted phrase, "There may be narrower scope for operation of the presumption of constitutionality when legislation appears on its face to be within a specific prohibition of the Constitution."[40]

"The limitation upon individual liberty must have appropriate relation to the safety of the state," said the Court in 1937.[41] The next year it added: "Mere legislative preferences or beliefs respecting matters of public convenience may well support regulation directed at other personal activities, but be insufficient to justify such as diminishes [guaranteed rights]."[42] And in 1945 the Court concluded: "For these reasons any attempt to restrain those liberties must be justified by clear public interest, threatened not doubtfully or remotely, but by clear and present danger."[43]

The historic test of the paramountcy of the freedom-of-expression guarantee might have been expected to be in the case of the Sedition Act of 1798,[44] but no direct challenge of that act was carried to the Supreme Court. Justice Story in his *Commentaries* said no more than that the law was "in the highest degree impolitic."[45] Another test, in the juristic chaos of the post-Civil War era, was not unequivocally answered because of the low estate to which the Court had fallen in public opinion.[46] Again, early in the twentieth century, the guarantee was subjected to the challenge of the contempt power as applied to newspaper reporting and commentary.[47] But the ultimate test of the scope of the First Amendment free-speech guarantee came with the so-called sedition cases of World War I, as pronounced by Justice Holmes: "The test in every case is whether the words used are used in such circumstances and are of such a nature as to create a clear and present danger that they will bring about the substantive evils that Congress has a right to prevent."[48] In the twenties the Court conceded that the First Amendment guarantee was "among the fundamental personal rights and liberties protected by the Fourteenth Amendment from impairment by the states,"[49] but added that a state's police power may properly be used to "punish those who abuse this freedom by utterances inimical to the public welfare."[50] Two years later the Court reiterated the incorporation of the free-speech guarantee and also the validity of a police power used to limit abuse of the guarantee.[51]

What constitutes a "clear and present danger"? The Court has given various answers, the principal one being the proof of an overt act which sought to convert advocacy into action.[52] On the eve of World War II, which produced a Federal law (the Smith Act[53]) and several companion statutes aimed at subversive activities, the Court under Chief Justice Vinson declared: "Speech is not an absolute, above and beyond control by the legislature when its judgment, subject to review here, is that certain kinds of speech are so undesirable as to warrant criminal action."[54] Six years later the majority opinion in Dennis was qualified by the requirement that a firm distinction be drawn between abstract doctrine and the advocacy of unlawful action.[55] In 1961 the Court held that membership in subversive organizations had to be evaluated as to "specific intent" of members to participate in unlawful actions.[56]

The Subversive Activities Control Act of 1950[57] and the Communist Control Act of 1954[58] were narrowly circumscribed by a succession of cases in the 1960s relying primarily on Fifth Amendment due process but substantially affecting First Amendment rights.[59] The end of the Warren Chief Justiceship found the Court moving back to the general libertarian doctrine of the 1930s.[60]

Time and Place of Public Expression

In 1919 Justice Holmes qualified the free-speech guarantee by warning that "the character of every act depends upon the circumstances in which it is done. The most stringent protection of free speech would not protect a man in falsely shouting fire in a theatre and causing panic."[61] The same words, in other circumstances, presumably would be permissible; thus in the same term of court Holmes was dissenting from the majority's finding of "clear and present danger": "Only the emergency that makes it immediately dangerous to leave the correction of evil counsels to time warrants any exception."[62] The lingering problem in this approach, of course, is the fact that the degree of danger appears in different magnitudes to different observers. Or the problem may be stated otherwise: The mere fact that speech is provocative may or may not justify its suppression; as Justice Douglas put it in 1949, "a function of free speech under our system of government is to invite dispute. It may indeed best serve its high purpose when it induces a condition of unrest, creates dissatisfaction with conditions as they are, or even stirs people to anger."[63]

Private rights as well as public rights may limit the circumstances under which the constitutional freedom may be exercised.[64] This general principle underlay the succession of "handbill cases" in the late 1930s and early 1940s, in which the Court groped for distinguishing criteria between the right to disseminate information on public streets,[65] reasonable regulations of the use of the streets under the police power[66] and the evidence of prior restraint.[67] While the right of a government to regulate the use of streets, parks and public buildings has been upheld as a general principle,[68] it has been denied where the effect was arbitrarily to suppress public discussion of public affairs.[69] Whether such discussion may be cut off by public authorities when it threatens to provoke violence has been vigorously debated—again in terms of the degree of individual discretion required to determine the imminence of a disturbance. In 1951 a divided Court held that where the evidence tended to establish the intent of the speaker to incite violence, the halting of the speech was permissible;[70] but the burden is on the state to establish the clear and present danger.[71]

The use of vagrancy or anti-loitering ordinances to deny or discourage expression in public places has been challenged as unconstitutionally vague and therefore too easily applicable to unpopular utterance or demonstration.[72] If the evidence shows both an unreasonable disruption of legitimate public business and a reasonable alternative course of action for the demonstrators, the right to clear the premises has been upheld.[73] But on the other hand, where the demonstration is orderly and appropriate to the location—e.g., picketing on private premises—it may not be forbidden if the premises are normally open to the general public.[74] In the related question of parade permits, the granting or withholding of the permits has been variously treated by the Court: Where a *bona fide* injunction has barred the parade, contempt citations for ignoring the injunction have been upheld.[75] Where the parade has been held in disregard of the denial of a permit, the cases have been treated more leniently,[76] usually on the ground that the administrative discretion involved in the decision on the permit is potentially arbitrary.

Common-Law Limitations: Libel, Obscenity, Contempt

The limitations of common-law libel, as already mentioned, have been incorporated into the constitutional provisions on free speech and press in many states and generally sustained against First Amendment attack. Traditionally the defenses against libel, either civil or criminal, have been proof of the truth of the published statement, proof of the privileged status of the original communication or, in certain circumstances, the right of fair comment. Against the latter defense, the sovereign right of courts (and legislatures) to punish for contempt has been cited and in due course reviewed and redefined. The basic guideline of the courts in all these instances has been the intent of American law to deny a government power of prior restraint, and the requirement that plaintiffs in civil suits or the state in criminal suits explicitly identify the injury and the injured interest.[77]

Thus the Court held unconstitutional a statute providing for the closing of allegedly scurrilous publications as a public nuisance, declaring that this constituted prepublication censorship forbidden by the First Amendment.[78] The threat to freedom inherent in a vaguely worded prohibition (e.g., "sacrilegious") has led to a striking down of a motion-picture censorship statute,[79] although the principle of film censorship has been upheld as within the police power of the state.[80] The censorship issue as it involves standards of obscenity is discussed further below.

Since World War II the Court has undertaken to restate the relationship between the First Amendment and the law of libel. In 1952 it upheld a state "group libel" law—a statute in derogation of the common law—which fixed liability for publications defamatory of racial or ethnic groups even though no individual claimed injury.[81] A decade later, in *New York Times v. Sullivan*,[82] the Court limited the right of public officials to recover damages "against critics of their official conduct." The social context of both cases, manifestly, was the increasing zeal to create an atmosphere of dignity for groups struggling for civil and social equality. However, the so-called "public official rule" has been broadened to include anyone in whose activities the public has a legitimate interest.[83] Whether a private person in a newsworthy situation may recover damages for a defamatory publication may depend, under the *Sullivan* doctrine, on the circumstances as well as on the intent of the publisher.[84]

In 1971 the Court in a divided majority of 5 to 3 extended the doctrine further by holding that where "a matter is a subject of public or general interest, it cannot suddenly become less so merely because a private individual is involved, or because in some sense the individual did not 'voluntarily' choose to become involved."[85] The Court has also held that in the interest of the broadest public information under the free-speech provision, radio and television broadcasters must provide equal time for both sides of current issues.[86]

Vagueness of standards has been the test by which laws against obscenity have been measured in the period since World War II. Beginning with *Winters v. New York*,[87] where the 6–3 majority found a statute unconstitutional for including "incidents within the guarantee of free speech," the Court in 1957 extended the First Amendment protection, through the Fourteenth, to all expressions "having even the slightest redeeming social importance" and defined obscenity as "material which deals with sex in a manner appealing to prurient interest."[88] Against the query whether these standards were vague in themselves, the Court in 1964 declared (with only Justices Brennan and Goldberg joining in the official opinion) in a 6–3 majority that the standard of contemporary taste had to be a national standard.[89] Two years later in another 6–3 holding (with three Justices joining in the official opinion) it was declared that only where "the dominant theme of the material taken as a whole appeals to prurient interest" can there be liability.[90]

But evidence that such publications were "commercially ex-

ploited for the sake of prurient appeal" led the Court in this
same term to uphold an obscenity conviction on the basis of
"deliberate representation of [the] publications as erotically arous-
ing," such representation being made to a general rather than a
professional audience.[91] Also in this term the Court upheld a conviction for publications aimed at "a clearly defined deviant sexual
group."[92] Two years later the Court upheld a state law prohibiting
the sale of material to minors even where the same matter sold to
adults would not necessarily incur liability for obscenity.[93] But
mere possession of obscene matter by a private person, it was then
declared, cannot in itself be a crime.[94]

The 1957 tests in *Roth v. United States,* said the Burger
Court in the spring of 1973, required restating in the light of the
sixteen years of increasingly confusing criteria designed to make
the tests more explicit. In *Miller v. California* and *Paris Adult
Theatre No. 1 v. Slaton,*[95] the Court accordingly (1) reasserted
the test of "prurient interest" set out originally in *Roth,* (2) returned from the national standard of community taste in *Jacobellis v. Ohio* to the "contemporary community standard" of *Roth,*
and (3) narrowed the *Roth* reference to the "slightest redeeming"
social importance to a requirement of "serious" social purpose.

The same judicial trend toward broad application of the
free-speech guarantee has led to a strict circumscription of the
contempt power. Although the older view was that utterances outside the courtroom could be punished summarily as jeopardizing
the objective conduct of judicial business, the liberalizing trend
began in 1941 with *Bridges v. California,*[96] limiting the power of
courts with reference to out-of-court utterances to standards meeting the "clear and present danger" rule.[97] Such danger, it was
subsequently averred, did not arise from mere carelessness in reporting or excessive vehemence in editorial comment,[98] even when
the publication related to a case currently under consideration.[99]

*Communications Generally: The Right to Speak and the Right
Not to Listen*

The general policy of the Court is to encourage and protect
the right of all persons to express a viewpoint or impart informa-

tion.[100] In most circumstances it is reasonable to infer that there is also the right of the reader or listener to receive information.[101] But occasionally the question has been presented of the right of the public not to have to listen, and this has been ambivalently answered. An ordinance regulating use of sound trucks and loud amplification of speakers was upheld as a reasonable accommodation of public convenience,[102] but subsequently the Court declined to find a constitutional bar to broadcasting within public buses to "captive audiences."[103] The right to impart information may override any competing public interests, as in cases where the audience consists of groups of laymen interested in knowing their legal rights,[104] and in this same vein the right of unions to picket or boycott has been defined as a form of guaranteed free expression.[105]

Free speech in labor disputes became an issue early in the history of the National Labor Relations Act[106] and resulted in a specific extension of the guarantee both to labor[107] and management.[108] The non-Communist affidavit required by the Taft-Hartley Act[109] was upheld in principle in 1950[110] against a First Amendment challenge, but fifteen years later it was held invalid as a bill of attainder.[111] Advocacy of Communism or other radical doctrines in the abstract, where there is no evidence of an attempt to incite subversion or violence, is protected by the First Amendment.[112] Freedom of conscience, while it involves both freedom of expression and freedom to be silent, has raised questions which may be more appropriately considered under the following clause on freedom of assembly.

Assembly and Association: Changing Standards

The security-conscious 1950s, and the politics of confrontation in the 1960s, cast this guarantee into new perspectives. While many confrontations appeared to stretch the meaning of "peaceable assembly," the courts have been reluctant to proscribe such activities as sit-ins, protest marches and loud demonstrations where these were part of a campaign to effectuate guaranteed civil rights. It has been declared that the rights of assembly and petition are "cognate to those of free speech and free press";[113] and separate guarantees of petition and assembly have been recognized.[114] To protect these rights in all circumstances has been difficult; attempts to break up unpopular assemblies have infrequently resulted in successful prosecutions.[115]

Loyalty tests, lists of subversive affiliations and the questioned right to private political belief were all put in issue in the security hysteria of the 1950s, as legislatures probed for evidence of under-cover conspiracies, cited recalcitrant witnesses for contempt and in consequence crossed swords with the Supreme Court over Fifth and First Amendment rights. Congressional concern with a nebulous but—to many persons—menacing disaffection had been expressed prior to World War II when the House Un-American Activities Committee was created, and in the cold war of the late 1940s the groping for a sinister movement which might be threatening national well-being continued in new Congressional enactments in the 1950s.[116] Guilt by association first climaxed in the issuances of the Attorney General's list of subversive organizations, the power to prepare such lists as an aid to loyalty review boards being affirmed.[117] The Court sought to circumscribe the loyalty issue by demanding evidence of knowing membership in such organizations[118] and struck down one city charter provision penalizing persons who availed themselves of the Fifth Amendment guarantee against self-incrimination.[119] This guarantee, however, was not considered in many cases where the Court chose alternative constitutional principles on which to review the cases, by narrow majorities upholding the right of government agencies to discharge employees on grounds of suspected loyalty which could hardly be expected to meet the normal requirements of proof beyond reasonable doubt.[120]

Uneasily, the Court continued to seek a balancing of interests between the right of privacy with reference to associations and beliefs and the reasonable need for public security and information. It sought, not without critical reaction to its efforts, to weigh the relative values involved; in a series of bar admission cases, it evolved the rule that prospective attorneys as officers of the courts had a primary obligation to divulge information which the examiners considered essential.[121] But where divulgence amounted to divesting civil-rights workers of an essential advantage in their legitimate effort to secure enforcement of these same civil rights, freedom of association was held to include the right to keep confidential the membership in such associations.[122] But it was not until the security hysteria waned that the Court, under the dominance of the libertarians in the 1960s, handed down a series of opinions narrowing the permissive doctrines of the previous decade.[123] A number of cases on legislative investigation—turning primarily on Fifth Amendment privileges against self-incrimination but involving as well the First Amendment freedom of association—ran a similar gamut from narrow to broad definition of the constitutional guarantee.[124]

1. One of the best summaries of the legal issues which have proliferated on this subject is Emerson, "Toward a General Theory of the First Amendment," 72 *Yale L. J.* 877 (1963).

2. The rationale of the incorporation doctrine, as well as the case against it, appears in the commentary under the Fourteenth Amendment.

3. *Gitlow v. New York*, 268 U.S. 652 (1925); *Whitney v. California*, 274 U.S. 375 (1927), overruled in *Brandenburg v. Ohio*, 395 U.S. 444 (1969).

4. *Cf.* McKay, "The Preference for Freedom," 34 *N.Y.U.L. Rev.* 1184 (1959); and *cf.* "Justice Black and First Amendment Absolutes," 37 *N.Y.U.L. Rev.* 549 (1962).

5. *United States v. Carolene Products*, 304 U.S. 144, 152 n. 4 (1944). *Cf.* also the comment of Frankfurter, J., in *Kovacs v. Cooper*, 336 U.S. 77, 89 (1949).

6. *Cf. Furman v. Georgia*, 408 U.S. 238 (1972), substantially incorporates the Eighth Amendment into the Fourteenth.

7. *Cf.* Frankfurter's enumeration in *Kovacs v. Cooper*, 336 U.S. at 89 (1949).

8. *Cf.* Black's opinion in *Everson v. Bd. of Education*, 330 U.S. 1, 11 (1947).

9. 2 *Commentaries on the Constitution*, ss. 1874, 1879.

10. But *cf.* the cases involving polygamy—*e.g.*, *Reynolds v. United States*, 98 U.S. 145 (1875).

11. *Everson v. Board of Education*, 330 U.S. 1 (1947); and *cf. Board of Education v. Allen*, 392 U.S. 236 (1968).

12. *Illinois ex rel. McCullom v. Board of Education*, 333 U.S. 203 (1948).

13. *Zorach v. Clauson*, 343 U.S. 306 (1952); and *cf. Cochran v. Louisiana Board*, 281 U.S. 370 (1930). But *cf.* dissent in *Zorach v. Clauson*, 343 U.S. at 320.

14. *Engel v. Vitale*, 370 U.S. 421 (1962.) *Cf.* also *Abingdon School District v. Schempp*, 374 U.S. 203 (1963).

15. On the flag salute cases, *cf. Minersville School District v. Gobitis*, 310 U.S. 624 (1940); *West Virginia Board v. Barnette*, 319 U.S. 105 (1943).

16. *Pierce v. Society of Sisters*, 268 U.S. 510 (1925).

17. *McGowan v. Maryland*, 366 U.S. 420 (1961); *Gallagher v. Crown Kosher Market*, 366 U.S. 617 (1961).

18. *Walz v. Tax Comm.*, 397 U.S. 664 (1970); *cf.* also *General Finance Corp. v. Archetto*, 369 U.S. 423 (1962); *Heiser v. County of Alameda*, 352 U.S. 921 (1952).

19. *Follett v. McCormick*, 321 U.S. 573 (1944). *Cf.* also *United States v. Ballard*, 322 U.S. 78 (1944); *Jones v. Opelika*, 316 U.S. 584 (1942); *Murdock v. Pennsylvania*, 319 U.S. 105 (1943); *Cantwell v. Connecticut*, 310 U.S. 296 (1941); *Martin v. Strothers*, 319 U.S. 141 (1943). For other problems of distribution of religious literature, see discussion under the freedom-of-expression clause below.

20. *Epperson v. Arkansas,* 393 U.S. 97 (1968).
21. *Presbyterian Church U.S.A. v. Memorial Presbyterian Church,* 393 U.S. 440 (1969); and *cf. Kedroff v. Cathedral,* 344 U.S. 94 (1952); *Kreshnik v. Cathedral,* 363 U.S. 190 (1960).
22. *Lemon v. Kuntzman,* 403 U.S. 602 (1971); *Tilton v. Richardson,* 403 U.S. 672 (1971).
23. *Davis v. Beason,* 133 U.S. 333, 342 (1890).
24. *Reynolds v. United States,* 98 U.S. 145 (1879); *Davis v. Beason,* 133 U.S. 333 (1890).
25. *Kunz v. New York,* 340 U.S. 290 (1951); *Niemótko v. Maryland,* 340 U.S. 268 (1951); *Fowler v. Rhode Island,* 345 U.S. 67 (1953).
26. *Poulos v. New Hampshire,* 345 U.S. 395 (1953).
27. *McGowan v. Maryland,* 366 U.S. 420 (1961); *Arlan's Dept. Store v. Kentucky,* 371 U.S. 218 (1962).
28. *Braunfeld v. Brown,* 366 U.S. 599 (1961).
29. *Scherbert v. Verner,* 374 U.S. 398 (1963); *In re Jenison,* 375 U.S. 14 (1963); and on a related issue, *cf. Wisconsin v. Yoder,* 406 U.S. (1972).
30. *Torcaso v. Watkins,* 367 U.S. 488 (1961).
31. *Jacobson v. Massachusetts,* 197 U.S. 11 (1905); *cf. Appl. of Georgetown College,* 331 F. 2d 1000 (1964), cert. den. 377 U.S. 978 (1964).
32. *People v. Woody,* 61 Calif. 2d 716 (1964).
33. *Arver v. United States,* 245 U.S. 366 (1918); *cf. Hamilton v. Regents,* 293 U.S. 245 (1935). An alien who is a conscientious objector but who is willing to perform non-military service may be admitted to citizenship. *Girouard v. United States,* 328 U.S. 61 (1946), overruling *United States v. Schwimmer,* 279 U.S. 644 (1929), and *United States v. MacIntosh,* 283 U.S. 605 (1931).
34. *United States v. Seeger,* 380 U.S. 163 (1965), decided on statutory rather than First Amendment grounds. *Cf.* also *Welsh v. United States,* 398 U.S. 333 (1970).
35. *Gillette v. United States,* 401 U.S. 437 (1971).
36. *Virginia Constitution,* I, 12.
37. 4 Blackstone's *Commentaries,* 145, 150.
38. *Associated Press v. National Labor Relations Board,* 301 U.S. 103 (1937).
39. *Cf.* Black, *loc. cit.,* n, 4 *supra.*
40. *United States v. Carolene Products,* 304 U.S. 144 (1938).
41. *Herndon v. Lowry,* 301 U.S. 242, 258 (1937)
42. *Schneider v. State,* 308 U.S. 147, 161 (1938).
43. *Thomas v. Collins,* 323 U.S. 516, 530 (1945).
44. 1 Stat. 596.
45. Story, *Commentaries,* III, 164.
46. *Cf. Ex parte McCardle,* 7 Wall. 506 (1869).
47. *Patterson v. Colorado,* 205 U.S. 454 (1907). *Cf.* also *Toledo Newspaper Co. v. United States,* 247 U.S. 402 (1918).
48. *Schenck v. United States,* 249 U.S. 47, 51 (1919); *Frohwerk v. United States,* 249 U.S. 204 (1919); *Debs v. United States,* 249 U.S. 211 (1919).
49. *Gitlow v. New York,* 268 U.S. 652 (1925).
50. *Id.,* at 669.
51. *Whitney v. California,* 274 U.S. 357 (1927); overruled in *Brandenburg v. Ohio,* 395 U.S. 444 (1969).
52. *Fiske v. Kansas,* 274 U.S. 380 (1927); *DeJonge v. Oregon,* 299 U.S. 353 (1937); *Herndon v. Lowry,* 301 U.S. 242 (1937).

53. 54 Stat. 670, 18 U.S.C. 2385.
54. *Dennis v. United States,* 341 U.S. 494 (1951).
55. *Yates v. United States,* 354 U.S. 298 (1957).
56. *Scales v. United States,* 367 U.S. 203 (1961); *cf.* also *Noto v. United States,* 367 U.S. 290 (1961).
57. 64 Stat. 987, 50 U.S.C. 781.
58. 68 Stat. 775, 50 U.S.C. 841.
59. *Communist Party of America v. Subversive Activities Control Board,* 367 U.S. 1 (1961); *Communist Party v. United States,* 331 F. 2d 807 (1963), cert. den. 377 U.S. 968 (1964); *Albertson v. Subversive Activities Control Board,* 382 U.S. 70 (1965); *DuBois Clubs v. Clark,* 389 U.S. 309 (1967).
60. *Cf. Aptheker v. Secretary of State,* 378 U.S. 500 (1964); *United States v. Robel,* 389 U.S. 258 (1967); *Brandenburg v. Ohio,* 395 U.S. 444 (1969).
61. *Schenck v. United States,* 249 U.S. 47, 52 (1919).
62. Dissent in *Abrams v. United States,* 250 U.S. 616, 624 (1919).
63. *Terminiello v. Chicago,* 337 U.S. 1, 4 (1949); but *cf. Chaplinsky v. New Hampshire,* 315 U.S. 568 (1942), and *Gooding v. Wilson,* 405 U.S. 518 (1972).
64. *Cf. Breard v. Alexandria,* 341 U.S. 622 (1951); *Martin v. Strothers,* 319 U.S. 141 (1943).
65. *Lovell v. Griffin,* 303 U.S. 444 (1938);*Schneider v. State,* 308 U.S. 147 (1938); *Cantwell v. Connecticut,* 310 U.S. 296 (1940); *Cox v. New Hampshire,* 312 U.S. 569 (1941); *Thomas v. Collins,* 323 U.S. 516 (1945).
66. *Cf. Prince v. Massachusetts,* 321 U.S. 158 (1944).
67. *Niemótko v. Maryland,* 340 U.S. 268 (1951); *Kunz v. New York,* 340 U.S. 290 (1951); *Feiner v. New York,* 340 U.S. 315 (1951).
68. *Cf. Cox v. New Hampshire,* 312 U.S. 569 (1941).
69. *Hague v. C.I.O.,* 307 U.S. 147 (1939).
70. *Feiner v. New York,* 340 U.S. 315 (1951). *Cf.* also *Colten v. Kentucky,* 407 U.S. 104 (1972).
71. *Bacheller v. Maryland,* 397 U.S. 564 (1970); *Coates v. Cincinnati,* 402 U.S. 611 (1971); *Gregory v. Chicago,* 394 U.S. 111 (1969); and *cf. Edwards v. South Carolina,* 372 U.S. 229 (1963).
72. *Edwards v. South Carolina,* 372 U.S. 229 (1963); *Brown v. Louisiana,* 383 U.S. 131 (1966); *Cox v. Louisiana,* 379 U.S. 536, 559 (1965).
73. *Adderley v. Florida,* 385 U.S. 39 (1966).
74. *Amalg. Food Employees v. Logan Valley Plaza,* 391 U.S. 308 (1968); but *cf. Lloyd Corp. v. Tanner,* 407 U.S. 551 (1972).
75. *Walker v. Birmingham,* 394 U.S. 147 (1969); but *cf. Carroll v. Pres. and Comm. of Princess Anne,* 393 U.S. 175 (1968).
76. *Shuttlesworth v. Birmingham,* 394 U.S. 147 (1969).
77. For a traditional view, *cf. Robertson v. Baldwin,* 165 U.S. 281 (1897); for a contemporary issue of prior restraint, *cf. New York Times v. United States* (Pentagon Papers), 403 U.S. 713 (1971).
78. *Near v. Minnesota ex rel. Olsen,* 283 U.S. 697 (1931); *Kingsley Books v. Brown,* 354 U.S. 436 (1957); *Bantam Books vs. Sullivan,* 372 U.S. 58 (1963).
79. *Burstyn v. Wilson,* 343 U.S. 495 (1952); *cf.* also *Winters v. New York,* 333 U.S. 507 (1948); *Commercial Printers v. Regents,* 346 U.S. 587 (1954).
80. *Times Film Corp. v. Chicago,* 365 U.S. 43 (1961); *cf. Freedman v. Maryland,* 380 U.S. 51 (1965).
81. *Beauharnais v. Illinois,* 343 U.S. 250 (1952).

82. 376 U.S. 254 (1964); cf. also *Garrison v. Louisiana,* 379 U.S. 64 (1964).
83. *Rosenblatt v. Baer,* 383 U.S. 75 (1966).
84. Cf. *Time, Inc. v. Hill,* 385 U.S. 374 (1967); *Curtis Pub. Co. v. Butts* and *Associated Press v. Walker,* both decided in 388 U.S. 130 (1969).
85. *Rosenbloom v. Metromedia,* 403 U.S. 29 (1971).
86. *Red Lion Broadcasting Co. v. F.C.C.,* 395 U.S. 367 (1969). Expressions may be symbolic as well as visual or vocal, and the Court in the recent era of protest has striven to distinguish between "communicative" and "non-communicative" acts. Where the "non-communicative" act can be distinguished, it may not claim First Amendment protection; *United States v. O'Brien,* 391 U.S. 367 (1968). But where it is "communicative" even though offensive, it may be protected; *Cohen v. California,* 403 U.S. 15 (1971): *Tinker v. Des Moines School Board,* 393 U.S. 503 (1969). The test of incitement of others may be applied to determine the "clear and present danger." *Street v. New York,* 394 U.S. 576 (1969). Cf. also *Columbia Broadcasting System v. Dem. Nat. Comm.,* 412 U.S. *** (1973).
87. 333 U.S. 507 (1948).
88. *Roth v. United States* and *Alberts v. California,* both in 354 U.S. 476 (1957); cf. also *Manual Enterprises v. Day,* 370 U.S. 478 (1962).
89. *Jacobellis v. Ohio,* 378 U.S. 184 (1964).
90. *Memoirs v. Attorney General* ("Fanny Hill case"), 383 U.S. 413 (1966).
91. *Ginzburg v. United States,* 383 U.S. 463 (1966).
92. *Mishkin v. New York,* 383 U.S. 502 (1966).
93. *Ginsberg v. New York,* 390 U.S. 629 (1969); and cf. *Smith v. California,* 361 U.S. 147 (1959).
94. *Stanley v. Georgia,* 394 U.S. 557 (1969); but cf. *United States v. Reidel,* 402 U.S. 351 (1971).
95. Cf. *Miller v. California,* 413 U.S. *** (1973) and *Paris Adult Theatre No. 1 v. Slaton,* 413 U.S. *** (1973).
96. 314 U.S. 252 (1941). Cf. also *Patterson v. Colorado,* 205 U.S. 454 (1907); *Toledo Newspaper Co. v. United States,* 247 U.S. 402 (1918).
97. Cf. also *Pennekamp v. Florida,* 328 U.S. 331 (1946).
98. *Craig v. Harney,* 331 U.S. 367 (1947).
99. *Wood v. Georgia,* 370 U.S. 375 (1962).
100. The guarantee is not "to be so circumscribed that it exists in principle but not in fact," *Tinker v. Des Moines School Dist.,* 393 U.S. 503 (1969).
101. Cf. cases cited in note 104 *infra.*
102. *Kovacs v. Cooper,* 336 U.S. 77 (1949); but cf. *Saia v. New York,* 334 U.S. 558 (1948). In two cases the Court was prepared to reject the claim that a vendor has the right to send unwanted material into another's home. *Rowan v. Post Office Department,* 397 U.S. 728 (1970). One who rejects such material for himself cannot seek to prevent its general distribution solely because he considers it objectionable. *Organization for a Better Austin v. Keefe,* 402 U.S. 415 (1971).
103. *Pub. Utility Comm. v. Pollak,* 343 U.S. 451 (1951).
104. *N.A.A.C.P. v. Button,* 371 U.S. 415 (1963); *Bro. R. Trainmen v. Virginia,* 377 U.S. 1 (1964).
105. *Teamsters v. Vogt, Inc.,* 354 U.S. 284 (1957). Cf. also *Thornhill v. Alabama,* 310 U.S. 88 (1939); *A.F.L. v. Swing,* 312 U.S. 321 (1941); *Giboney v. Empire Storage & Ice Co.,* 336 U.S. 490 (1949).

106. 49 Stat. 449, 290 U.S.C. 151.
107. *Thomas v. Collins*, 323 U.S. 516 (1945); *Hague v. C.I.O.*, 307 U.S. 496 (1939).
108. *May Dept. Stores v. N.L.R.B.*, 326 U.S. 376 (1945).
109. 61 Stat. 136, 29 U.S.C. 151.
110. *Am. Comm. Assn. v. Douds*, 339 U.S. 382 (1950).
111. *United States v. Brown*, 381 U.S. 437 (1965).
112. *Harisiades v. Shaughnessy*, 342 U.S. 580 (1952); *Kingsley Pictures v. Regents*, 360 U.S. 684 (1959); *Dennis v. United States*, 341 U.S. 491 (1951). And *cf. Yates v. United States*, 354 U.S. 298 (1957).
113. *DeJonge v. Oregon*, 299 U.S. 353 (1937); *Herndon v. Lowry*, 301 U.S. 242 (1937).
114. *Cruikshank v. United States*, 92 U.S. 542 (1876). And *cf. United States v. Rumeley*, 345 U..S 41 (1953); *United States v. Harris*, 347 U.S. 612 (1954).
115. *Cf. Collins v. Hardyman*, 341 U.S. 651 (1951); *Hague v. C.I.O.*, 307 U.S. 496 (1939).
116. *Cf.* 64 Stat. 987, 8 U.S.C. 1102; 69 Stat. 539, 50 U.S.C. 791.
117. *Joint Anti-Fascist Comm. v. McGrath*, 341 U.S. 123 (1951).
118. *Garner v. Board of Pub. Works*, 341 U.S. 716 (1951); *Adler v. Board of Education*, 342 U.S. 485 (1952); *Wieman v. Updegraf*, 344 U.S. 183 (1952).
119. *Slochower v. Board of Education*, 350 U.S. 551 (1956).
120. *Service v. Dulles*, 354 U.S. 363 (1957); *Lerner v. Casey*, 357 U.S. 468 (1958); *Becker v. Board of Education*, 357 U.S. 399 (1958); *Green v. McElroy*, 360 U.S. 474 (1959); *Nelson v. County of Los Angeles*, 360 U.S. 1 (1960).
121. *Schware v. Board of Bar Exam.*, 353 U.S. 232 (1957); *Konigsburg v. State Bar* (I), 353 U.S. 252 (1957); same (II), 366 U.S. (1961); *In re Anastalpo*, 366 U.S. 82 (1961); but *cf. Spevak v. Klein*, 385 U.S. 511 (1967).
122. *N.A.A.C.P. v. Patterson*, 357 U.S. 449 (1958).
123. *Cf. Shelton v. Tucker*, 364 U.S. 479 (1960); *Cramp v. Board of Pub. Instr.*, 368 U.S. 278 (1961); *Baggett v. Bullitt*, 377 U.S. 360 (1964); *Elfbrandt v. Russell*, 384 U.S. 11 (1966); *Whitehill v. Elkins*, 389 U.S. 54 (1967).
124. *Cf. Watkins v. United States*, 354 U.S. 178 (1957); *Sweezy v. New Hampshire*, 354 U.S. 234 (1957); *Barenblatt v. United States*, 360 U.S. 109 (1959); *Gibson v. Florida Legis. Inv. Comm.*, 372 U.S. 539 (1963); *DeGregory v. Attorney General*, 383 U.S. 825 (1966); *Branzburg v. Hayes*, 408 U.S. 665 (1972).

Amendment II. The Right to Bear Arms

A well-regulated militia, being necessary to the security of a free state, the right of the people to keep and bear arms shall not be infringed.

The language of the Amendment clearly indicates that the right to keep and bear arms is derived from the public need for a citizen reserve—i.e., a militia.[1] An emphasis on this criterion of constitutionality conceivably might have cut off a certain amount of the debate which has chronically revolved about this "right." The manifest necessity of possessing weapons for hunting and defense in the frontier era made this "right" part of national folklore (along with the legendary gunslinging of the Old West). In the twentieth century, the zeal of sportsmen hunters has been augmented by a vociferous gun lobby eager to limit the police power of government by their own version of the meaning of the Amendment.[2]

Yet state and Federal governments, when the presumed right to keep and bear arms has been exploited into a threat to public safety, have used the police power to limit the possession of weapons to lawful purposes. In 1886 the Court sustained a state statute forbidding groups of armed men to drill in military formations and to parade in public streets with weapons.[3] In 1934 Congress passed the National Firearms Act,[4] which was concerned especially with particular types of weapons presumed to be favored by professional criminals; and in upholding the constitutionality of this statute the Court suggested, although not very forcefully, that the burden was on the individual to show that possession of firearms bore some reasonable relationship to the maintenance of a well-regulated militia.[5]

With the growth in violent crime after World War II (following an urbanizing trend which accelerated after World War I), Congress has periodically been urged to enact more stringent gun-control laws.[6] It has also been persuaded to water down the enactments by two converse arguments—that citizens should not be deprived of instruments of self-defense in an age of violence and that gun-control laws will not significantly deter professional criminals bent on acquiring weapons. While no statistical documentation of either argument has been convincingly advanced, the basic fact is that the question is essentially one of public policy concerning the use of the police power and not one concerning an individual right which is constitutionally insulated from the police power.

No attempt has been made to the present to incorporate the Second Amendment into the Fourteenth as has been undertaken with reference to most of the elements of the Bill of Rights.

1. *Cf. United States v. Miller*, 307 U.S. 174 (1939).
2. *Cf. Presser v. Illinois*, 116 U.S. 252 (1886); and *cf.* also *United States v. Cruik-shank*, 92 U.S. 533 (1875), declaring somewhat gratuitously that the Amendment left matters of regulation and control of firearms to the states. The typical view of state courts, that the right to keep and bear arms antedated the Federal Constitution, is expounded in *Moore v. Gallup*, 45 N.Y.S. 2d 63 (1943); and *cf.* also *Eckart v. City of Philadelphia*, 329 F.S. 845 (1971).
3. *Presser v. Illinois*, 116 U.S. 252 (1886).
4. 48 Stat. 1236.
5. *United States v. Miller*, 307 U.S. 174 (1939).
6. *Cf.* Federal Firearms Act of 1934, n. 4 *supra;* National Firearms Act of 1950, 74 Stat. 149, 26 U.S.C. 5801; National Gun Control Act of 1968, 82 Stat. 1227, 42 U.S.C. 1401.

Amendment III
Prohibition of Quartering of Troops

No soldier shall, in time of peace, be quartered in any house without the consent of the owner, nor in time of war, but in a manner to be prescribed by law.

The quartering of troops in private premises, one of the abuses of government power explicitly forbidden by the English Bill of Rights and the earlier Petition of Right,[1] was one of the fundamental "rights of Englishmen" which the American colonists saw as being flouted in the years leading up to the Revolution. Since the policy had, in the main, been accepted by the mother country as an unequivocal limitation on the government, the drafters of the first state constitutions insisted on its inclusion in various state bills of rights and then in the basic Amendments to the Federal Constitution.[2] As in England, so in the United States it has become a self-evident truth which has not occasioned any modern attempt at infringement.

Taken with the Fourth Amendment, the Third has been suggested as establishing a constitutional principle of privacy in the business of the individual generally.[3] To the degree that the Court has cautiously examined this proposition, it has done so in the context of the Ninth and Tenth Amendments rather than the Third and Fourth. It is safe to say, however, that this subject, as exemplified in the security of private premises from government trespass, is in the nature of what the British call a constitutional convention rather than a rule of constitutional construction.

1. 9 Stat. at 1 (Gr. Brit.) 67; 7 *id.*, 317.
2. *Cf.* Swindler, ed., *Constitutional Documents of the American Revolution* (Dobbs Ferry, N.Y., 1974).
3. *Cf.* Douglas, J., in *Griswold v. Connecticut*, 381 U.S. 479, 481 (1965).

Amendment IV
Unreasonable Searches and Seizures

The right of the people to be secure in their persons, houses, papers, and effects, against unreasonable searches and seizures, shall not be violated, and no warrants shall issue, but upon probable cause, supported by oath or affirmation, and particularly describing the place to be searched, and the persons or things to be seized.

This Amendment (1) prohibits searches and seizures which are unreasonable, and a primary safeguard of reasonableness is (2) the stipulation that no general warrant shall issue but only a warrant setting out probable cause; while (3) the particular party or objects to be seized, and the site where the search may be carried out, must also be identified. In construction of this Amendment, the courts accordingly have addressed themselves to the breadth of the subject covered by these provisions, the sufficiency of warrants as issued, the circumstances of search and seizure and— most important of all, in the final analysis—the admissibility of evidence based on these procedures.

General Coverage of the Amendment

Two cases, in 1886 and 1914, emphasized the closeness of the relationship between the Fourth and Fifth Amendments, "as running 'almost into each other,'" as Justice Tom Clark expressed it in 1961.[1] The first case, *Boyd v. United States*, established that unreasonable searches and seizures amount to potential if not actual self-incrimination as prohibited by the Fifth Amendment;[2] while the second, *Weeks v. United States,* held that the Fourth Amendment barred the Federal courts from admitting evidence obtained in violation of the constitutional immunities defined in *Boyd.*[3] The purpose of the two Amendments (to which the Sixth was also joined in subsequent cases), said Justice Clark, in this context was to prohibit "all invasion on the part of the government and its employees of the sanctity of a man's home and the privacies of life."[4] The rule in *Boyd* had followed on an earlier ruling in 1878 that personal letters in the United States mails might not be opened by postal authorities without authorization of a magistrate,[5] and *Weeks* was broadened, in 1921, by a holding that Fourth Amendment safeguards apply even to premises which are opened voluntarily to officers without warrants.[6]

Wiretapping and related techniques of electronic eavesdropping are issues which have had a turbulent judicial history. The 1928 case of *Olmstead v. United States*[7] held (5–4) that wiretapping was not within the concepts of the drafters of the Amendment; search and seizure did not include hearing and sight, as Chief Justice Taft put it. Not until 1967 did the Court discard the *Olmstead* doctrine and restate the constitutional conditions required for such surveillance.[8] Prior to this, Congress had undertaken to proscribe the introduction of intercepted messages into evidence in cases arising under Section 605 of the Federal Communications Act of 1934.[9] The Court sustained the exclusionary rule deriving from this statute in *Nardone v. United States;*[10] and in 1951 it barred introduction of evidence obtained by penetrating a wall of defendant's premises with a listening device, holding this to be impermissible entry.[11]

Because a major portion of criminal cases involving searches and seizures come under state jurisdiction, the Court in recent decades has been increasingly concerned with the applicability of the Fourth Amendment criteria to the states through the Fourteenth Amendment. From *Wolf v. Colorado* in 1949[12] to *Mapp v. Ohio* in 1961,[13] the struggle to incorporate the Fourth Amendment standards into the Fourteenth was carried on, with the Supreme Court ultimately concluding that to refrain from applying the Fourth Amendment exclusionary rule to the state courts would ultimately undermine the *Weeks* standard in Federal courts.[14] The incorporation of the Fourth Amendment standards into the Fourteenth is discussed under that Amendment.

Sufficiency of Warrant; Conditions of Search

How explicit the statement of probable cause must be has been a question of more importance than the question of who issues the warrant.[15] A mere statement that "affiant has reason to believe," or that complainant concludes that a particular person has committed a criminal act, has usually been held invalid.[16] The circumstances and facts must justify the action; if apparent facts are set out, or if the information is gathered from sources previously proved to have been reliable, the definition of probable cause is satisfied.[17] Since the purpose of the requirement of probable cause is to avoid empowering the investigator to appropriate one thing while searching for another, the courts have denied discretion to the searcher.[18]

Search without warrant is permissible under certain conditions. A moving vehicle, obviously capable of carrying evidence out of reach, may be intercepted and searched if probable cause can be established (even though, as a practical matter, the establishing takes place after the search).[19] In 1900 the courts declared that anyone witnessing an attempted felony may make an arrest and that a qualified peace officer may arrest on suspicion of felony.[20] In 1925 courts added that arrest of a person in the act of committing a crime justified the contemporaneous search of the immediate premises.[21] Between 1947 and 1950 there was a sequence of cases in which the judiciary grasped for criteria for reasonable search either with or without warrant. Chief Justice Vinson sustained a prolonged search after entry with warrant, when the specific evidence indicated in the warrant was turned up.[22] The following year the search was invalidated, even though incident to arrest, and resulting in a finding of relevant evidence, because a warrant had not been obtained.[23] Two years later this doctrine was overruled in an opinion which sought to establish standards of reasonableness: valid arrest, premises accessible to the public and under respondent's complete control, limitation of search to these premises.[24]

From this sequence of cases the Court was led logically to the need to qualify, if not nullify, the *Olmstead* doctrine and to restate criteria of reasonableness relating to wiretapping. In a return to the essentials of probable cause, electronic surveillance was limited to cases where an appropriate magistrate was "properly notified of the need for such investigation, specifically informed of the basis on which it was to proceed, and clearly apprised of the precise intrusion it would entail."[25] In a related problem area, "third-party bugging" (respondent speaking to informant whose concealed device relayed the speech to outside agents), the surveillance had first been held permissible,[26] then cast into doubt by the *Katz* doctrine, then reaffirmed by a divided court on the ground that *Katz*, not having retroactive effect,[27] did not concern the earlier holding.[28] But the Court continued to require a modicum of Fourth Amendment safeguards in "bugging" generally—particularly when these activities were frequently conducted without issuance of warrant and more particularly since they have tended to raise questions of national security.[29]

The Exclusionary Rule: Federal Courts

With the extension of the Federal exclusionary rule to state courts in *Mapp*, even though the Court subsequently declared that this did not compel state courts to conform to general procedural practice in Federal courts,[30] the uniformity of standards set out in a succession of state cases has suggested that this uniformity extend also to the Federal cases.[31] Earlier in the twentieth century, Federal authorities were enjoined not to use evidence gathered by state authorities which would be excluded if gathered on the initiative of Federal officers.[32] Since 1927 it has been held that state officers enforcing Federal law could not use illegally seized evidence,[33] and in 1956 it was held that a defendant in a state court could have injunctive relief from attempts by Federal officers to turn over illegal evidence to state prosecutors.[34] The Court has held that Federal officers may not subpoena incriminating records whose existence had been discovered through illegal search.[35] But where the knowledge of the existence of the records derives from legal sources, such evidence is admissible.[36]

Under Chief Justice Burger the Court began in 1971 a general re-examination of the exclusionary rule, dramatized by an elaborate dissent by the Chief Justice in *Bivens v. Six Unknown Agents*.[37] Among other things, the dissent pointed out that the rule penalized the prosecutor rather than the peace officer who committed the illegal act and who is not subject to the prosecutor's control; and, conversely, that many investigatory acts which may jeopardize or flout constitutional rights never reach a prosecution stage where the rule might act as the safeguard it was intended to be.[38] Essentially related to the exclusionary rule is the judicial policy of prospective as against retrospective overruling, discussed under Article III. Since the Court first sought to come to grips with this matter in 1965,[39] the interrelated rights covered in the Fourth, Fifth and Sixth Amendments have inevitably raised the issue of retroactivity and have divided the Court in a succession of opinions.[40] The effort of the Burger Court to restate the exclusionary rule, whether by inviting Congressional code reform or by judicial initiative, ultimately may involve a restatement of the rule of prospectivity as well.

1. *Mapp v. Ohio*, 367 U.S. 643, 646 (1961).
2. 116 U.S. 616, 630 (1886).
3. 232 U.S. 383 (1914).
4. *Mapp v. Ohio*, 367 U.S. at 646, 647.
5. *Ex parte Jackson*, 96 U.S. 727 (1878).
6. *Amos v. United States*, 255 U.S. 313 (1921); *Miller v. United States*, 357 U.S. 301 (1958); but *cf.* qualifications of this rule in *Carroll v. United States*, 354 U.S. 394 (1957), and see also *Brinegar v. United States*, 338 U.S. 160 (1949).
7. 277 U.S. 438 (1928); and *cf. Goldman v. United States*, 316 U.S. 129 (1942).
8. *Katz v. United States*, 389 U.S. 347 (1967).
9. 48 Stat. 1064, 47 U.S.C. 605 as amended.
10. *Nardone v. United States*, 302 U.S. 379 (1937); 308 U.S. 338 (1939). In the first case, the general principle in Section 605 of the statute was affirmed, but in the second the Court held that the defendant had the burden of proving the fact of wiretapping and the materiality of this fact to the case against him. But see the discussion under n. 31 below.
11. *Silverman v. United States*, 365 U.S. 505 (1951).
12. 388 U.S. 25 (1949).
13. 367 U.S. 643 (1961).
14. Compare, in this same time period, *Lustig v. United States*, 338 U.S. 74 (1949), which the Court found it necessary to overrule in *Elkins v. United States*, 364 U.S. 206 (1960), because admissibility of evidence illegally obtained by state officers and turned over to Federal prosecutors, as permitted by *Lustig*, would reopen the avenue of circumvention of the exclusionary rule presumably closed by *Wolf v. Colorado*.

15. *Cf. McGrain v. Daugherty,* 273 U.S. 135 (1927).
16. *Byars v. United States,* 273 U.S. 28 (1927); *Giordinello v. United States,* 357 U.S. 480 (1958).
17. *Steele v. United States,* 267 U.S. 498 (1925); and *cf. Jones v. United States,* 362 U.S. 257 (1960).
18. *Marron v. United States,* 275 U.S. 192 (1927); and *cf. Kremen v. United States,* 353 U.S. 346 (1957).
19. *Carroll v. United States,* 354 U.S. 394 (1957); *Brinegar v. United States,* 338 U.S. 160 (1949). But *cf.* also *Scher v. United States,* 305 U.S. 251 (1938).
20. *Bad Elk v. United States,* 177 U.S. 529 (1900).
21. *Agnello v. United States,* 269 U.S. 20 (1925); but *cf. United States v. Lefkowitz,* 285 U.S. 452 (1932).
22. *Harris v. United States,* 331 U.S. 145 (1947).
23. *Trupiano v. United States,* 334 U.S. 699 (1948).
24. *United States v. Rabinowitz,* 339 U.S. 56 (1950).
25. *Katz v. United States,* 389 U.S. 347 (1968). Congress undertook a legislative broadening of the criteria in Title III of the Omnibus Crime and Safe Streets Act of 1968, 82 Stat. 197, 18 U.S.C. 921. *Cf.* generally, *Alderman v. United States,* 394 U.S. 165 (1969).
26. *On Lee v. United States,* 343 U.S. 747 (1952).
27. *Cf. Desist v. United States,* 394 U.S. 244 (1969).
28. *United States v. White,* 401 U.S. 745 (1971).
29. *United States v. District Court,* 407 U.S. 297 (1972); and *cf. United States v. Ventresca,* 380 U.S. 102 (1965). See also Ruffin, "Out on a Limb of the Poisonous Tree: The Tainted Witness," 15 *U.C.L.A. L. Rev.* 32 (1967).
30. *Ker v. California,* 374 U.S. 23 (1963).
31. Admissibility in state courts of wiretap evidence was upheld as to Section 605 of the Communications Act of 1964 in *Schwartz v. Texas,* 344 U.S. 149 (1952), but barred from use in Federal courts in *Benanti v. United States,* 355 U.S. 96 (1957); *Schwartz* was then overruled in *Lee v. Florida,* 391 U.S. 378 (1968).
32. *Elkins v. United States,* 364 U.S. 206 (1960); and see *Preston v. United States,* 376 U.S. 364 (1964).
33. *Gambino v. United States,* 275 U.S. 310 (1927); *Lustig v. United States,* 338 U.S. 74 (1949); and *cf. McGuire v. United States,* 273 U.S. 95 (1927).
34. *Rea v. United States,* 350 U.S. 214 (1956); but see *Wilson v. Schnettler,* 365 U.S. 381 (1961).
35. *Silverthorne Lumber Co. v. United States,* 251 U.S. 385 (1920).
36. *United States v. Wallace,* 336 U.S. 793 (1949); *Zap v. United States,* 328 U.S. 624 (1946); *Am. Tobacco Co. v. Werckmeister,* 207 U.S. 284 (1907).
37. 403 U.S. 388 (1971); and see Oakes, "Studying the Exclusionary Rule in Search and Seizure," 37 *U. Chi. L. Rev.* 665 (1970).
38. 403 U.S. at 425.
39. *Linkletter v. Walker,* 381 U.S. 618 (1965).
40. *Cf. Williams v. United States,* 401 U.S. 646 (1971); *Mackey v. United States,* 401 U.S. 667 (1971); *United States v. White,* 401 U.S. 745 (1971).

Amendment V. Due Process of Law

No person shall be held to answer for a capital or otherwise infamous crime, unless on a presentment or indictment of a grand jury, except in cases arising in the land or naval forces, or in the militia, when in actual service in time of war or public danger; nor shall any person be subject for the same offense to be twice put in jeopardy of life or limb; nor shall be compelled in any criminal case to be a witness against himself, nor be deprived of life, liberty or property, without due process of law; nor shall private property be taken for public use without just compensation.

This Amendment covers five essentials of due process and incorporates guarantees of English liberty extending back to Magna Carta (*cf.* p. 28 *supra*): (1) grand-jury process; (2) double jeopardy; (3) self-incrimination; (4) the safeguarding of life, liberty and property; and (5) limitations on eminent domain.

Grand-Jury Process

There are several exacting questions raised by the first clause of this Amendment: What is an "infamous crime"? Is there a public policy involved in any choice between presentment (charging of a crime on the initiative of the grand jury) and indictment (charging of a crime on evidence laid before the grand jury by the prosecutor)? What are cases "arising" in the military service and what is a "time . . . of public danger"? Added to these questions is the ultimate question of the role of the common law—inferred in or imputed to the term "grand jury" in this Amendment and repeatedly mentioned in reference to civil trials in the Seventh Amendment.[1]

An "infamous crime" is generally treated as a synonym for felony.[2] As early as 1885, however, the Court conceded that the concept "may be affected by the changes of public opinion from one age to another,"[3] and, under a familiar rule of statutory construction, the term has been defined in relationship to capital offenses (the specific term preceding it in the clause) and to the requirement of grand-jury action (the provision following it in the clause).[4] It is immaterial how Congress has classified the crime.[5]

While a grand jury's power to initiate a charge of crime is of ancient origin, the modern Court requires that a presentment, like an indictment, must be specific in its allegations so that it may inform the defendant of the charges he must face and defend against. A general statement that the grand jury has concluded that a named defendant is to be charged with grand larceny, without further detail, has been declared constitutionally inadequate.[6] An indictment in Federal felony cases is a matter of constitutional right,[7] and although states may proceed to prosecute on an information rather than a grand-jury action, this alternative is not open to Federal prosecutors;[8] and an indictment cannot be amended except by resubmission to a grand jury unless the change is obviously no more than a matter of form.[9]

While the Court has long acknowledged that "cases arising" in military service are excepted from the grand-jury safeguard,[10] in recent years it has limited the jurisdiction of military tribunals to "service-connected" crimes.[11] The ambivalent position of the Court in the matter of civilians' liability to military trial was illustrated in the two cases of *Reid v. Covert*,[12] where three Justices dissented and one "reserved judgment" in the first disposition, upholding military jurisdiction, while in the second, denying jurisdiction, there was a majority of four plus two separate concurring opinions. Justice Black, for the majority in the second case, held that if no court-martial liability would apply domestically it could not apply overseas; Justice Frankfurter simply found no "service-connected" crime in the acts of the civilians.[13] In earlier cases the Court had first asserted that ex-servicemen were liable to court-martial for crimes committed in service,[14] then retreated from that position.[15] In 1957 the Court upheld a treaty provision under which servicemen charged with crime in another country could be tried in the courts of that country.[16]

Double Jeopardy

This clause is directly related in purpose to the provision on grand-jury process—the latter is intended to insure a precise, detailed charge to which a defendant is required to answer, and the former is intended to insure that he need answer only once.[17] At the same time, the safeguard of specificity set out in the first clause enables the government to prosecute for separate violations of separate provisions deriving from the same act of the defendant.[18] A hung jury does not bar retrial of the case under this clause,[19] but where a jury had been impaneled and then dismissed, a second trial was construed as double jeopardy.[20] In the same vein, the Court has held that a successful appeal from conviction at a first trial (charge of second-degree murder) bars a new trial on first-degree murder, since the charge in the first trial was "an implicit acquittal" of the first-degree charge.[21] But where a defendant voluntarily avails himself of a trial *de novo* in a court of record after a first trial in a court not of record, no double jeopardy attaches.[22]

Separate prosecutions in state and Federal courts do not create double jeopardy.[23] The test of double jeopardy in the same court is whether the same evidence is required to sustain the charge in the second trial.[24] The fact that Congress has imposed both civil and criminal sanctions in reference to the same act does not establish double jeopardy.[25] Where the civil action to recover taxes is punitive in nature, however, it may be barred by a prior criminal conviction in the same case where the defendant was convicted.[26] But where a defendant is charged with both civil and criminal contempt, the purposes of the charges being different (one to compel action, the other to punish refusal to act), the Court in a 4–3 decision dismissed the constitutional plea.[27]

The quashing of an indictment does not create double jeopardy on reindictment.[28] Nor does *nolle prosequi* under one indictment bar a second indictment.[29] A motion for a new trial after the first trial has been set aside for improper instructions is not double jeopardy,[30] nor is there double jeopardy in a resentencing where the defendant on his own motion has succeeded in having the first sentence set aside.[31] The constitutional immunity in this clause is a personal right, and the lower Federal courts have consistently held that it may be waived impliedly or expressly.[32]

Self-Incrimination

This privilege should always be broadly construed, said Justice Frankfurter in 1956, in view of the policy that it is better to let an occasional crime go unpunished than to permit prosecutors to extort disclosures from defendants.[33] On the other hand, said Justice Cardozo in 1937, "today as in the past there are students of our penal system who look upon the immunity [from compulsory self-incrimination] as a mischief rather than a benefit, and who would limit its scope, or destroy it altogether."[34] These represent the two poles between which the alternating currents of constitutional theory have flowed now for more than half a century. While the readiness of defendants or witnesses to "take the Fifth" in the security hysteria of the 1950s developed a sense of frustration among prosecutors and legislators,[35] the excesses of McCarthyism in this period re-emphasized the dangers of extortionate interrogation which the Amendment had historically been intended to guard against. When, in the 1960s, the succession of defendants' rights cases carried to its logical extreme the containment of government agents' powers to obtain confessions,[36] a new sense of frustration was professed by law-enforcement interests.

These decisions, seeking to develop standards limiting processes of self-incrimination, unequivocally incorporated this Fifth Amendment provision into the Fourteenth: The "third degree" had been held unconstitutional as early as 1937;[37] psychological pressure as well as physical intimidation was added to the prohibited list in 1944;[38] and in 1952 the Court broadened the safeguard by declaring generally that coerced confessions obtained under any circumstances "offend the community's sense of fair play and decency."[39] Judicial development of the self-incrimination clause with reference to Federal agencies kept pace with the Court's doctrines as applied to the states; in 1943 it was held that even voluntary confessions, if made under circumstances of illegal detention, were inadmissible as evidence,[40] and in 1957 it was added that unnecessary delay in bringing a suspect before a magistrate would invalidate any evidence obtained from the suspect.[41] These sweeping rules applied to Federal courts accelerated the trend of the doctrine applied to state courts[42] and successively overturned contrary rules in a number of cases.[43]

Finally, in *Miranda v. Arizona*,[44] the Court summarized the various cases on self-incrimination in a declaration that "the Fifth Amendment privilege . . . serves to protect persons in all settings in which their freedom of action is curtailed from being compelled to incriminate themselves."[45] Amid a tumultuous reaction to this declaration, Congress sought to circumscribe it in the Omnibus Crime Control and Safe Streets Act of 1968[46] by declaring that voluntary confessions were admissible in evidence in Federal courts and directing Federal trial judges to determine voluntariness on the basis of certain statutory criteria.[47] In 1971, in a case widely discussed as a limitation on the *Miranda* principle,[48] Chief Justice Burger for the Court held that even if a statement could not be admitted as evidence as part of the prosecution's case in chief, because of its having been obtained without complying with *Miranda* standards,[49] it could be introduced to impeach defendant's credibility.[50]

An equally fundamental practice of prosecutors—but presumably less fraught with opportunity for abuse—is "plea bargaining," the invitation to a plea of guilty to a reduced charge or in consideration of some other inducement. In cases where such procedure may chill the constitutional right to plead not guilty and demand a jury trial,[51] or where the prosecutor fails to keep the bargain,[52] the Court is prepared to invalidate the transaction. But in general, where the guilty plea is voluntary and made in anticipation of a reduced penalty, it will be sustained.[53] In the same general category is the practice of encouraging incriminating testimony under state or Federal immunity statutes. Since 1892 the rule of transactional immunity has obtained in the Federal courts, covering all circumstances in which the witness might subsequently be prosecuted;[54] but in 1972 the Court qualified this rule by holding that a witness was only constitutionally immune from prosecutors' use of the testimony given, not from prosecution based on evidence independently gathered.[55] Disclosure of records of corporations as may be required by law cannot be refused by agents on self-incrimination grounds; the privilege is a personal one and cannot be asserted on behalf of an institution.[56]

Life, Liberty or Property

Due process of law is essentially made up of all of the particular provisions of this Amendment, the Fourth, Sixth and Eighth—and more. It has been exhaustively defined[57] and traces its fundamentals to the earliest records of the common law. Its fundamental objective, as the language of this clause indicates, is to safeguard the individual in his well-being—i.e., his life, his independence of action and his possessions. It is the basic standard of conduct in government's dealing with individuals, requiring that government abide by the required limits and procedures which the people have set up as guidelines to its actions. In the twentieth century it has been distinguished both as a procedural and a substantive right,[58] and in terms of contemporary American life it has alternately been a shield for private enterprise from government regulation and a sword for civil rights (see, generally, Amendment XIV).

Due process as an element in testing the legitimacy of the regulatory powers of government has been discussed under the commerce and contract clauses, and it has become routine to raise it as an issue in constitutional cases arising under various Amendments. The relationship which it bears to the identical phrase in the Fourteenth Amendment, and the ultimate possibility of counterbalancing incorporation from the Fourteenth to the Fifth (i.e., in the matter of the equal-protection clause), has attracted some judicial attention.[59]

In the course of the security cases in the 1950s, the Court was constrained to set out the details of procedural due process, most of which were Sixth Amendment provisions (*q.v.*).[60] The accused is to be recorded as pleading, or having a plea of not guilty entered on his behalf:[61] and where, as in the 1950s, charges involved informers' reports to the government, the prosecutor must either produce relevant papers for examination by the defense, or the action will be dismissed.[62] Where Congress has provided for judicial review of administrative regulations, due process is insured by such review even if national emergency conditions justify the promulgation of the regulations without hearing.[63] The basic requirement is that a defendant be assured of a hearing at some ultimate, essential stage of the proceeding.[64]

Substantive due process guards against discrimination between defendants or litigants by requiring a rational basis for liability.[65] Related to this is the rule against deprivation of liberty, a doctrine which meant liberty of contract in favor of management in the *laissez-faire* era and the opposite after the New Deal revolution.[66] Deprivation of property has frequently been at issue in the matter of retroactive legislation; the test is whether the Constitution expressly preserves certain rights, or whether instead the constitutional power of the legislature to enact laws on a given subject may qualify a previously acquired private right.[67] All private contracts are made subject to the freedom of the sovereign to amend the general laws, however such amendments may affect the interests of contracting parties.[68]

Whereas, in the heyday of *laissez-faire*, due process was treated virtually as a property right guaranteeing through the Constitution the insulation of private enterprise from all but minimum regulation, the Court since the New Deal era has viewed due process essentially as the guideline for the use of police power. The pivotal case of *National Labor Relations Board v. Jones & Laughlin Steel Corp.*[69] identified the legitimate interest of government under the commerce clause in the regulation of labor-management interests and rejected the theretofore standard argument that such regulation deprived management of liberty without due process.[70] The question is no longer whether such regulation is within the constitutional powers of government but whether the manner of its implementation is just and reasonable.[71] This has been a distinction which the Court has made increasingly clear in the twentieth century, as the power of government in interstate commerce[72] and in the exercise of the tax power[73] has steadily broadened.

Limitations on Eminent Domain

Eminent domain, the taking of private property for public use, is one of the inherent attributes of sovereignty, and this final clause of the Fifth Amendment is merely a limitation on a pre-existing power.[74] Federal power of eminent domain extends to state interests as well, and the fact that this type of taking may impair state revenues or projects does not in itself inhibit the

Federal power.[75] While the decision as to how much property to take for public use is a matter of legislative discretion,[76] Justice Holmes once described the process as a "petty larceny of the police power"[77] which the Fifth and Fourteenth Amendments were intended to keep within equitable bounds. Yet Holmes—with Brandeis dissenting—read an opinion setting aside a state legislative act which was intended to prevent a mining company from taking subsurface coal to which it had a contract right where this undermined the surface structures of the other contracting party; where the public interest was not affected, said Holmes, the police power should not be exercised in favor of one party as against another in a private contract.[78]

Private public service corporations (e.g., utilities) are usually vested with a right to take certain private property if duly compensated; whether this right, if curtailed by subsequent government restraint, has been taken and is compensable, or whether the public convenience and necessity which warrants the exercise of the police power is overriding, has been variously answered in the courts.[79] It has consistently been held that where the government requisitions or otherwise appropriates all of the product of a private operator, valid private rights dependent thereon must be compensated.[80] However, this rule applies only to direct appropriation and not to consequential injuries: if the injury is the by-product of the exercises of a valid government power for a valid public purpose—e.g., injury to rights of private users of public waters when the government is constitutionally empowered to improve navigable waters—the injury is not compensable.[81] Finally, where a taking does require compensation, the test of what is "just compensation" has usually been the reasonable equivalent of the value of the interest directly affected.[82]

---

1. The Fifth Amendment has been the subject of many studies, one of the first of the recent works being Griswold, *The Fifth Amendment Today* (New York, 1955); *cf.* also Rogge, *The First and the Fifth* (New York, 1960); Levy, *Origins of the Fifth Amendment* (New York, 1968).

2. *Green v. United States*, 356 U.S. 165 (1958); *Parkinson v. United States*, 121 U.S. 281 (1887).

3. *Ex parte Wilson*, 114 U.S. 417, 427 (1885); *Macklin v. United States*, 117 U.S. 348, 352 (1886).

4. *Ex parte Wilson*, 114 U.S. 417, 423 (1885); *Dicke v. United States*, 301 U.S. 492 (1937); *Lawn v. United States*, 355 U.S. 339 (1958); *Stirone v. United States*, 361 U.S. 212 (1960).

5. *Ex parte Wilson*, 114 U.S. 417, 426 (1885).

6. *Gaither v. United States*, 413 F. 2d 1061 (1969).

7. *Michel v. Louisiana*, 350 U.S. 91 (1955); *Heisler v. United States*, 394 F. 2d 692 (1968), cert. den. 393 U.S. 986 (1968). This provision of the Fifth Amendment has not been extended to the states; cf. *Martin v. Beto*, 397 F. 2d 741 (1968), cert. den. 394 U.S. 906 (1968).

8. *Beavers v. Henkel*, 194 U.S. 84 (1904).

9. *Stewart v. United States*, 395 F. 2d 484 (1968).

10. *Kurtz v. Moffitt*, 115 U.S. 500 (1885).

11. *Relford v. Commandant*, 401 U.S. 355 (1971); *O'Callahan v. Parker*, 395 U.S. 258 (1969); *United States ex rel. Toth v. Quarles*, 350 U.S. 11 (1955).

12. 351 U.S. 497 (1956); 354 U.S. 1 (1957).

13. 354 U.S. at 41. and cf. *Kinsella v. United States, ex rel. Singleton*, 361 U.S. 234 (1960); *McElroy v. United States*, 361 U.S. 278 (1960).

14. *Burns v. Wilson*, 346 U.S. 147 (1953); *Jackson v. Taylor*, 353 U.S. 569 (1957); *Ex parte Quirin*, 317 U.S. 1 (1943).

15. *United States ex rel. Toth v. Quarles*, 350 U.S. 11 (1955).

16. *Wilson v. Girouard*, 354 U.S. 514 (1957).

17. Cf. *Benton v. Maryland*, 395 U.S. 784 (1969); *United States v. Sabella*, 272 F. 2d 206 (1959); *United States v. Jorn*, 440 U.S. 470 (1971); *Ashe v. Swenson*, 397 U.S. 436 (1970); *Green v. United States*, 355 U.S. 184 (1957).

18. *Gore v. United States*, 357 U.S. 386 (1958); *Blockburger v. United States*, 284 U.S. 299 (1932); *Will v. United States*, 389 U.S. 90 (1967).

19. *Wade v. Hunter*, 336 U.S. 684 (1949).

20. *Downum v. United States*, 372 U.S. 734 (1963).

21. *Green v. United States*, 355 U.S. 184 (1957). A unanimous Court broadened the rule in *Price v. Georgia*, 398 U.S. 323 (1970).

22. *Colten v. Kentucky*, 407 U.S. 104 (1972); *North Carolina v. Pearce*, 395 U.S. 711 (1969).

23. *Bartkus v. Illinois*, 359 U.S. 121 (1959); *Abbate v. United States*, 359 U.S. 187 (1959); *United States v. Lanza*, 260 U.S. 377 (1922).

24. *Morgan v. Devine*, 237 U.S. 632 (1915); *Carter v. McLaughry*, 183 U.S. 365 (1902).

25. *Rex Trailer Co. v. United States*, 350 U.S. 148 (1956); and cf. *United States ex rel. Marcus v. Hess*, 317 U.S. 537 (1940); *United States v. Ewell*, 383 U.S. 116 (1966).

26. *United States v. LaFranca*, 282 U.S. 568 (1931); and cf. *Coffey v. United States*, 116 U.S. 443 (1886).

27. *Yates v. United States*, 355 U.S. 66 (1957).

28. *United States v. Kimbrew*, 380 F. 2d 536 (1967).

29. *Newman v. United States*, 410 F. 2d 259 (1969).

30. *Forman v. United States*, 361 U.S. 416 (1960).

31. *North Carolina v. Pearce*, 395 U.S. 711 (1969); and cf. *Bozza v. United States*, 330 U.S. 160 (1947).

32. *Harris v. United States*, 237 F. 2d 274 (1956); *United States v. Reeves*, 203 F. 2d 213 (1968); *Levin v. United States*, 5 F. 2d 598 (1925), cert. den. 269 U.S. 562 (1925).

33. *Ullmann v. United States*, 350 U.S. 422, 429 (1956).

34. *Palko v. Connecticut*, 302 U.S. 319, 325 (1937).

35. *Cf. Blau v. United States,* 340 U.S. 159 (1950); *Quinn v. United States,* 349 U.S. 155 (1955). *Cf.* also *Hoffman v. United States,* 341 U.S. 479 (1951); *Rogers v. United States,* 340 U.S. 367 (1951); *Emspak v. United States,* 349 U.S. 190 (1955).
36. *Brown v. Mississippi,* 297 U.S. 278 (1937).
37. *Id.,* at 286.
38. 322 U.S. 143 (1944); *cf.* also *Watts v. Indiana,* 338 U.S. 49 (1949); *Hoby v. Ohio,* 332 U.S. 596 (1948).
39. 342 U.S. 165 (1952); *Stein v. New York,* 346 U.S. 156 (1953); *Spano v. New York,* 360 U.S. 315 (1959); *Rogers v. Richmond,* 365 U.S. 354 (1961); and *cf. Fikes v. Alabama,* 352 U.S. 191 (1956) and *Thomas v. Arizona,* 356 U.S. 390 (1958).
40. *McNabb v. United States,* 318 U.S. 332 (1943).
41. *Mallory v. United States,* 354 U.S. 49 (1957). *Cf.* also *Ullman v. United States,* 350 U.S. 422 (1956), holding the Federal immunity statute to cover state as well as Federal investigators.
42. *Malloy v. Hogan,* 378 U.S. 1 (1964); and *cf. Murphy v. Waterfront Commission,* 378 U.S. 52 (1964).
43. *Twining v. New Jersey,* 211 U.S. 78 (1908), sustaining state practices permitting comment on defendants' failure to testify; *United States v. Murdock,* 284 U.S. 141 (1931), denying defendants' right to remain silent under Federal interrogation because of possible incrimination under state law; *Feldman v. United States,* 322 U.S. 487 (1944), sustaining a Federal conviction based on testimony taken under a state immunity statute; *Adamson v. California,* 332 U.S. 46 (1947), upholding the Twining doctrine; *Knapp v. Schweitzer,* 357 U.S. 371 (1958), upholding a state contempt conviction as against claim that statement would render defendant liable to Federal prosecution.
44. 384 U.S. 436 (1966).
45. *Id.,* at 445. *Cf. Lego v. Toomey,* 404 U.S. 477 (1972).
46. 82 Stat. 197, 18 U.S.C. 921.
47. For comment on Title II of the statute, see Burt, "Miranda and Title II: A Morganatic Marriage," 1969 *Sup. Court Rev.* 81.
48. *Harris v. New York,* 401 U.S. 222 (1971).
49. These were set out by the Court in *Miranda* as follows: (1) Advising the suspect of his right to remain silent; (2) further advising suspect that anything he does say may be used against him; (3) providing of counsel during interrogation; (4) clear evidence that any right to counsel has been knowingly waived; (5) assurance that counsel will be appointed if accused is unable to retain one; and (6) carrying of burden of proof by the government that defendant has knowingly and intelligently waived his rights against self-incrimination. 384 U.S. at 467.
50. *Harris v. New York,* 401 U.S. 222 (1971).
51. *United States v. Jackson,* 390 U.S. 570 (1968).
52. *Santobello v. New York,* 404 U.S. 257 (1971).
53. *Brady v. United States,* 397 U.S. 742 (1970); *cf. Parker v. North Carolina,* 397 U.S. 790 (1970).
54. *Counselman v. Hitchcock,* 142 U.S. 547 (1892).
55. *Kastigar v. United States,* 406 U.S. 441 (1972).
56. *Rogers v. United States,* 340 U.S. 367 (1951); *California v. Byers,* 402 U.S. 424 (1971).
57. *Cf.* Mott, *Due Process of Law* (Indianapolis, 1926); and *cf. Hurtado v. California,* 110 U.S. 535 (1884).

58. *Cf.*, generally, *Lincoln Fed. Union v. Northwestern I & S. Co.*, 335 U.S. 525 (1948).

59. *Shapiro v. Thompson*, 394 U.S. 618 (1969); *Schneider v. Rusk*, 377 U.S. 173 (1964); *Hirabayashi v. United States*, 320 U.S. 81 (1943); *Bolling v. Sharpe*, 347 U.S. 497 (1954).

60. E.g., *Jencks v. United States*, 353 U.S. 657 (1957); *Watkins v. United States*, 354 U.S. 178 (1957), *Service v. Dulles*, 354 U.S. 363 (1957); *Barenblatt v. United States*, 360 U.S. 109 (1958).

61. *Crain v. United States*, 162 U.S. 625 (1896); and *cf. Hardy v. United States*, 250 F. 2d 580 (1958), cert. den., 357 U.S. 921 (1958).

62. *Jencks v. United States*, 353 U.S. 657 (1957); *Palermo v. United States*, 360 U.S. 343 (1959); and on the furore over the Jencks case, see Swindler, *The New Legality*, 242–49. For Congressional efforts to safeguard informants' identity, *cf.* 71 Stat. 595, 18 U.S.C. 3500, and the judicial construction of the provision in *Rosenberg v. United States*, 360 U.S. 367 (1959); *Campbell v. United States*, 365 U.S. 85 (1961).

63. *Bowles v. Willingham*, 321 U.S. 503 (1944); and *cf. Opp Cotton Mills v. Administrator*, 312 U.S. 126 (1941).

64. *Cf. Springer v. United States*, 102 U.S. 586 (1881); *Morgan v. United States*, 304 U.S. 1 (1938).

65. *Stewart Machine Co. v. Davis*, 301 U.S. 548, 584 (1937); *Currin v. Wallace*, 306 U.S. 1, 14 (1939); *Sunshine Coal Co. v. Atkins*, 310 U.S. 381, 401 (1940); *Railway Express Agency v. New York*, 336 U.S. 106, 112 (1949).

66. *Cf. Adair v. United States*, 208 U.S. 161 (1908), overruled in effect in *Phelps Dodge Corp. v. N.L.R.B.*, 313 U.S. 177 (1941); *Adkins v. Children's Hospital*, 261 U.S. 525 (1923), overruled in *West Coast Hotel Co. v. Parrish*, 300 U.S. 379 (1937).

67. *Fleming v. Rhodes*, 331 U.S. 100 (1947).

68. *Norman v. B.& O. R. Co.*, 294 U.S. 240 (1935).

69. 301 U.S. 1 (1937).

70. *Cf.* also *Virginia R. Co. v. System Federation*, 300 U.S. 515 (1937); *Railway Employees Dept. v. Hanson*, 351 U.S. 225 (1956).

71. *St. Joseph Stockyards v. United States*, 304 U.S. 470 (1938); *F.P.C. v. Hope Natural Gas Co.*, 320 U.S. 591 (1944).

72. *Cf.* Swindler, *The Old Legality*, p. 247.

73. *Id.*, p. 293.

74. *Cf. United States v. Carmack*, 329 U.S. 230, 241 (1946). For a similar limit on states under the Fourteenth Amendment, *cf. C.B. & Q., R. Co. v. Chicago*, 166 U.S. 226 (1897).

75. *Oklahoma v. Atkinson County*, 313 U.S. 508, 534 (1941).

76. *Shoemaker v. United States*, 147 U.S. 282 (1893).

77. *Cf.* draft opinion in *Jackson v. Rosenbaum Co.*, 260 U.S. 22 (1922), described in Howe, ed., *Holmes-Laski Letters* (Boston, 1953), p. 456.

78. *Pennsylvania Coal Co. v. Mahon*, 260 U.S. 393 (1922). A different standard was applied where the statute provided for the destruction of one type of property (ornamental red cedars) to protect another type (apple orchards threatened with blister rust from the cedars). *Miller v. Schoene*, 276 U.S. 272 (1928).

79. *Cf. Causby v. Griggs*, 328 U.S. 256 (1940), concerning damage to chicken farm caused by noise of low-flying aircraft; *A.T. & S. F. R. Co., v. P.U.C.*, 346 U.S. 346 (1952), requiring railroads to eliminate grade crossings at their own expense;

Euclid v. Ambler Realty Co., 272 U.S. 365 (1926), denying land developer a remedy where the police power of municipality validly preserved residential zoning and thus blocked industrial construction. *Cf.* also *Goldblatt v. Hempstead,* 369 U.S. 590 (1962); *United States ex rel. T.V.A. v. Welch,* 327 U.S. 546 (1946); *Berman v. Parker,* 348 U.S. 26 (1954).

80. *Int. Paper Co. v. United States,* 282 U.S. 399 (1931); *Armstrong v. United States,* 364 U.S. 40 (1960); *Hannibal Bridge Co. v. United States,* 221 U.S. 194 (1911).

81. *United States v. Central Eureka Mining Co.,* 357 U.S. 155 (1958); *cf.* also *Gibson v. United States,* 166 U.S. 269 (1897); *United States v. Appalachian Power Co.,* 311 U.S. 377 (1940); *United States v. Commodore Park,* 324 U.S. 386 (1945); *Lewis Blue Point Oyster Co. v. Briggs,* 229 U.S. 82 (1913).

82. *Monongahela Nav. Co. v. United States,* 148 U.S. 312 (1893); *United States v. New River Collieries Co.,* 262 U.S. 341 (1923).

Amendment VI. Rights of the Accused

In all criminal prosecutions, the accused shall enjoy the right to a speedy and public trial, by an impartial jury of the state and district wherein the crime shall have been committed, which district shall have been previously ascertained by law, and to be informed of the nature and cause of the accusation; to be confronted with the witnesses against him; to have compulsory process for obtaining witnesses in his favor, and to have the assistance of counsel for his defense.

This Amendment completes the sequence of guarantees which form a continuum from the Fourth through the Fifth to the Sixth, and like its associates this Amendment has attracted substantial adjudication in the activism of the mid-century. The paragraph covers half a dozen fundamental rights: (1) speedy and public trials, (2) local juries, (3) full advice of charges against the accused, (4) confrontation of prosecution witnesses, (5) compulsory process to summon defense witnesses and (6) assistance of counsel.

Speedy and Public Trial

This provision was intended to prevent prolonged threat of prosecution and, in some instances, detention.[1] It was also intended to insure that witnesses would be readily available and memories fresh—something which defendants often have found working as much against them as for them.[2] Speed, in the final analysis, is a relative matter; it does not require the prosecution to take up indictments in order, and it assumes that a reasonable time is needed by both sides to prepare the case.[3] While the provision applies only to criminal charges,[4] it may include judicial review of administrative actions which are penal in nature.[5] Whether a delay in trial is unreasonable ultimately depends on the court's findings on the length of time involved, reasons for the prolongation, and whether the accused has in fact waived the right to a speedy trial.[6] Congested court calendars, as much as calculated delaying tactics by either side, have accounted for the length of pending trials in many jurisdictions.[7]

Public trials are intended to promote fair dealing.[8] Defendants may in certain circumstances waive the right to a public trial, but they have no correlative constitutional right to demand a private trial.[9] The trial judge may in his discretion clear a courtroom for sufficient grounds, such as intimidation of a witness by someone present,[10] or occasionally because of the nature of the testimony. Although an old state case[11] held that a trial remained public, even when the courtroom was cleared, if press representatives were allowed to remain, the better rule today is that media representation is not a matter of First Amendment privilege but of general public right.[12]

Jury Trials: Changing Criteria

The twelve-member jury and the unanimous verdict have been regarded as immemorial traditions of the common law,[13] while the venire from the vicinage is traceable back to Magna Carta. But in the 1970 and 1971 terms the Supreme Court treated both jury size and unanimity as "assumptions" which, at least with reference to state courts, were not constitutionally required. In *Williams v. Florida*[14] Justice White for the majority upheld a trial by a jury of less than twelve persons, since "we find little reason to think that [fair deliberations] are in any meaningful sense less likely to be achieved."[15] In two other cases,[16] the Court, again speaking through Justice White, upheld non-unanimous jury verdicts. While Justice Powell concurred as to the rule in state courts, he declared a conviction that unanimity was still required in Federal trials, "not because unanimity is necessarily fundamental to the function performed by the jury, but because that result is mandated by history."[17] As a matter of fact, however, some of the new doctrine has already been applied to the Federal trial courts—e.g., in the succession of orders permitting juries of less than twelve in various circuits.[18]

In 1968 the Sixth Amendment guarantee of jury trial had been applied to the states through the Fourteenth.[19] The jury requirement, however, is not *per se* a requirement of every part of the criminal process,[20] so long as there is ultimate opportunity for examination and cross-examination of testimony in a public courtroom before a jury.[21] The right to jury trial may be waived, but the courts are admonished to insure that the waiver is knowingly and intelligently made.[22] The right extends to all but "petty" offenses,[23] or to contempt cases which are traditionally subject to summary disposition by the court; but the ultimate fairness of the contempt doctrine has come increasingly under scrutiny.[24]

Impartiality and non-discrimination in selection of jurors has been reviewed by the courts in recent years.[25] While the prosecution may not hand-pick a site for the trial which enhances the prospect for conviction,[26] a trial in the vicinity of the crime is the most practical venue in most circumstances,[27] and courts are reluctant to grant motions for change of venue unless evidence of serious prejudice to the defense is substantial.[28] Related to the general jury question is the matter of impartiality of the trial judge and the proper behavior of the prosecutor: A judge who is shown to have any kind of interest in a criminal case jeopardizes the provisions for fairness imputed to the Fourteenth Amendment;[29] and the Supreme Court similarly admonished Federal judges to disqualify themselves in such cases.[30] Where the prosecutor is excessive in his charges and general conduct in the courtroom, this fact may be ground for reversal.[31]

Precise Charge of Crime

"Void for vagueness" is a standard rule of construction in criminal statutes; legislation imposing criminal liability must not leave it to "variant views of the different courts and juries which may be called on to enforce it."[32] But what is vague or general depends on different factual situations—and, inevitably, on dif-

ferent reviewing tribunals. The term "unreasonable" sounded unconstitutional to the Court in 1921, but not to the Court in 1963,[33]
in the later case the 6–3 majority finding that the statute actually
directed the administrator to make explicit definitions of the prohibited conduct.[34] In 1945 the Court divided unhappily over the
vagueness of the term "willfully" and remanded the case to the
trial court to be tried on a narrower interpretation of the statute.[35]
An equally divided Court in 1951 sought to rehabilitate the same
statute (making it a crime willfully to deprive one of his civil
rights[36]) by finding a specific right which had been specifically—
and, hence, constructively, willfully—violated.[37]

The problem—bound up with the problem of enforcement
of civil rights themselves—continued to agitate the Court in the
1960s. In *Monroe v. Pape*,[38] the majority found that such statutes
related to sufficiently definite acts to support a prosecution and
adhered to this position in two 1966 cases.[39] The continuing purpose of the constitutional requirement, as courts repeatedly
asserted, is to insure that the accused will clearly understand the
charge he is expected to answer.[40] Where defendants fail to move
for dismissal before trial, or demand a bill of particulars, and proceed to trial thereafter, a reviewing court may conclude that the
charges were definite enough to present a defense of former
jeopardy, which is a corollary purpose of the clause.[41]

Witnesses, For and Against

Faceless accusers have been decried by all advocates of fair
judicial process,[42] and in the cold-war hysteria of the 1950s the
issue was frequently raised but never squarely faced in terms of
this clause.[43] In 1968 the Court reiterated the basic principle that
the purpose of the confrontation right is to permit defense counsel to test the substance and veracity of an accusing witness's testimony.[44] Confrontation is a trial right and does not relate to out-
of-court statements until their author has been brought to the
stand.[45] While defendants in criminal cases are normally required
to be present at any stage where incriminating evidence is introduced into the trial,[46] a disruptive defendant who refuses to comply with reasonable rules for orderly conduct may be excluded

from the courtroom until he undertakes to behave according to accepted standards.[47]

The right of confrontation was extended to the states through the Fourteenth Amendment in 1965,[48] and the right to summon witnesses for the defense was similarly extended in 1967.[49] However, the right is limited by public policy or by the immunity of certain offices—thus, ambassadors, members of Congress, foreign citizens and others outside the jurisdiction may not be reached by such writs.[50] And where a witness declines to testify because of his own privilege against self-incrimination, the refusal of the writ is not a denial of the constitutional right of the defendant in the principal case.[51]

Assistance of Counsel

The 1963 case of *Gideon v. Wainwright*[52] dramatized this guarantee at the same time that it greatly broadened its application to the states, a process which had begun with *Powell v. Alabama* in 1932.[53] The later case settled the debate over the basic principle of incorporation which had continued since *Betts v. Brady*[54] in 1942, which *Gideon* now overruled. As for the Federal courts, the general judicial application of the guarantee dates from 1938[55] and developed rapidly during the period in which incorporation and application to the states was under debate.[56] The right is broadly asserted in all phases of Federal criminal procedure,[57] and Congress in the Criminal Justice Act of 1964[58] incorporated into legislation the right-to-counsel principle first enunicated in detail in *Zerbst*.

The proliferation of cases touched off by *Gideon* has affected both state and Federal constitutional law and criminal procedure. The right to counsel had already been applied to appellate stages of a case[59] and then was extended back before trial to the moment of police interrogation.[60] Since 1967 it has been applied specifically to a wide number of other investigatory or accusatory situations: police lineups,[61] certain juvenile-court proceedings,[62] inmate assistance after imprisonment ("jailhouse lawyers")[63] and preliminary hearings.[64] While *Miranda v. Arizona*[65] raised a substantial amount of debate over the broad linkage of the Sixth Amendment and

Fifth Amendment guarantees (see Amendment V, *supra*), with resulting efforts at limitation by both Congress and Court, the continuing tenor of judicial application of the specific clause in this Amendment suggests that it has become accepted as a fundamental and pervasive right.

1. *Cf. Dickey v. Florida,* 398 U.S. 30 (1970); *Will v. United States,* 389 U.S. 90 (1967); *United States v. Ewell,* 383 U.S. 116 (1966); *Smith v. Hooey,* 393 U.S. 374 (1969). The "speedy trial" requirement was incorporated into the Fourteenth Amendment in *Klopfer v. North Carolina,* 386 U.S. 213 (1967).
2. *Cf.* generally, Downie, *Justice Denied* (New York, 1971); Frank, *American Law: The Case for Radical Reform* (New York, 1969); Swindler, ed., *Justice in the States* (St. Paul, 1972), p. 189.
3. *Beaver v. Haubert,* 198 U.S. 77 (1905); *Pollard v. United States,* 352 U.S. 354 (1957). *Cf.* also *United States v. Marion,* 404 U.S. 307 (1971), holding that the speedy-trial guarantee becomes applicable only on arrest or indictment.
4. *United States v. Zucker,* 161 U.S. 481 (1896).
5. *Cf. Greene v. McElroy,* 360 U.S. 474 (1959).
6. *Cf. Brooks v. United States,* 423 F. 2d 1149 (1970), cert. den. 400 U.S. 872 (1971). In *Barker v. Wingo,* 407 U.S. 514 (1972), Justice Powell rejected as "insensitive" to a fundamental right the "demand-waiver" rule that if a speedy trial was not demanded it was deemed waived.
7. Swindler, ed., *Justice in the States* (St. Paul, 1972), p. 140.
8. *Estes v. Texas,* 381 U.S. 532 (1965). *Cf. In re Oliver,* 333 U.S. 257 (1948), invalidating a state law permitting a "one-man grand jury" to conduct secret hearings in which defendants could be convicted of contempt for allegedly evasive responses.
9. *Singer v. United States,* 380 U.S. 24 (1965); and *cf. Levine v. United States,* 362 U.S. 610 (1960).
10. *Cf. United States ex parte Bruno v. Herold,* 408 F. 2d 125 (1969), cert. den. 397 U.S. 957 (1970).
11. *Keddington v. Arizona,* 172 P. 273 (1918).
12. *Cf. Craemer v. Superior Court . . . Marin County,* 71 Calif. Reptr. 193 (1968). For jeopardy to fair trial from news media, *cf. Irvin v. Dowd,* 366 U.S. 717 (1961); *Estes v. Texas,* 381 U.S. 532 (1965); *Sheppard v. Maxwell,* 384 U.S. 333 (1966); *Groppi v. Wisconsin,* 400 U.S. 505 (1971).
13. *Cf. Patton v. United States,* 281 U.S. 276 (1930); *Rasmussen v. United States,* 197 U.S. 518 (1905); and see also *Berra v. United States,* 351 U.S. 131 (1956).
14. 399 U.S. 78 (1970).
15. *Id.,* at 86. *Cf.* also *Baldwin v. New York,* 399 U.S. 66 (1970), holding unconstitutional a state law dispensing with juries in misdemeanor cases. *Cf.* also *Schick v. United States,* 195 U.S. 64 (1904), considering the possible conflict between the Fifth Amendment and the provision in Article III, 2. Cl. 3 that "the trial of all crimes, except in cases of impeachment, shall be by jury."
16. *Apodaca v. Oregon,* 406 U.S. 404 (1972); *Johnson v. Louisiana,* 406 U.S. 356 (1972).
17. 406 U.S., at 366.

18. A current list from November 12, 1970 to September 27, 1972 appears in 56 *F.R.D.* at 535 (1972).
19. *Duncan v. Louisiana*, 391 U.S. 148 (1968).
20. *McKeiver v. Pennsylvania*, 403 U.S. 528 (1971).
21. *Cf. Turner v. Louisiana*, 399 U.S. 466 (1965).
22. *Cf.* generally *Baldwin v. New York*, 399 U.S. 66 (1970).
23. *Frank v. United States*, 395 U.S. 147 (1969); but *cf. Baldwin v. New York*, 399 U.S. 66 (1970).
24. *Cf. United States v. Barnett*, 376 U.S. 681 (1964); *Frank v. United States*, 395 U.S. 147 (1969).
25. *Fay v. New York*, 332 U.S. 261 (1947); *Ballard v. United States*, 329 U.S. 187 (1946); *Frazier v. United States*, 335 U.S. 497 (1948). Note Congressional efforts to meet this issue in the Jury Selection and Service Act of 1964, 82 Stat. 53, 28 U.S.C. 1821.
26. *Travis v. United States*, 364 U.S. 631 (1961); *United States v. Johnson*, 323 U.S. 273 (1944).
27. *Platt v. Minn. Min. & Mfg. Co.*, 376 U.S. 240 (1964); *cf.* also *Salinger v. Loisel*, 265 U.S. 224 (1924).
28. *Cf. United States v. Bourassa*, 411 F. 2d 69 (1969), cert. den. 396 U.S. 915 (1969); *State v. Beckus*, 229 Atl. 2d 216 (1967), cert. den. 389 U.S. 870 (1967).
29. *Tumey v. Ohio*, 273 U.S. 510 (1927).
30. On contempt cases, *cf. Offutt v. United States*, 348 U.S. 11 (1954); *Sachs v. United States*, 343 U.S. 1 (1952); *Mayberry v. Pennsylvania*, 400 U.S. 455 (1971).
31. *Berger v. United States*, 295 U.S. 78 (1935); *Mooney v. Holohan*, 294 U.S. 103 (1935); *Brady v. Maryland*, 373 U.S. 83 (1963); *Giles v. Maryland*, 386 U.S. 66 (1967).
32. *United States v. Cohen Gro. Co.*, 255 U.S. 81 (1921); *cf. Viereck v. United States*, 318 U.S. 236 (1943).
33. *United States v. Cohen Gro. Co.*, 255 U.S. 81, 89 (1921); *United States v. National Dairy Corp.*, 372 U.S. 29, 31, 34 (1963).
34. 372 U.S., at 32. and see *United States v. Cardiff*, 344 U.S. 174 (1952); *United States v. Spector*, 343 U.S. 169 (1952).
35. *Screws v. United States*, 325 U.S. 91 (1945).
36. 62 Stat., 686, 18 U.S.C. 242.
37. *Williams v. United States*, 341 U.S. 97 (1951); and see *United States v. Williams*, 341 U.S. 70 (1951) and *Collins v. Hardyman*, 341 U.S. 651 (1951).
38. 365 U.S. 167 (1961).
39. *United States v. Guest*, 383 U.S. 745 (1966); *United States v. Price*, 383 U.S. 787 (1966).
40. *Rosen v. United States*, 161 U.S. 40 (1896); *Logan v. United States*, 144 U.S. 263 (1892). *Cf.* also *Van Lieuw v. United States*, 321 F. 2d 664 (1963); *United States v. Strauss*, 283 U.S. 155 (1960).
41. *Vasquez v. United States*, 229 F. 2d 288 (1956), cert. den. 351 U.S. 950 (1956).
42. *Cf. Salinger v. United States*, 272 U.S. 542, 548 (1926).
43. Swindler, *The New Legality*, Ch. 8. And see especially *Greene v. McElroy*, 360 U.S. 474 (1959); *Hannah v. Larche*, 363 U.S. 420 (1960); *Jenkins v. McKeithen*, 395 U.S. 411 (1969); and also *McCray v. Illinois*, 386 U.S. 300 (1967); *Barber v. Page*, 390 U.S. 719 (1968); *United States v. Gibbs*, 435 F. 2d 621 (1970), cert. den. 401 U.S. 994 (1970).
44. *Bruton v. United States*, 391 U.S. 193 (1968), holding that in a joint trial a

confession by one defendant implicating codefendant violates codefendant's right of confrontation; and see *Barber v. Page*, 390 U.S. 719 (1968); *Douglas v. Alabama*, 380 U.S. 415 (1965); but *cf. Frazier v. Culp*, 394 U.S. 731 (1969).

45. *Nelson v. O'Neill*, 402 U.S. 622 (1971).
46. *United States v. Hayman*, 342 U.S. 205 (1952).
47. *Illinois v. Allen*, 397 U.S. 337 (1970).
48. *Pointer v. Texas*, 380 U.S. 400 (1965); *Snyder v. Massachusetts*, 291 U.S. 97 (1934).
49. *Washington v. Texas*, 388 U.S. 14 (1967).
50. *Cf.* generally *Washington v. Texas*, 388 U.S. 14 (1967); *People v. Cavanaugh*, 70 Calif. Reptr. 438 (1968), cert. den. 395 U.S. 981 (1968); *United States v. Davenport*, 312 F. 2d 303 (1963); *In re Dillon*, Fed. Cas. No. 3,914 (1845); *United States v. Cooper*, 4 U.S. 341 (1800).
51. *Murdock v. United States*, 283 F. 2d 585 (1960), cert. den. 366 U.S. 953 (1960).
52. 372 U.S. 335 (1963).
53. 287 U.S. 45 (1932).
54. 316 U.S. 455 (1942). And *cf. Pickenhimer v. Wainwright*, 375 U.S. 2 (1963); *Winter v. Peck*, 385 U.S. 907 (1966); *Heller v. Connecticut*, 389 U.S. 902 (1967).
55. *Johnson v. Zerbst*, 304 U.S. 458 (1938).
56. *Cf. Walker v. Johnston*, 312 U.S. 275 (1941), failure of defendant to waive right; *Glasser v. United States*, 315 U.S. 60 (1942), compelling both defendants to accept same counsel; *Adams v. United States*, 317 U.S. 269 (1942), criteria for a knowing waiver; *United States v. Hayman*, 342 U.S. 205 (1952), broadening the prohibition in *Glasser; Massiah v. United States*, 377 U.S. 201 (1964), eavesdropping on defendant's comments to confederate in absence of lawyer.
57. *United States v. Wade*, 388 U.S. 218 (1967); *C.I.R. v. Teller*, 383 U.S. 687 (1966).
58. 78 Stat. 552, 18 U.S.C. 3006A.
59. *Douglas v. California*, 372 U.S. 353 (1963); *Mempa v. Rhay*, 389 U.S. 128 (1967); and in a related constitutional area *cf. Griffin v. Illinois*, 351 U.S. 12 (1956), and *Mayer v. Chicago*, 404 U.S. 189 (1971).
60. *Escobedo v. Illinois*, 378 U.S. 478 (1964); and see *Crooker v. California*, 357 U.S. 433 (1958); *Massiah v. United States*, 377 U.S. 201 (1964).
61. *United States v. Wade*, 388 U.S. 218 (1967); *Gilbert v. California*, 388 U.S. 263 (1967); *Cf.* also *Stovall v. Denno*, 388 U.S. 293 (1967); *Johnson v. New Jersey*, 384 U.S. 719 (1966).
62. *In re Gault*, 387 U.S. 1 (1967).
63. *Johnson v. Avery*, 393 U.S. 483 (1969).
64. *Coleman v. Alabama*, 399 U.S. 1 (1970). *Cf.* also *Adams v. Illinois*, 405 U.S. 278 (1972).
65. 384 U.S. 436 (1966).

Amendment VII. Jury Trial in Civil Cases

In suits at common law, where the value in controversy shall exceed twenty dollars, the right of trial by jury shall be preserved, and no fact tried by a jury shall be otherwise reexamined in any court of the United States, than according to the rules of the common law.

This Amendment has been explicitly confined to Federal courts, and no incorporation into the Fourteenth has been suggested.[1] Justice Frankfurter's argument against incorporation *per se,* that this tended to fix on the states the values of the eighteenth century as applied to the Bill of Rights,[2] is most telling in relation to this Amendment, in which it has been held (1) that the common law to which the paragraph refers is the common law as established at the time of the adoption of this Amendment,[3] and (2) that the jury provided for in this paragraph is fixed by the common law at twelve men[4] and that a unanimous verdict is required.[5] The purpose of the Amendment, the Court has concluded, was to preserve the substance of the common-law distinction between the judge's province in resolving matters of law and the jury's province of determining matters of fact.[6]

While the Amendment thus applies only to Federal courts, it also extends to cases in which a right created under Federal law is being enforced.[7] Since the common law of 1791 (when the Amendment was adopted) is construed as controlling, it has been held that cases which at that time involved only equitable remedies were not within the Amendment,[8] nor were cases arising from statutes concerning subjects unknown to the common law.[9] There have been various judicial references to types of actions which were not within the purview of the Amendment.[10] Although law and equity have been merged under the Federal Rules of Civil Procedure, the type of issues which were originally triable at common law are still under the guarantee.[11]

The steady decline in the number of civil cases tried by juries in Federal courts[12] has to a degree reduced the significance of this Amendment. The fact that the common law may be modified by statute and that the common law of England, to which the reference in this Amendment looked in 1791, has substantially changed since then further suggests that the guarantee may be modified by legislation or court order as to certain details without affecting the original purpose.

1. *Cf. Olesen v. Trust Co.,* 245 F. 2d 522 (1957), cert. den. 355 U.S. 896 (1957).
2. *Cf. Adamson v. California,* 332 U.S. 46, 59 (1947).
3. *Dimick v. Schiedt,* 293 U.S. 474 (1935); *United States v. Louisiana,* 339 U.S. 699 (1950).
4. *Capital Traction Co. v. Hof.* 174 U.S. 1, 13 (1899).

5. *Maxwell v. Dow*, 176 U.S. 581 (1900); and *cf. Andres v. United States*, 333 U.S. 740 (1948).
6. *Baltimore & Carolina Lines v. Redman*, 295 U.S. 654 (1935).
7. *Dice v. Akron, C. & Y. R. Co.*, 342 U.S. 359 (1952). On the other hand, Federal courts enforcing state-created rights apply their own rules on the subject. *Byrd v. Blue Ridge Co-op.*, 356 U.S. 525 (1958); *Simmler v. Conner*, 372 U.S. 221 (1963).
8. *Pease v. Rathburn-Jones Eng. Co.*, 243 U.S. 273 (1917); but *cf. Dairy Queen v. Wood*, 369 U.S. 469 (1962).
9. *Yakus v. United States*, 321 U.S. 414 (1944); *N.L.R.B. v. Jones & Laughlin Steel Corp.*, 301 U.S. 1 (1937).
10. *Galloway v. United States*, 319 U.S. 372 (1943), suits to enforce claims against the United States; *Crowell v. Benson*, 285 U.S. 22 (1932), suits based on a Federal statute; *In re Wood and Henderson*, 210 U.S. 246 (1908), jurisdiction of bankruptcy courts; and *cf.* the statute authorizing the Supreme Court to promulgate Federal Rules of Civil Procedure, 48 Stat. 1064, 28 U.S.C. 2072.
11. *Beacon Theaters v. Westover*, 359 U.S. 500 (1959); *Dairy Queen v. Wood*, 369 U.S. 469 (1962). *Cf.* the recent discussion in *Ross v. Berhard*, 369 U.S. 531 (1970). It is the principle of a jury trial, rather than the details of common-law procedure, which is preserved by the Amendment. *Galloway v. United States*, 319 U.S. 372 (1943).
12. *Cf.*, generally, annual *Report* of the Director of the Administrative Office of the United States Courts, e.g., 1970-date.

Amendment VIII. Excessive Bail or Punishment

Excessive bail shall not be required, nor excessive fines imposed, nor cruel and unusual punishments inflicted.

In 1958 Chief Justice Warren, conceding the vagueness of the term "excessive" in relation to bail and fines and of the term "cruel and unusual" in relation to punishment, observed that the particular definition of these terms in the Eighth Amendment must necessarily change with "the evolving standards of decency that mark the progress of a maturing society."[1] This reasoning ultimately led, in 1972, to the Court's declaration in a 5–4 *per curiam* order that the death penalty, in the circumstances of the cases then before it, amounted to cruel and unusual punishment in violation of the Eighth and Fourteenth Amendments.[2] Thus the Eighth, only sporadically considered by the Court over most of its history, not only has become a significant source of fundamental rights subjoined to the Fourth, Fifth and Sixth but has in consequence been incorporated into the Fourteenth as well.

Excessive Bail

In the security-conscious 1950s, the Court was several times requested to define the circumstances under which bail could be held to be excessive. In these cases, the Court did not go further than to suggest that the term had to be measured by what was reasonable in the circumstances. In some of the so-called subversive conspiracy cases, the Court declared that the amount of bail deemed reasonable was the amount calculated to insure the presence of a defendant at his trial—a time-honored standard which in these cases simply re-emphasized that the prosecution was required to show that an unusually high figure was justified.[3] Denial of bail in certain cases, as with alien radicals awaiting deportation, has been held to be within the sovereign power of the government and not *ipso facto* under the prohibition of the Amendment.[4]

More recently, the question has shifted to equal-protection standards as affecting bail-reform movements in the states[5] and the rights of indigents in bailable situations.[6] But the basic criteria have not as yet been substantially altered; the essential purpose of the provision in the Amendment is to insure that no one is to be capriciously held by setting bail so high as effectively to deny bail altogether.[7] The Amendment has never been construed to mean that everyone charged with an offense is entitled to bail;[8] if in the opinion of the court the safety of the community would be jeopardized, bail may be denied.[9] Cases of doubt, it has been said, ought to be resolved in favor of the defendant;[10] and both of these propositions—community safety and bail reform—have been considered by Congress in the "preventive detention" and bail reform acts for the District of Columbia in recent years.[11]

Excessive Fines

Even less than in the case of bail has the Court been disposed to define a measure of excessiveness for fines. While the monumental fine of $29,240,000 levied against the Standard Oil Company in the trust-busting era[12] had been dismissed on appeal,[13] and the fine of $3,500,000 against the United Mine Workers under the Taft-Hartley Act was ultimately reduced to a figure of less than half that amount,[14] these did not involve a constitutional issue but rather were routine consequences of appellate review and compromise involved in final disposition of the cases. Fines may constitute cruel and unusual punishment in themselves;[15] but a statute which provides for incarceration on refusal to pay a fine is not in conflict with the Amendment,[16] nor is inability to pay acceptable proof of the excessiveness of the fine.[17]

Cruel and Unusual Punishment

It has been in this clause of the Amendment that Chief Justice Warren's dynamic standard of evolving social conscience has been urged on the Court by a succession of eloquent counsel. Since most criminal cases are under the jurisdiction of the states, the application of Eighth Amendment limitations might have incorporated this part of the Bill of Rights into the Fourteenth had there been, in the nineteenth century, many cases testing the issue. Even so narrow a constructionist as Justice Field dissented in 1892 from a majority refusal to apply the Amendment to the states, contending that the prohibition extended to "all punishments which . . . are greatly disproportioned to the offenses charged."[18] As a general principle, the Court in 1910 declared that a punishment much greater than that imposed for more serious crimes was barred by the Amendment,[19] but in 1948 it was held that charging a separate offense for each piece of unmailable matter actually placed in the mails did not automatically invoke the Amendment,[20] and in 1947 the renewal of an attempted execution after initial mechanical failure was also upheld.[21]

In the activist humanitarianism of the 1960s, a broadening of the Eighth Amendment protection was a logical ingredient in the general broadening of Bill of Rights protections. Thus the Court invalidated a California statute defining narcotics addiction *ipso facto* as a crime[22] and suggested that in some circumstances the same would be true of statutes concerning alcoholism.[23] Expatriation, as a punishment for nonconformity, was decried by various members of the Court without crystallizing into a firm majority doctrine,[24] as were certain other formulae of penalty. But the primary target of the activists was the death penalty, an issue which was skirted several times before it finally was adjudicated in 1972.[25]

The ambivalence of the Court in *Furman v. Georgia*[26] attests to the basic problem of construing general terms in the Constitution. The only consensus in the five concurring opinions of the majority and the four dissenting opinions was that capital punishment was not "cruel and unusual" at the time the Amendment was adopted. But several of the majority and all of the dissenters had misgivings as to the logical consequence of the consensus: that any contemporary definition of the term is also temporary and tentative.[27] Without focussing at length on that fact, individual Justices offered their individual criteria: Punishment is cruel and unusual when "a capriciously selected random handful" of persons convicted of the same capital offense are sentenced to death, said Justice Stewart.[28] The increasing infrequency of imposition of the punishment suggested its unusual character to Justice White,[29] while Justices Brennan, Douglas and Marshall concluded, for varying reasons, that the death penalty was potentially and perhaps actually discriminatory and shocked the moral sense of modern men.[30]

1. *Trop v. Dulles*, 356 U.S. 86, 99 (1958).
2. *Furman v. Georgia, et al.*, 408 U.S. 238 (1972). *Cf.* the earlier decision of the California supreme court holding capital punishment unconstitutional in all cases. *People v. Anderson*, 100 Calif. Rep. 152, 493 P. 2d 880 (1972).
3. *Stack v. Boyle*, 342 U.S. 1 (1951).
4. *Carlisle v. Landon*, 342 U.S. 524 (1952).
5. *Cf.* discussion of this subject in *Rehman v. California*, 95 S. Ct. 8 (1964).
6. *Cf. Schilb v. Kuebel*, 404 U.S. 357 (1971). While poverty should not in itself deny a defendant the right to bail, his inability to raise the amount of the bail is not *prima facie* evidence of unconstitutionally excessive bail. *Hadgdon v. United States*, 365 F. 2d 679 (1966), cert. den. 385 U.S. 1029 (1966).
7. *Carlisle v. Landon*, 342 U.S. 524 (1952).
8. *Cf. Mastrion v. Hedman*, 326 F. 2d 708 (1964), cert. den. 376 U.S. 965 (1964); and *cf. United States ex rel. Fink v. Heyd*, 287 F.S. 716 (1968), aff'd. 408 F. 2d 7 (1969), cert. den. 396 U.S. 895 (1969).
9. *Rehman v. California*, 95 S. Ct. 8 (1964).
10. *Herzog v. United States*, 75 S. Ct. 349 (1955).
11. *Cf.* 80 Stat. 217, 18 U.S.C. 3041; 84 Stat. 473.
12. *Cf.* Swindler, *The Old Legality*, p. 130.
13. *Id.*, p. 151.
14. *Cf.* Swindler, *The New Legality*, p. 165.

15. *Whitney Stores, Inc., v. Summerford,* 280 F.S. 406 (1968), aff'd. 393 U.S. 9 (1968).
16. *Morris v. Schoonfield,* 310 F.S. 554 (1969).
17. *United States ex rel. Privitera v. Kross,* 239 F.S. 118 (1965), aff'd. 345 F. 2d 533 (1965), cert. den. 382 U.S. 911 (1965).
18. *O'Neil v. Vermont,* 144 U.S. 323, 340 (1892).
19. *Weems v. United States,* 217 U.S. 349 (1910).
20. *Donaldson v. Read Magazine,* 333 U.S. 178 (1948).
21. *Louisiana v. Resweber,* 329 U.S. 459 (1947).
22. *Robinson v. California,* 370 U.S. 660 (1962).
23. *Powell v. Texas,* 392 U.S. 514 (1968).
24. *Trop v. Dulles,* 356 U.S. 86, 124 (1958); *Kennedy v. Mendoza-Martinez,* 372 U.S. 144, 187 (1963).
25. *Rudolph v. Alabama,* 375 U.S. 889, 891 (1963); *Boykin v. Alabama,* 395 U.S. 238 (1969); *United States v. Jackson,* 390 U.S. 570 (1968); *McGautha v. California,* 402 U.S. 183 (1971).
26. 408 U.S. 238 (1972).
27. *Id.,* at 240. Thus Chief Justice Burger, in dissent, paraphrased Justice Holmes in warning not to "seize upon the enigmatic character" of the Amendment "to enact our personal predilections into law," while Justice Powell echoed the late Justices Frankfurter and Harlan in decrying the "shattering effect" of the majority construction on "the root principles of *stare decisis,* federalism, judicial restraint and—most importantly—separation of powers." For the dissents of Justices Blackmun and Rehnquist, see 408 U.S. at 375.
28. *Id.,* at 306.
29. *Id.,* at 310.
30. *Id.,* at 257, 314. Cruel and unusual punishment has been held to include prison conditions, in Eighth Amendment cases applied to state agencies, *e.g.: Cruz v. Beto,* 405 U.S. 319 (1972), the denial of religious services for certain defendants; *Haines v. Kerner,* 404 U.S. 519 (1972), solitary confinement resulting in injuries and indignities; *Younger v. Gilmore,* 404 U.S. 15 (1971), limitation of access to prison library facilities.

Amendment IX
Preservation of Unenumerated Rights

The enumeration in the Constitution of certain rights, shall not be construed to deny or disparage others retained by the people.

The "forgotten Ninth Amendment," as one writer has called it,[1] is essentially hortatory in its language. Its hypothetical basis is the denial of the applicability of the common-law rule of construction, *expressio unius est exclusio alterius.* It was included in the Bill of Rights, Justice Goldberg observed, "to quiet expressed fears that a bill of specifically enumerated rights could not be sufficiently broad to cover all essential rights and that the specific mention of certain rights would be interpreted as a denial that others were protected."[2] It led Justice Douglas, delivering the opinion of the Court in the same case, to urge that "specific guarantees in the Bill of Rights have penumbras, formed by emanations from those guarantees that help give them life and substance."[3] Such inchoate rights may find a shelter under the Ninth Amendment until such time as they are recognizable as matters germane to other, more explicit Amendments.[4]

Since 1965 the Court has not pursued the line of reasoning suggested by the Goldberg and Douglas opinions, although it approached the subject in two cases in the 1971 term.[5] Since these cases concerned private rights of abortion, whereas *Griswold* concerned private rights to obtaining medically guided contraception, they manifestly invited the development of the privacy doctrine under the Ninth Amendment. In the few earlier cases seeming to fall under the Amendment, the Court rejected in 1939 an argument that private property rights were among rights "retained by the people"[6] and in 1947 accepted the argument that the right to engage in political activity was a "retained" right.[7]

1. Patterson, *The Forgotten Ninth Amendment* (Indianapolis, 1955); *cf.* esp. Ch. 8.
2. Concurring opinion in *Griswold v. Connecticut*, 381 U.S. 479, 486 (1965).
3. *Id.*, at 499.
4. *Cf.* Redlich, "Are There 'Certain Rights . . . Retained by the People'?" 37 *N.Y.U.L. Rev.* 787 (1962).
5. *United States v. Vuitch*, 402 U.S. 62 (1971); *Eisenstadt v. Baird*, 405 U.S. 438 (1972).
6. *Tennessee Power Co. v. T.V.A.*, 306 U.S. 118 (1939); and *cf. Ashwander v.T.V.A.*, 297 U.S. 118 (1939).
7. *United Public Workers v. Mitchell*, 330 U.S. 75 (1947).

Amendment X
Reserved Powers of States or People

The powers not delegated to the United States by the Constitution, nor prohibited by it to the states, are reserved to the states respectively, or to the people.

While constitutional conservatives have recurrently grasped at this generality as a means of challenging Federal authority, the courts have consistently recognized that it "added nothing to the [Constitution] as originally ratified."[1] In the desegregation cases of the late 1950s, a quixotic attempt was made to "interpose" the sovereign power of the states when, it was contended, the Federal government had assumed authority over a subject (public education) which was reserved to the states.[2] The preposterous nature of the interposition doctrine, said the Court, would amount to a continual inhibition of Federal action whenever the states, rather than the courts, determined that the action was contrary to their own self-interest.[3]

The question of reserved power has periodically been threshed out, usually in a case involving some other specific provision of the Constitution such as the commerce clause. In 1819 Chief Justice Marshall noted that, whereas an equivalent section of the Articles of Confederation had referred to "*expressly* delegated" powers, the absence of the qualifying adverb in the Amendment left the question of the locus of a particular power "to depend upon a fair construction of the whole instrument."[4] That construction, as it turned out, was subject to changing concepts of Federal power generally. From the progressive era to the first New Deal, the Court worked itself into a 180-degree turn in a number of cases;[5] but even while the Court of the *laissez-faire* period was declaring a categorical limit to Federal power in some subject areas, it was readily confirming Federal powers which were hardly distinguishable.[6] With few exceptions, twentieth-century cases have tended to establish that any "necessary and proper" power, or any definition of a Federal interest growing out of a specific power, is not compromised by the reservation expressed in the language of this Amendment.[7]

1. *United States v. Sprague*, 282 U.S. 716, 733 (1931); *Knapp v. Schweizer*, 357 U.S. 371 (1958).
2. *Cooper v. Aaron*, 358 U.S. 1, 18 (1958).
3. *Bush v. Orleans School Board*, 364 U.S. 500 (1960).
4. *McCulloch v. Maryland*, 4 Wheat. 316, 406 (1819).
5. *Cf.* Swindler, *The Old Legality*, Ch. 14; *The New Legality*, Ch. 6.
6. *Cf. Hammer v. Dagenhart*, 247 U.S. 251 (1918), overruled in *United States v. Darby*, 312 U.S. 100 (1941); *Schechter Corp. v. United States*, 295 U.S. 495 (1935); *United States v. Butler*, 297 U.S. 1 (1936); *Carter v. Carter Coal Co.*, 298 U.S. 238 (1936); *Stewart Machine Co. v. Davis*, 301 U.S. 548 (1937); *Champion v. Ames*, 188 U.S. 321 (1903); *Houston, etc. R. Co. v. United States* (Shreveport Rate Case), 234 U.S. 342 (1914); *Thornton v. United States*, 271 U.S. 414 (1926). Justice Stone concluded in the *Darby* case that the Tenth Amendment "states but a truism that all is retained which has not been surrendered." 312 U.S. 100, 124 (1941).
7. "There is no general doctrine implied in the Federal Constitution that the two governments, national and state, are each to exercise its powers so as not to interfere with the free and full exercise of the powers of the other." *Maryland v. Wirtz*, 392 U.S. 183 (1968). It may be pointed out that one major opinion of the Court has pointed in the other direction: In *Erie R. Co. v. Tompkins*, it was held that for Federal courts to entertain their independent judgment of what the common law of a state was or ought to be was an invasion of a reserved right of a state to effect uniformity in the construction and application of its own law. 304 U.S. 64 (1938); *cf.* also *United States v. Constantine*, 296 U.S. 287 (1938). *Cf.* also *New York v. O'Neill*, 359 U.S. 1 (1959); *Sperry v. Florida ex rel. State Bar*, 373 U.S. 379 (1963); *Zwickler v. Koota*, 389 U.S. 24 (1967).

Amendment XI. Immunity of States

The judicial power of the United States shall not be construed to extend to any suit in law or equity, commenced or prosecuted against one of the United States by citizens of another state, or by citizens or subjects of any foreign state.

This was one of three instances—the Thirteenth and Sixteenth Amendments being others—in which an Amendment was adopted specifically overriding a specific decision of the Supreme Court. In 1793 the Court, vindicating the worst fears of anti-Federalists, had held that a state could be sued by residents of another state, as in this instance, in a common-law action on assumpsit.[1] Congress, on the vociferous petitions of the states, drafted the Amendment and it was ratified, as Justice Frankfurter later put it, with "vehement speed."[2] In 1824 the Court laid down a rule of application of the Amendment which still is followed: that a state official does not have the benefit of the state's immunity when acting under color of authority of an unconstitutional statute.[3]

State officials are liable when acting in excess of their authority,[4] under an unconstitutional statute (see above),[5] or in committing a personal injury while acting under a valid state law.[6] Subdivisions of the state—counties and municipalities—and state-created public corporations are suable in the Federal courts,[7] but a state may not be sued in Federal courts by its own citizens[8] nor by a foreign state.[9] The test of immunity is whether the ultimate effect of a judgment runs against the state itself.[10] In the 1890s, in its zeal to protect railroad promoters from defaulting governments which had issued bonds to finance lines which had never been constructed,[11] the Court condoned injunctive relief against state agents even when they were carrying out constitutional duties,[12] and this laissez-faire judicial attitude continued in varying forms up through the first New Deal.[13]

Sovereign immunity of states as parts of the United States derives from principles of international law as well as the specific exemption of this Amendment[14] and bars a Federal court from entertaining suits against a state by private parties without the state's consent.[15] But local governments and their officers may be sued to enforce Federally guaranteed rights.[16] A state may be sued by another state under Article III. 2,[17] and may also be sued by the United States.[18] A state may waive immunity in cases directed against itself as a sovereign[19] or in creating public corporations in which it vests the right to sue and be sued.[20]

1. *Chisholm v. Georgia*, 2 Dall. 419 (1793). But one state may sue another on private claims which have been assigned to it as sovereign. *South Dakota v. South Carolina*, 192 U.S. 286 (1904).
2. Dissent in *Larson v. Dom. & For. Corp.*, 337 U.S. 682, 708 (1949). *Cf. Hans v. Louisiana*, 134 U.S. 1 (1890).
3. *Osborn v. Bank of United States*, 9 Wheat. 738, 858 (1824).
4. *L. &N. R. Co. v. Greene*, 244 U.S. 522 (1917).

5. *Sterling v. Constantine,* 287 U.S. 378 (1932); *Ex parte Young,* 209 U.S. 123 (1908).
6. *South Carolina v. Wesley,* 155 U.S. 542 (1895); *Tindal v. Wesley,* 167 U.S. 204 (1897).
7. *Lincoln County v. Luning,* 133 U.S. 529 (1890).
8. *Parden v. Alabama State Docks Dept.,* 377 U.S. 184 (1964); *Georgia R. & Banking Co. v. Redwine,* 342 U.S. 299 (1952); *Diehne v. New Jersey,* 251 U.S. 311 (1920); *Hans v. Louisiana,* 134 U.S. 1 (1890).
9. *Monaco v. Mississippi,* 292 U.S. 313 (1934).
10. *Sully v. Bird,* 209 U.S. 481 (1908); *Illinois Cent. R. Co. v. Adams,* 180 U.S. 37 (1901); *Pennoyer v. McConnaughy,* 140 U.S. 1 (1880); and *cf. Louisiana v. Jumel,* 107 U.S. 711 (1876).
11. *Cf.* Swindler, *The Old Legality,* Ch. 4.
12. *Cf. Reagan v. Farmers' Loan & Trust Co.,* 154 U.S. 362 (1894); *Smyth v. Ames,* 169 U.S. 466 (1898).
13. *Cf. Home Tel. & Tel. Co. v. Los Angeles,* 227 U.S. 278 (1913); *Truax v. Raich,* 239 U.S. 33 (1915); *Terrace v. Thompson,* 263 U.S. 197 (1923); *Fenner v. Boykin,* 271 U.S. 240 (1926); *Hawkes v. Hamill,* 258 U.S. 52 (1933).
14. *Cf. National City Bank v. Republic of China,* 348 U.S. 356 (1955); *Missouri v. Fiske,* 290 U.S. 18 (1933).
15. *Ford Motor Co. v. Dept. Treas. of Indiana,* 323 U.S. 459 (1945).
16 *Griffin v. Prince Edward County School District,* 337 U.S. 218 (1964) ; *cf. Graham v. Folsom,* 200 U.S. 248 (1906); *Lincoln County v. Luning,* 133 U.S. 530 (1890).
17. *Cf. New Jersey v. New York,* 345 U.S. 369 (1953); *South Dakota v. North Carolina,* 192 U.S. 286 (1904).
18. *United States v. Louisiana,* 225 F. 2d 353 (1963), aff'd. 380 U.S. 145 (1964).
19. *Great Northern Ins. Co. v. Read,* 322 U.S. 47 (1944); *Kennecott Copper Corp. v. Tax Commission,* 327 U.S. 573 (1946).
20. *Petty v. Tennessee-Missouri Commission,* 359 U.S. 275 (1959); and *cf. Hopkins v. Clemson College,* 221 U.S. 636 (1911); *Ashton v. Cameron County District,* 298 U.S. 513 (1936).

Amendment XII
The Presidential Electoral Process

The electors shall meet in their respective states and vote by ballot for President and Vice President, one of whom, at least, shall not be an inhabitant of the same state with themselves; they shall name in their ballots the person voted for as President, and in distinct ballots the person voted for as Vice President, and they shall make distinct lists of all persons voted for as President, and of all persons voted for as Vice President, and of the number of votes for each, which lists they shall sign and certify, and transmit sealed to the seat of the govern-

ment of the United States, directed to the President of the Senate;—
The President of the Senate shall, in presence of the Senate and House
of Representatives, open all the certificates and the votes shall then
be counted;—The person having the greatest number of votes for
President, shall be the President, if such number be a majority of the
whole number of electors appointed; and if no person have such majority, then from the persons having the highest numbers not exceeding three on the list of those voted for as President, the House of
Representatives shall choose immediately, by ballot, the President. But
in choosing the President, the votes shall be taken by states, the representation from each state having one vote; a quorum for this purpose shall consist of a member or members from two thirds of the
states, and a majority of all the states shall be necessary to a choice.
And if the House of Representatives shall not choose a President
whenever the right of choice shall devolve upon them, before the
fourth day of March next following, then the Vice President shall act
as President, as in the case of the death or other constitutional disability of the President.—The person having the greatest number of
votes as Vice President, shall be the Vice President, if such number be
a majority of the whole number of electors appointed, and if no person have a majority, then from the two highest numbers on the list,
the Senate shall choose the Vice President; a quorum for the purpose
shall consist of two thirds of the whole number of Senators, and a
majority of the whole number shall be necessary to a choice. But no
person constitutionally ineligible to the office of President shall be
eligible to that of Vice President of the United States.

The long-drawn-out contest between Aaron Burr and Thomas
Jefferson in the deadlocked election of 1800, even when finally
settled, created an anomaly with a Vice President who was dia-
metrically opposed to many of the views and plans of the President. This Amendment was accordingly drafted, submitted to the
states and ratified by the summer of 1804, superseding Article I.
§1. Cl. 3. In due time, the provisions in this Amendment respecting the time of inauguration, and the function of the Vice Presidency if the President shall not have qualified, were changed in
1933 with the adoption of the Twentieth Amendment.

The function of the Electoral College, as suggested under
Article II *supra,* has never followed the theory on which it was
based by the Founding Fathers, and sporadically there have been
proposals for amending the Constitution to abolish it altogether.

Inertia, and the dislike of the prospect of changing a system to which both major political parties have accommodated themselves, appear to be the major impediments to action. An alternative, providing for a division of the electoral vote in proportion to the votes cast within a state, is constitutionally feasible[1] but has not stirred any interest. Theoretically, too, electors are free agents when once elected; but the occasions when electors have exercised their own independent choice, following election on a party slate, are rare. Moreover, where state law requires an elector to pledge, as a condition of appearing on the party slate, to support the party nominee, he is not free to exercise his own initiative.[2] An effort to relate the Presidential electoral process to the reapportionment question was unsuccessful in 1948[3] and has not been revived in the later reapportionment cases.

1. *McPherson v. Blocker,* 146 U.S. 27 (1892).
2. *Ray v. Blair,* 343 U.S. 214 (1952).
3. *MacDougall v. Green,* 335 U.S. 281 (1948).

Amendment XIII. Abolition of Slavery

Section 1. Neither slavery nor involuntary servitude, except as a punishment for crime whereof the party shall have been duly convicted, shall exist within the United States, or any place subject to their jurisdiction.

Section 2. Congress shall have power to enforce this article by appropriate legislation.

The language of the opening section of this Amendment "reproduced the historic words of the Ordinance of 1787 for the government of the Northwest Territory, and gave them unrestricted application within the United States."[1] While the Amendment specifically overrode the majority holding in *Dred Scott v. Sandford,*[2] and while it was common knowledge that the original purpose of the Amendment was "to forbid all shades and conditions of African Negro slavery,"[3] the Court has also brought under the abolition rule all state laws which created involuntary servitudes through a practice of requiring defaulting debtors to "work out" their contractual obligations; this was an improper use of a criminal process to enforce a civil obligation.[4] But selective military service does not come within the definition of involuntary servitude,[5] nor do certain provisions limiting labor-union activities.[6] Servitudes attaching to real property are not *per se* subject to this Amendment.[7]

This is the first Amendment to have a separate section providing for statutory implementation. While the Amendment itself is self-executing *vis-à-vis* the abolition of slavery and legally defined forms of involuntary servitude, the courts have held that by this second section Congress may by legislation reach certain individual acts as well.[8] Correlatively, Congress has authority under this section of the Thirteenth Amendment to complement the powers vested in it by the Fourteenth Amendment.[9]

1. *Bailey v. Alabama*, 219 U.S. 219, 240 (1911).
2. 19 How. 393 (1857).
3. *Slaughterhouse Cases*, 16 Wall. 36 (1873).
4. *Peonage Cases*, 123 F. 2d 67 (1903); *Bailey v. Alabama*, 219 U.S. 219 (1911); *Clyatt v. United States*, 197 U.S. 207 (1905); *United States v. Reynolds*, 235 U.S. 133 (1914); *Taylor v. Georgia*, 315 U.S. 25 (1942); *Pollock v. Williams*, 322 U.S. 4 (1944); *United States v. Gaskin*, 320 U.S. 527 (1944).
5. *Butler v. Perry*, 240 U.S. 328 (1916); *Arver v. United States*, 245 U.S. 366 (1917); *United States v. Brooks*, 54 F.S. 995 (1944); aff'd. 147 F. 2d 134 (1945); cert. den. 324 U.S. 878 (1945).
6. *United States v. Petrillo*, 332 U.S. 1 (1947); *United Auto Workers v. Wisconsin Board*, 336 U.S. 245 (1949).
7. *Marcus Brown Co. v. Feldman*, 256 U.S. 170 (1921); but see *Jones v. Alfred H. Mayer Co.*, 392 U.S. 409 (1964).
8. *Jones v. Alfred H. Meyer Co.*, 392 U.S. 409 (1964); *Clyatt v. United States*, 197 U.S. 207, 218 (1905).
9. *United States v. Jefferson County Board*, 372 F. 2d 836 (1966), 380 F. 2d 385 (1967); cert. den. 389 U.S. 840 (1967).

Amendment XIV. National Citizenship; Protection from State Infringement

Section 1. All persons born or naturalized in the United States and subject to the jurisdiction thereof are citizens of the United States and of the state wherein they reside. No state shall make or enforce any law which shall abridge the privileges or immunities of citizens of the United States; or shall any state deprive any person of life, liberty or property, without due process of law; nor deny to any person within its jurisdiction the equal protection of the laws.

Section 2. Representatives shall be apportioned among the several states according to their respective numbers, counting the whole number of persons in each state, excluding Indians not taxed. But when the right to vote at any election for the choice of electors for President and Vice President of the United States, Representatives in Congress, the Executive and Judicial officers of a state, or the members of the legislature thereof, is denied to any of the male inhabitants of such state, being twenty-one years of age, and citizens of the United States, or in any way abridged, except for participation in rebellion, or other crime, the basis of representation therein shall be reduced in the proportion which the number of such male citizens shall bear to the whole number of male citizens twenty-one years of age in such state.

Section 3. No person shall be a Senator or Representative in Congress, or elector of President and Vice President, or hold any office, civil or military, under the United States, or under any state, who, having previously taken an oath, as a member of Congress, or as an officer of the United States, or as a member of any state legislature, or as an executive or judicial officer of any state, to support the Constitution of the United States, shall have engaged in insurrection or rebellion against the same, or given aid or comfort to the enemies thereof. But Congress may by a vote of two-thirds of each House, remove such disability.

Section 4. The validity of the public debt of the United States, authorized by law, including debts incurred for payment of pensions and bounties for services in suppressing insurrection or rebellion, shall not be questioned. But neither the United States nor any state shall assume or pay any debt or obligation incurred in aid of insurrection or rebellion against the United States, or any claim for the loss or emancipation of any slave; but all such debts, obligations and claims shall be held illegal and void.

Section 5. The Congress shall have power to enforce, by appropriate legislation, the provisions of this article.

The pivotal concept in the modern Constitution is in this section; it fundamentally reoriented the relationship of the individual American and the several states to the Federal authority. Much has been written about the circumstances of the drafting and early construction of this Amendment, and the principal issues have been concisely reviewed earlier in this volume.[1] The basic importance of the section derives from (1) the fact that it restated in more explicit terms the qualifications for national and state citizenship;[2] (2) the fact that it enumerated the rights of citizens ("privileges and immunities") and declared all persons (living and "legal") entitled to due process and the equal protection of the laws; (3) the fact that the courts in the beginning, for better or for worse, extended the provisions of the Amendment to a broad spectrum of national economic life quite distinct from the purposes for which the Amendment obviously had been first drafted; (4) the fact that, in the mid-years of the twentieth century, virtually all of the Bill of Rights provisions were incorporated into this Amendment and applied with the enforcing authority of the Federal government as against the states; and (5) the fact that as a part of this incorporation the equal-protection clause was defined by the Court as having self-executing effect in certain circumstances.[3]

Foreword: The Pros and Cons of Incorporation

Incorporation of the principal provisions of the Bill of Rights was the ultimate achievement of the Warren Court, not unattended, before or since, by vigorous disputes of its propriety. While the eloquence of Justices Frankfurter and Harlan provided elaborate warnings against either general or selective incorporation, the fact remains that even since the Warren Court the trend has continued, although perhaps at a decelerating rate.[4]

The incorporation doctrine may be based, in whole or in part, on any of the three basic guarantees of this section—privileges or immunities, due process, or equal protection. Of the three, the due-process clause for a long period seemed the most logical point of entry, since Fourteenth Amendment due process could arguably be equated with Fifth Amendment due process, and the guarantees in the other phrases of the Bill of Rights—particularly the specific provisions of the Fourth, Fifth and Sixth Amendments—would, according to this line of reasoning, establish the standards of due process in the Fourteenth.[5] On the other hand, in the latter years of the Warren Court the equal-protection clause became an even more persuasive avenue of incorporation, as the Court became increasingly disposed to declare certain rights to be absolute or universal and hence logically to be extended to all persons.[6]

Justice Cardozo, in his eloquent argument against incorporation in *Palko v. Connecticut,* conceded that certain guarantees within the first eight Amendments were "of the very essence of a scheme of ordered liberty" and urged that the Fourteenth Amendment should incorporate only those specific rights which reason and experience concluded were so fundamental that "neither liberty nor justice would exist if they were sacrificed."[7] Thus, in 1937, the Court had declared against general incorporation, citing with approval a case of long standing which had said the same thing, in 1908.[8] The specific issue in the earlier case—the constitutionality of comment on a defendant's failure to testify in his own defense—was reaffirmed in another case in 1947,[9] with Justice Frankfurter making his own argument against incorporation: "The Amendment neither comprehends the specific provisions by which the founders deemed it appropriate to restrict the Federal government, nor is it confined to them. . . . A construction which gives to due process no independent function but turns it into a summary of the Bill of Rights would assume that no other abuses would reveal themselves in the course of time than those which had become manifest in 1791."[10]

Frankfurter felt that this was an inescapable conclusion because he firmly maintained that the guarantees of the Bill of Rights were definable only in eighteenth-century terms. Justice Black, in dissent, complained that Frankfurter's "natural law" theory not only froze the definition of these rights but rejected the assumption made at the time of adoption of the Fourteenth Amendment that this clause did in fact protect from state infringement "the privileges and protections of the Bill of Rights."[11] When, twenty-one years later, *Duncan v. Louisiana*[12] recited the general incorporation of most of the provisions of the Bill of Rights, by citing the major opinions relating to one specific guarantee after another,[13] the Frankfurter argument appeared to have become academic. Three years earlier, in *Griswold v. Connecticut*,[14] Justice Douglas had suggested that "specific guarantees in the Bill of Rights have penumbras, formed by emanations from those guarantees that help give them life and substance"[15]—a bold idea that provoked critical comment both in the concurring and dissenting opinions.[16]

On occasion the Warren Court justified incorporation in terms of the preponderance of jurisdictions, state and Federal, which applied the particular Bill of Rights principle, the argument being that this suggested a trend toward general acceptance of the principle which ought accordingly to be established as the general constitutional rule. Thus in *Mapp v. Ohio*, overruling *Wolf v. Colorado*,[17] Justice Clark found that the Federal exclusionary rule of the Fourth Amendment had been disparately applied by the states at the time of *Wolf*, but that by the time of *Mapp*, sixteen years later, "time had set its face against" the *Wolf* doctrine, as indicated by the preponderance of states which by then had adopted and applied the Federal rule.

The criticism of the incorporation doctrine has been twofold: There is, first, the Frankfurter premise that Bill of Rights guarantees are limited to eighteenth-century values. There is, second, the complaint that selective incorporation creates a double standard of constitutional rights, with "preferred freedoms" defined at the option of a majority of the Court as being universal values limiting all government powers while other freedoms are disparately enforced at different state and national levels.[18] There has also been the ultimate question of whether incorporation could work both ways, with certain principles developed from the judicial construction of the Fourteenth Amendment being applied back to the Fifth, as against Federal powers. The answer to this may depend on the readiness of the Court to extricate itself from the "original meaning," eighteenth-century limitations on the Bill of Rights guarantees themselves. Whether the Burger Court, in freeing the states from the common-law doctrine of twelve-man juries and unanimous verdicts,[19] has deliberately or inevitably freed the Federal courts from this same common-law doctrine remains to be seen.[20] In other areas, the Burger Court has followed precedents in the Warren Court incorporation cases, whether or not this amounts to a reciprocity between the Fourteenth and Fifth Amendments.[21]

National Citizenship; Privileges and Immunities

Duality of citizenship is a natural result of a Federal system of government such as that of the United States, but it was not until the opening clause of this section of the Fourteenth Amendment that it was explicitly distinguished. As Justice Miller pointed out, a citizen of the United States was one "born or naturalized in the United States, and subject to the jurisdiction thereof," and the definition vested, or had the effect of vesting, certain rights which "depend upon different characteristics or circumstances of the individual."[22] Nearly half a century later, Chief Justice White held that this distinction was intended to make the national citizenship "paramount and dominant."[23] Such citizenship, as well as state citizenship, was held to be limited to natural persons and not to extend to artificial or "legal" persons (i.e., corporations).[24]

The definition of national citizenship, by the language of the next clause in this section, also recognizes "privileges and immunities" of citizens of the United States which states are admonished not to abridge. Whether the privileges and immunities of the Fourteenth Amendment are analogous or complementary to the privileges and immunities of state citizens in Article IV. §2. Cl. 1 has never been categorically decided, although the older cases cited under the "comity clause" of Article IV have been qualified by more recent decisions (*cf.* pp. 155–58 *supra*). Miller, in the *Slaughterhouse Cases*, undertook to give examples of those "which owe their existence to the Federal government, its national character, its Constitution, or its laws": right of access to the seats of state or national governments, right to protection as an American national under international law, and at least certain rights as set out in the Bill of Rights.[25] In 1908[26] the Court recapitulated the rights as recognized in opinions in the intervening years: the right of unrestricted travel from state to state,[27] the right to petition Congress for redress of grievances,[28] the right to vote in national elections,[29] to enter public lands[30] and to be protected in the operation of law.[31]

In the years of *laissez-faire* dominance, the Court was not inclined to treat the clause dynamically,[32] and even when, in 1935, it did invoke "privileges and immunities" as a rule of decision, it was to limit state powers of regulation of private enterprise;[33] and the overriding of this case in 1940 had the effect of further restricting the force of the words.[34] In 1939 a case decided primarily on First Amendment grounds nevertheless did aver that the right to use public premises as a site for communicating views was one of the privileges of a citizen of the United States.[35] In 1941 a concurring opinion of four Justices, in a case invalidating a California migrant control law, urged that national citizenship was a sounder basis for the decision than was the commerce clause relied on by the majority opinion.[36] And in 1948 the Court affirmed a challenge to a California alien land control law, where a native-born Japanese-American contended that as a citizen of the United States he could not be barred from land ownership by the state law.[37] The main thrust of the case, however, was that the right was grounded on the equal-protection clause.[38]

While the Court in 1900 had categorically denied that privileges of the Bill of Rights were within the definition of "privileges and immunities of citizens of the United States,"[39] recent cases on incorporation have modified the view, although joining this clause with due process and equal protection. Freedom of association, as read into the First Amendment, was included among "privileges and immunities" in 1966.[40] So was the Fifth Amendment prohibition against self-incrimination.[41] But merely calling some recognized benefit a "privilege" does not conclusively vest in it a constitutional status, the Court warned in 1971,[42] and the protection of this clause can be invoked only when state action clearly deprives one of a constitutionally guaranteed right.[43] As these rights have been progressively broadened by judicial definition, the restraint of the clause on the states has broadened.[44] The fact remains, however, that the Court has avoided developing to their full potential dimensions either the concept of national citizenship or the privileges and immunities which attach to this status, partly because the terms are too general and partly because, conversely, the due-process and equal-protection clauses have offered more viable alternatives.

Due Process in This Amendment

Although the Court early in the twentieth century conceded that Fourteenth Amendment due process "operates to extend . . . the same protection against arbitrary state legislation affecting life, liberty and property, as is offered by the Fifth Amendment,"[45] and further that "if an act of Congress is valid under the Fifth Amendment it would be hard to say that a state law in like terms was void under the Fourteenth,"[46] the development of the latter clause in the nineteenth century was disparate. The *Slaughterhouse Cases,* significant as they were for diverting the Amendment as a whole into areas distinct from the civil rights to which it was originally addressed,[47] treated due process as essentially procedural. In 1887 the Court suggested that the substantive reasonableness of state regulation of private enterprise might also be a constitutional question,[48] a doctrine which reached fruition a decade later when the Court invalidated a state law on the ground that it deprived individuals (insurance companies) of liberty without due process[49] and defined liberty as including an individual's freedom of contract and added: "although it may be conceded that this right . . . may be regulated and sometimes prohibited when the contracts or business conflict with the policy of the state as contained in its statutes, yet the power does not and cannot extend to prohibiting a citizen from making contracts . . . outside the limits and jurisdiction of the state."[50]

This doctrine, elaborately developed by Justice Peckham in the insurance case, rapidly led to a long list of decisions insulating private enterprise from public surveillance on the ground that substantive due process empowered the courts to evaluate the state's public policy in legislating the regulations as well as the procedural safeguards in applying the regulations.[51] Although now discredited, the rule was confidently followed for nearly half a century and generally hampered state and national governments from implementing social and economic policies which informed and objective opinion strongly supported. With the collapse of *laissez-faire* in the 1930s, the doctrine's force deteriorated, and in the course of the following decade most of the restrictive cases of the prior era came to be overturned.[52] In 1949 Justice Black summarized the judicial reorientation in his statement that "the due process clause is no longer to be so broadly construed that Congress and state legislatures are put in a strait jacket when they attempt to suppress business and industrial conditions which they regard as offensive to the public welfare."[53]

After the Court's about-face in the later New Deal years, substantive due process metamorphosed into a standard for broad rather than narrow government power and extended specifically to theretofore judicially disapproved regulations of labor conditions,[54] utility rate-making[55] and other utility activities,[56] various business practices,[57] the general use of the state police power[58] and the use of other constitutional power in implementation thereof.[59] More significantly, in terms of the emerging constitutionalism of the post-World War II period, substantive and procedural due process tended to merge and, as a result, to prepare the way for the incorporation of Bill of Rights provisions into this Amendment.

Although the Court had sought to bar the general incorporation of the Fourth, Fifth and Sixth Amendments in 1937,[60] an entering wedge was inserted in 1948 when the provisions for public trial and informing of charges against defendants were extended from the Fifth to the Fourteenth.[61] The next year, however, the Court majority, speaking through Justice Frankfurter, firmly declared that due process was "a gradual and empiric process of 'inclusion and exclusion'"[62] and that the Fourth Amendment prohibition of unreasonable search and seizure did not extend the Federal rule, excluding evidence so obtained,[63] to the states. In *Rochin v. California*,[64] Frankfurter conceded that state rules on admissibility of evidence must "respect certain decencies of civilized conduct," but insisted that the Fourth Amendment prohibition should not be treated as a universal standard.[65] The Frankfurter view was confirmed by an opinion by Justice Jackson in 1954,[66] while the Sixth Amendment provision on right to counsel, limited in 1932 to capital cases,[67] also came under the Frankfurter–Jackson policy against general incorporation.[68]

The restrictive rule in *Wolf* fell in 1961 and the rule in

Betts in 1963; with these breaches in the major points of the non-incorporation barricade, incorporation itself proceeded steadily thereafter. *Mapp v. Ohio*[69] extended the exclusionary rule on evidence gathered through unreasonable search and seizure; *Gideon v. Wainwright*[70] extended the Sixth Amendment right to counsel to all felony cases and touched off a long series of subsequent decisions refining the details of the doctrine.[71] In 1964 the Fifth Amendment guarantee against self-incrimination[72] and general procedural safeguards within the due-process concept[73] were extended to the Fourteenth; the next year there was the Sixth's provision for confrontation of witnesses,[74] with the speedy trial[75] and power of summoning defense witnesses[76] added in 1967. The double-jeopardy rule of the Fifth, incorporated in 1969,[77] virtually completed the process.

Incorporation, or its equivalent, had really begun long before the dazzling activism of the 1960s, insofar as it amounted to judicial recognition of certain universal standards of public and private behavior. Thus the eminent-domain provision of the Fifth Amendment was cited as a restraint against arbitrary taking of property for state use, without adequate compensation, as early as 1897[78] and was extended generally in 1920[79] and by 1946 was unequivocally incorporated.[80] First Amendment provisions on freedom of expression were somewhat obliquely incorporated in the 1920s,[81] and from the "handbill cases" of the late 1930s to the latter 1960s, other guarantees of the First were added to the Fourteenth.[82] While there is some ambivalence concerning the Court's recent holdings on Seventh Amendment guarantees *vis-à-vis* the states,[83] the Eighth Amendment guarantees have been generally extended.[84] The invitation to extend, indefinitely, both Federal and state guarantees through the Ninth Amendment, urged on the Court by Justice Douglas in 1965,[85] has not been taken up.

The basic principles of Fourteenth Amendment due process, on which incorporationists and non-incorporationists can generally agree, is that "it is of the very nature of a free society to advance in its standards of what is deemed reasonable and right" and that the concept of due process is not to be limited to "a permanent catalogue" of unchangeable rights.[86] Like Fifth Amendment due process, this clause has as its elemental objective the protection of the individual from arbitrary acts.[87] While it has been broadened to include new concepts of racial equality, considerably beyond the civil-rights concepts of the generation in which it was adopted,[88] the impracticality of making it indefinitely retroactive has been recognized.[89]

Equal Protection of the Laws

Until the Warren Court, the final clause in this section was so seldom treated as viable in its own right that it seemed to merit Justice Holmes's denigrating reference to it as "the usual last resort of constitutional arguments,"[90] thrown into counsels' briefs as an afterthought or superficial makeweight. While lawyers and jurists were disposed to treat the clause as a somewhat vague complement to the due-process clause,[91] an elementary basis for its application developed in the context of legislative classification formulae—a standard procedure by which statutory rights or obligations were applied (and limited) to members of a defined class.[92] The power to classify, said the Court in 1911, is reviewable only on the question of its reasonable basis;[93] but rather obviously this question turns on the matter of equal protection.[94]

From such general issues of political economy, the Court in the 1960s moved quickly to define and extend equal-protection standards to social issues: Where, in 1937, a state poll tax had been upheld so long as indiscriminately applied,[95] a 6–3 majority in 1966 held that "a state violates the equal protection clause . . . whenever it makes the affluence of the voter or payment of any fee an electoral standard."[96] While literacy tests were upheld in 1959,[97] the power of Congress to prohibit tests which were limited to the English language in Spanish-speaking areas was also affirmed in 1966.[98] Property qualifications for special bond elections were struck down in 1969.[99] Limitations on the right of minority parties to gain places on election ballots,[100] and on state filing-fee requirements,[101] have been recently and critically reviewed under equal-protection standards.

While many of the defendants'-rights cases, incorporating portions of the Fifth and Sixth Amendments into Fourteeth Amendment due process, also alleged a constitutional question of equal protection, the leading cases have inferred rather than stated the logical conclusion: Where a right—e.g., to counsel, to appeal, etc.—is fundamental, it is guaranteed to all persons from the time and place at which the right begins.[102] The second Justice Harlan protested against general reliance on the equal-protection clause lest it "read into the Constitution a philosophy of leveling that would be foreign to many of our basic concepts. . . . The state may have a moral obligation to eliminate the evils of poverty, but it is not required by the equal-protection clause to give to some what others can afford."[103] Harlan reviewed his objections at length in a dissent in *Shapiro v. Thompson,*[104] a 1969 case in which a 6–3 majority held invalid a state law denying welfare assistance to those who had not fulfilled a minimum residence requirement.[105]

The Warren Court devised, although it did not in all respects originate, what Justice Harlan described as "the rule that statutory classifications which are either based on certain 'suspect' criteria or affect certain 'fundamental rights' will be held to deny equal protection unless justified by a 'compelling' governmental interest."[106] This was applied to various situations—e.g., rights of illegitimate as distinguished from legitimate children;[107] discrimination against indigents by requiring them to "work off" fines;[108] and denial of the right to file papers for lack of funds for the filing fee.[109] In its first term, the Burger Court suggested that a "reasonable basis" for state action ought to dispose of the "suspect" standard and need not require proof of a " 'compelling' governmental interest."[110]

The equal-protection clause has attained its greatest jurisdiction as a constitutional standard in the areas of racial and electoral equality. It is here, in the issues of integration and reapportionment, that the jurisprudence of the Warren Court reached its apogee—and also made the most fundamental changes in the constitutional orientation of the United States since the crises of 1937. There was ironic coincidence in the fact that racial segregation had come to rest on a doctrine of "separate but equal" facilities and the fact that the cases which began with *Brown v. Board of Education*[111] should base their rule on the test of equality. In 1896, dissenting from the first enunciation of the "separate but equal" doctrine, the first Justice Harlan made his famous remark, "Our Constitution is color-blind, and neither knows nor tolerates classes among citizens," thereafter concluding: "The arbitrary separation of citizens, on the basis of race," when they are claiming a right to which all persons are entitled, "is a badge of servitude wholly inconsistent with . . . the equality before the law established by the Constitution."[112]

The first *Brown* decision, like its implementing decision the following year,[113] set off a chain reaction of desegregation cases with respect to other public facilities,[114] led to a series of Congressional statutes over the next fifteen years and finally brought the nation to an apparent impasse on the issue of compulsory busing of school children to offset *de facto* segregation of neighborhood schools.[115] Out of the welter of socially explosive decisions in this subject area, only one fundamental constitutional principle remained stubbornly dominant: the clause compelling all government to enforce equal protection (i.e., beneficial effect) of constitutional rights.

A decade after the first desegregation case, the Court again invoked the equal-protection clause to establish the doctrine of "one man, one vote." A 6–2 majority held that the failure of a state legislature to reapportion its voting districts equitably with population amounted to state action denying equal protection.[116] From the question of Tennessee's legislative representation the Court proceeded swiftly to extend the principle to Georgia's unit system for statewide voting,[117] to Congressional districting[118] and then to all state representation in a variety of cases.[119] The full vitality of the equal-protection clause was expressed in *Reynolds v. Sims,* where the Court, speaking through Chief Justice Warren, declared that it "requires that a state make an honest and good faith effort to construct districts, in both houses of its legislature, as nearly of equal population as is practicable.[120]

By 1969 the Court had dispelled virtually all of the Frankfurter arguments against involvement in apportionment questions, made in the 1948 holding (3+1—3) in *MacDougall v. Green,*[121] and had extended its equal-protection standard into local government as well.[122] While the Burger Court undertook to revise and restate the formulae for applying the equal-protection doctrine to apportionment,[123] it is unlikely that the doctrine itself will be abandoned.

1. *Cf.* pp. 35–38 *supra.*
2. *Cf.* Justice Miller's recapitulation in the *Slaughterhouse Cases,* 16 Wall. 36, 74 (1873).
3. Representative law-review discussion of recent developments on this Amendment are: Dixon, "Reapportionment in the Supreme Court and Congress: Constitutional Struggle for Fair Representation," 63 *Mich. L. Rev.* 209 (1964); Fairman, "Does the Fourteenth Amendment Incorporate the Bill of Rights? The Original Understanding," 2 *Stanf. L. Rev.* 5 (1949); Frantz, "Congressional Power to Enforce the Fourteenth Amendment Against Private Persons," 73 *Yale L. J.* 1353 (1964); Hale, "Unconstitutional Conditions and Constitutional Rights," 35 *Colum. L. Rev.* 321 (1935); Swindler, "The Warren Court: Completion of a Constitutional Revolution," 23 *Vand. L. Rev.* 205 (1970).
4. *Cf.* opinions in *Williams v. Florida,* 399 U.S. 78 (1970); *Apodaca v. Oregon,* 406 U.S. 404 (1972); *Johnson v. Louisiana,* 406 U.S. 356 (1972).
5. But *cf.* Justice Cardozo's distinctions between Fifth and Fourteenth Amendment due process in *Palko v. Connecticut,* 302 U.S. 319, 332 (1937).
6. Among representative articles, *cf.* Henkin, " 'Selective Incorporation' in the Fourteenth Amendment," 73 *Yale L. J.* 74 (1963); Kadish, "Methodology and Criteria of Due Process Litigation: A Survey and Criticism," 66 *Yale L. J.* 319 (1958).
7. 302 U.S., at 326. This case was overruled in 1969 in *Benton v. Maryland,* 395 U.S. 789.
8. *Twining v. New Jersey,* 211 U.S. 78, overruled in *Malloy v. Hogan,* 378 U.S. 1 (1964).
9. *Adamson v. California,* 332 U.S. 46 (1947), also overruled in *Malloy v. Hogan,* 378 U.S. 1 (1964).
10. 332 U.S., at 59.
11. *Id.,* at 66. *Cf.,* in criticism of Black's view, Fairman, "Does the Fourteenth Amendment Incorporate the Bill of Rights? The Original Understanding," 2 *Stanf. L. Rev.* 5 (1949); and *cf.* also Bickel, "The Original Understanding and the Segregation Decision," 69 *Harv. L. Rev.* 1 (1955).
12. 391 U.S. 145 (1968).
13. In a concurring opinion, Justice Black replied to Professor Fairman's article cited in note 11 *supra;* Justices Harlan and Stewart dissented, reiterating the Frankfurter arguments.
14. 381 U.S. 479 (1965).
15. *Id.,* at 482.
16. *Id.,* at 499, 527. Among many law-review commentaries, *cf.* esp. Kauper, "Penumbras, Peripheries and Emanations: Things Fundamental and Things Forgotten; the Griswold Case," 64 *Mich. L. Rev.* 235 (1965).
17. *Mapp v. Ohio,* 367 U.S. 643 (1961); *Wolf v. Colorado,* 338 U.S. 25 (1949).
18. *Cf.* Harlan's dissent in *Duncan v. Louisiana,* 391 U.S. 145, 171 (1968), and in *Benton v. Maryland,* 395 U.S. 784 (1969).
19. *Cf. Williams v. Florida,* 399 U.S. 78 (1970); *Apodaca v. Oregon,* 406 U.S. 404 (1972); *Johnson v. Louisiana,* 406 U.S. 356 (1972).
20. *Cf.* report on Federal juries of less than twelve members provided for in orders approved in various circuits; *cf.* most recent list of fifty-four Federal districts in 56 *F.R.D.* 535 (1972); and *cf.* the criticism of the trend in Gibbons, "The New Minijuries: Panacea or Pandora's Box?" 58 *A.B.A.J.* 594 (June 1972). *Cf.*

also a rebuttal in Fisher, "The Seventh Amendment and the Common Law: No Magic in Numbers," 56 *F.R.D.* 507 (1972).

21. E.g., *Swann v. Charlotte-Mecklenburg Board of Education,* 402 U.S. 1 (1971); *North Carolina State Board v. Swann,* 402 U.S. 43 (1971); *Wisconsin v. Yoder,* 406 U.S. 205 (1972); but *cf.* also *Palmer v. Thompson,* 403 U.S. 217 (1971).

22. *Slaughterhouse Cases,* 16 Wall. 36, 74 (1875).

23. *Arver v. United States,* 245 U.S. 389 (1918).

24. *Orient Ins. Co. v. Daggs,* 172 U.S. 557, 561 (1879); *Berea College v. Kentucky,* 211 U.S. 45 (1908); *Grosjean v. Am. Press Co.,* 297 U.S. 233, 244 (1936).

25. 16 Wall., at 78, 97.

26. *Twining v. New Jersey,* 211 U.S. 78 (1908).

27. *Crandall v. Nevada,* 6 Wall. 35 (1868); but *cf. United States v. Wheeler,* 254 U.S. 281, 299 (1920).

28. *United States v. Cruikshank,* 92 U.S. 541 (1876).

29. *Ex parte Yarbrough,* 110 U.S. 651 (1884); *Wiley v. Sinkler,* 179 U.S. 58 (1900).

30. *United States v. Waddell,* 112 U.S. 76 (1884).

31. *Logan v. United States,* 144 U.S. 263 (1892); *In re Quarles,* 158 U.S. 532 (1895).

32. *Cf. Presser v. Illinois,* 116 U.S. 252 (1886); *Holden v. Hardy,* 169 U.S. 366 (1898); *Crane v. New York,* 239 U.S. 195 (1915); *Bryant v. Zimmer,* 278 U.S. 63 (1928); *Breedlove v. Suttles,* 302 U.S. 277 (1937); *Snowden v. Hughes,* 321 U.S. 1 (1944).

33. *Colgate v. Harvey,* 296 U.S. 404 (1935).

34. *Madden v. Kentucky,* 309 U.S. 83 (1940).

35. *Hague v. C.I.O.,* 307 U.S. 496 (1939).

36. *Edwards v. California,* 314 U.S. 160, 177 (1941).

37. *Oyama v. California,* 332 U.S. 633 (1948).

38. *Id.,* 635.

39. *Maxwell v. Dow,* 176 U.S. 601 (1900).

40. *Elfbrandt v. Russell,* 384 U.S. 11 (1966).

41. *Tehan v. United States ex rel. Shott,* 382 U.S. 406 (1966).

42. *Sailer v. Leger,* 403 U.S. 365 (1971); and *cf. Snowden v. Hughes,* 132 F. 2d 416 (1943), aff'd. 321 U.S. 1 (1944).

43. *Rice v. Sioux City Mem. Park Cem.,* 349 U.S. 70 (1955).

44. *West Virginia Board of Education v. Barnette,* 319 U.S. 624 (1943); *Murdock v. Pennsylvania,* 319 U.S. 105 (1943). The state action must be against Federal rights, not against state rights. *Hamilton v. Regents,* 293 U.S. 245 (1934); *Prud. Ins. Co. v. Check,* 259 U.S. 530 (1922).

45. *Hibben v. Smith,* 191 U.S. 310, 325 (1903).

46. *Carroll v. Greenwich Ins. Co.,* 199 U.S. 401, 410 (1905).

47. 16 Wall. 36 (1873); *cf. Davidson v. New Orleans,* 96 U.S. 97 (1878); *Chi., Milw. & St. P. R. Co. v. Minnesota,* 134 U.S. 418 (1890).

48. *Mugler v. Kansas,* 123 U.S. 613 (1887).

49. *Allgeyer v. Louisiana,* 165 U.S. 578 (1897).

50. *Id.,* at 582.

51. *Nebbia v. New York,* 291 U.S. 502 (1934). *Cf.,* generally, Swindler, *The Old Legality,* Ch. 14.

52. *Cf.* Swindler, *The New Legality,* Chs. 6, 7.

53. *Lincoln Fed. Labor Union v. N.W. Iron & Metal Co.,* 335 U.S. 525, 533 (1949).

54. *West Coast Hotel Co. v. Parrish,* 300 U.S. 379 (1937); *N.L.R.B. v. Jones & Laughlin Steel Corp.,* 301 U.S. 1 (1937); *A.F.L. v. American Sash Co.,* 335 U.S. 538 (1949); *Auto Workers v. Wisconsin Board,* 336 U.S. 245 (1949); *Day-Brite Lighting Co. v. Missouri,* 342 U.S. 421 (1952).

55. *F.P.C. v. Pipeline Co.*, 315 U.S. 575 (1942); *F.P.C. v. Hope Natural Gas Co.*, 320 U.S. 591 (1944).

56. *Atchison R. Co. v. Commission*, 346 U.S. 346 (1953).

57. *State Farm Ins. Co. v. Duel*, 324 U.S. 154 (1945); *Daniel v. Family Life Ins. Co.*, 336 U.S. 220 (1949); *Williamson v. Lee Optical Co.*, 348 U.S. 438 (1955); *Safeway Stores v. Oklahoma Grocers*, 360 U.S. 334 (1959).

58. *Thompson v. Consol. Gas Co.*, 300 U.S. 55 (1937); *Railway Express Agency v. New York*, 336 U.S. 106 (1949).

59. *Carmichael v. So. Coal & Coke Co.*, 300 U.S. 644 (1937); *Whitney v. Tax Commission*, 309 U.S. 530 (1940).

60. *Palko v. Connecticut*, 302 U.S. 319 (1937).

61. *In re Oliver*, 333 U.S. 257 (1948); *Winters v. New York*, 333 U.S. 507 (1948); and *cf. Edelman v. California*, 344 U.S. 357 (1953).

62. *Wolf v. Colorado*, 338 U.S. 25 (1949); and *cf. Adamson v. California*, 332 U.S. 46 (1947).

63. *Weeks v. United States*, 232 U.S. 383 (1914).

64. 342 U.S. 165 (1952).

65. *Id.*, at 172. "The faculties of the due-process clause may be indefinite and vague, but the mode of their ascertainment is not self-willed. In each case 'due process of law' requires an evaluation based on a disinterested inquiry pursued in the spirit of science, on a balanced order of facts exactly and fairly stated, on the detached consideration of conflicting claims, on a judgment not *ad hoc* and episodic but duly mindful of reconciling the needs both of continuity and of change in a progressive society."

66. *Irvine v. California*, 347 U.S. 128 (1954).

67. *Powell v. Alabama*, 287 U.S. 45 (1932).

68. *Betts v. Brady*, 316 U.S. 455 (1942).

69. 367 U.S. 643 (1961).

70. 372 U.S. 335 (1963).

71. *Cf. Massiah v. United States*, 377 U.S. 201 (1964); *Escobedo v. Illinois*, 378 U.S. 478 (1964); *United States v. Wade*, 388 U.S. 218 (1967); *Gilbert v. California*, 388 U.S. 263 (1967).

72. *Malloy v. Hogan*, 378 U.S. 1 (1964).

73. *Baggett v. Bullitt*, 377 U.S. 360 (1964).

74. *Pointer v. Texas*, 380 U.S. 400 (1965).

75. *Klopfer v. North Carolina*, 386 U.S. 213 (1967).

76. *Washington v. Texas*, 388 U.S. 14 (1967).

77. *Benton v. Maryland*, 395 U.S. 784 (1969).

78. *Chi., Burl. & Q. R. Co. v. Chicago*, 166 U.S. 226 (1897), nullifying, if not overruling, *Davidson v. New Orleans*, 96 U.S. 397 (1878).

79. *Green v. Frazier*, 253 U.S. 233 (1920); *Cincinnati v. Vester*, 281 U.S. 439 (1930).

80. *United States ex rel. T.V.A. v. Welch*, 327 U.S. 546 (1946); *Case v. Bowles*, 327 U.S. 92 (1946); *New York v. United States*, 326 U.S. 572 (1940).

81. *Gitlow v. New York*, 268 U.S. 652 (1925); *Whitney v. California*, 274 U.S. 357 (1927); *Near v. Minnesota*, 283 U.S. 697 (1931).

82. *Cf.* annotations to Amendment I, *supra*, pp. 172–87.

83. *Cf.* annotations to Amendment VII, *supra*, pp. 214–16.

84. *Cf.* annotations to Amendment VIII, *supra*, pp. 216–20.

85. *Griswold v. Connecticut*, 381 U.S. 479 (1965).

86. *Frank v. Maryland*, 359 U.S. 360 (1959); *cf.* also *Munn v. Illinois*, 94 U.S. 123 (1876).

87. Tot v. United States, 319 U.S. 463 (1943); Curry v. McCanless, 307 U.S. 357 (1931); and cf. Hurtado v. California, 110 U.S. 535 (1884).
88. Cf. Loving v. Virginia, 388 U.S. 1 (1966).
89. Stovall v. Denno, 388 U.S. 293 (1967); Johnson v. New Jersey, 384 U.S. 719 (1966).
90. Buck v. Bell, 274 U.S. 200, 208 (1927).
91. Guano Co. v. Virginia, 253 U.S. 412 (1920).
92. Cf. Railway Express Agency v. New York, 336 U.S. 106 (1949); Goesart v. Cleary, 335 U.S. 464 (1948); Daniel v. Family Life Ins. Co., 336 U.S. 20 (1949).
93. Lindsley v. Natural Carbonic Gas Co., 220 U.S. 61, 78 (1911); Louisville Gas Co. v. Coleman, 277 U.S. 32, 37 (1928); Williamson v. Lee Optical Co., 348 U.S. 483 (1955).
94. An exhaustive analysis of the subject appears in Tussman and tenBroek, "The Equal Protection of the Laws," 37 Calif. L. Rev. 341 (1949).
95. Breedlove v. Suttles, 302 U.S. 277 (1937).
96. Harper v. Board of Elections, 383 U.S. 663, 666 (1966).
97. Lassiter v. Northampton County Board, 360 U.S. 45 (1959).
98. Katzenbach v. Morgan, 384 U.S. 641 (1966).
99. Kramer v. Union Free Sch. Dist., 395 U.S. 621 (1969); Cipriano v. Houma, 395 U.S. 701 (1969).
100. Williams v. Rhodes, 393 U.S. 23 (1968); but cf. Jenness v. Fortson, 403 U.S. 431 (1971).
101. Bullock v. Carter, 405 U.S. 134 (1972).
102. Cf. Kamisar, "The Right to Counsel and the Fourteenth Amendment," 30 U. Chicago L. Rev. 1 (1962). Cf. also Griffin v. Illinois, 351 U.S. 12 (1956); Douglas v. California, 372 U.S. 353 (1963).
103. 372 U.S., at 362.
104. 394 U.S. 618, 655 (1969).
105. Id., at 638.
106. Levy v. Louisiana, 391 U.S. 68 (1968); Labine v. Vincent, 401 U.S. 532 (1971); Weber v. Aetna Cas. & Sur. Co., 406 U.S. 164 (1972).
107. Williams v. Illinois, 399 U.S. 335 (1970); Tate v. Short, 401 U.S. 395 (1971).
108. Peonage Cases, 123 F. 2d 67 (1903).
109. Boddie v. Connecticut, 401 U.S. 371 (1971), decided on due process, although the concurring opinions urged equal-protection grounds.
110. Dandridge v. Williams, 397 U.S. 471 (1970); cf. also Richardson v. Belcher, 404 U.S. 78 (1971). But discrimination against aliens in welfare eligibility was barred by the equal-protection clause. Graham v. Richardson, 403 U.S. 365 (1971).
111. 347 U.S. 483 (1954). "Separate educational facilities are inherently unequal," and persons denied equal (i.e., integrated) facilities are "deprived of the equal protection of the laws." Id., at 493.
112. Plessy v. Ferguson, 163 U.S. 537 (1896). Cf. footnote by the Court in the Brown case, 347 U.S. at 491, citing the 1849 case of Roberts v. Boston, 59 Mass. 198, 206.
113. Brown v. Board of Education (II), 349 U.S. 294 (1955).
114. Cf. Gayle v. Browder, 352 U.S. 903 (1956); Goss v. Board of Education, 373 U.S. 683 (1963); Rogers v. Paul, 382 U.S. 198 (1966); Evans v. Newton, 382 U.S. 296 (1966); Lee v. Washington, 390 U.S. 333 (1968); Alexander v. Holmes County, 396 U.S. 19 (1969).

115. *Cf. Carter v. School Board,* 396 U.S. 290 (1970); *Swann v. Charlotte-Mecklenburg Board of Education,* 402 U.S. 1 (1971); *North Carolina State Board of Education v. Swann,* 402 U.S. 43 (1971); *Wright v. Emporia,* 407 U.S. 451 (1972).
116. *Baker v. Carr,* 369 U.S. 186 (1963).
117. *Gray v. Sanders,* 372 U.S. 368 (1963); but *cf. Fortson v. Morris,* 385 U.S. 231 (1966).
118. *Wesberry v. Sanders,* 376 U.S. 1 (1964).
119. *Reynolds v. Sims,* 377 U.S. 533 (1964); *WMCA, Inc., v. Lomenzo,* 377 U.S. 633 (1964); *Maryland Comm. for Fair Representation v. Tawes,* 377 U.S. 656 (1964); *Davis v. Mann,* 377 U.S. 678 (1964); *Roman v. Sincock,* 377 U.S. 695 (1964); *Lucas v. General Assembly,* 377 U.S. 713 (1964).
120. 377 U.S., at 585.
121. 335 U.S. 381 (1948); *Moore v. Ogilvie,* 394 U.S. 814 (1968).
122. *Avery v. Midland County,* 390 U.S. 474 (1968). For apportionment at administrative district levels, *cf. Hadley v. Junior College District,* 397 U.S. 50 (1970).
123. *Gordon v. Lowe,* 403 U.S. 1 (1971); *Whitcomb v. Chavis,* 403 U.S. 124 (1971); *Abate v. Mundt,* 403 U.S. 182 (1971).

Amendment XV. Universal Manhood Suffrage

Section 1. The right of citizens of the United States to vote shall not be denied or abridged by the United States or by any state on account of race, color or previous condition of servitude.

Section 2. The Congress shall have power to enforce this article by appropriate legislation.

Although this Amendment was adopted in 1870 and implemented by "appropriate legislation" in the same year, nearly a century was to pass until, in the concerted drive for civil rights in the 1960s, it began to take on its full but latent force. Early adjudication was negative; the Amendment did "not confer the right [to vote] upon anyone"[1] and merely extended manhood suffrage to all eligible persons regardless of race.[2] In 1884 Justice Miller urged that the clause should be read as affirmative and self-executing,[3] and in the course of the years the words of the Amendment were used as a measure of constitutionality of discriminatory laws and a means of invalidating them.[4] In part this limited reliance on this Amendment was due to the greater practical force of the Fourteenth Amendment due-process and equal-protection clauses, which could be made to dispose of many issues which nominally might come under the Fifteenth.[5] In larger part, however, it was due to the steady diminishing of national zeal for universal manhood suffrage as a constitutional principle, reflected in the desuetude which befell the Civil Rights Act of 1870.[6]

The Fifteenth Amendment standards began to be applied in their own right by the Court in 1953, when the device of a private club (from which, of course, blacks were excluded) to select the panel of candidates for public office was struck down as a denial of voting rights.[7] While literacy tests as a qualification for voting have been upheld in the absence of a showing of discriminatory purpose or effect,[8] any ambiguity or vagueness in the provisions for such tests will render them invalid.[9] Thus a statute requiring one to "interpret" a part of the state constitution was held in violation of both the Fourteenth and Fifteenth Amendments because it was manifestly liable to arbitrary application.[10] Frustration of voting privileges by gerrymandering[11] or by segregated ethnic districts[12] have been held contrary to the intention of the Amendment.

Emboldened by the judicial initiative of the early 1950s, Congress in 1957, 1960 and 1964 adopted progressively more detailed civil-rights acts, with specific provisions for the protection of voting rights. While the fact-finding authority vested in special commissions by the original act was strengthened by criminal sanctions against violators in 1960, and specific acts of interference with the franchise were identified in 1964, this piecemeal approach was replaced by the Voting Rights Act of 1965,[13] which undertook a full-scale implementation of the Fifteenth Amendment under the authority of its Section 2. The Department of Justice was given broad enforcement authority in the matter of guaranteed suffrage, and the law authorized the suspension of local authority over elections on a finding by the courts of a systematic denial of voting rights. Literacy tests confined to the English language were also forbidden.[14]

The general constitutional question of the power of Congress to enact the stringent provisions of the 1965 statute was tested in an original suit brought by South Carolina the following year.[15] By an 8–1 majority, with Justice Black concurring in part and dissenting in part, Chief Justice Warren rejected the argument that Congress "may appropriately do no more than

forbid violation of the Fifteenth Amendment in general terms"
while the states are left with the responsibility of drafting affirmative remedies.[16] "This may have been an uncommon exercise of
Congressional power," the Chief Justice acknowledged, "but the
Court has recognized that exceptional conditions can justify
measures not otherwise appropriate. . . . Congress had reason to
suppose that these States might try . . . to evade the remedies for
voting discrimination contained in the act itself. Under the com-
pulsion of these unique circumstances, Congress responded in a
permissively decisive manner."[17]

1. *United States v. Reese,* 92 U.S. 214, 217 (1876).
2. *United States v. Cruikshank,* 92 U.S. 542, 556 (1876).
3. *Ex parte Yarbrough,* 110 U.S. 651 (1884); *Neal v. Delaware,* 103 U.S. 370 (1881).
4. *Gwinn v. United States,* 238 U.S. 347 (1915); *Lane v. Wilson,* 307 U.S. 268 (1939).
5. *Cf. United States v. Classic,* 313 U.S. 299 (1941); *Smith v. Allwright,* 321 U.S. 649 (1944), reversing *Grovey v. Townsend,* 295 U.S. 45 (1935); and *cf. Nixon v. Herndon,* 273 U.S. 536 (1937); *Nixon v. Condon,* 286 U.S. 73 (1932).
6. *Cf.* the review of the ebb and flow of Congressional interest in the subject in Sen. Rep. No. 162, III, 89th Cong., 1st Sess., 1965.
7. *Terry v. Adams,* 345 U.S. 461 (1953).
8. *Lassiter v. Northampton El. Board,* 360 U.S. 45 (1960); *cf. Williams v. Mississippi,* 170 U.S. 213 (1898).
9. *Davis v. Schnell,* 81 F.S. 872 (1949), aff'd. 336 U.S. 933 (1949).
10. *Louisiana v. United States,* 380 U.S. 145 (1965).
11. *Gomillion v. Lightfoot,* 364 U.S. 339 (1960).
12. *Wright v. Rockefeller,* 376 U.S. 52 (1964), although the majority simply held that the plaintiffs had failed to make out their case.
13. Earlier cases had limited liability under the Fifteenth Amendment to "state action"; *cf. United States v. Reese,* 92 U.S. 214 (1876); *James v. Bowman,* 190 U.S. 197 (1903). The Court did not directly answer the allegation that the 1957 statute overturned the rule in these cases; *cf. United States v. Raines,* 362 U.S. 17 (1960); *United States v. Thomas,* 362 U.S. 58 (1960); *United States v. Alabama,* 362 U.S. 602 (1960). *Cf.* 71 Stat. 634; 74 Stat. 86; 78 Stat. 241; 79 Stat. 437.
14. The English-language prohibition was upheld in *Katzenbach v. Morgan,* 384 U.S. 641 (1966).
15. *South Carolina v. Katzenbach,* 383 U.S. 301 (1966).
16. *Id.,* at 326.
17. *Id.,* at 329; *cf.* also *Allen v. State Board,* 393 U.S. 544 (1969); *Gaston County v. United States,* 395 U.S. 285 (1969).

Amendment XVI. The Income Tax Power

The Congress shall have power to lay and collect taxes on incomes, from whatever source derived, without apportionment among the several states, and without regard to any census or enumeration.

This Amendment, like the Eleventh and Thirteenth, overturned a specific rule of the Supreme Court.[1] That rule in turn had overturned prior rules,[2] with a 5–4 holding that a Federal tax on income was a direct tax and hence required to be apportioned equally among the states.[3] While the Court had subsequently retreated from this 1895 holding,[4] President Taft insisted that the preferred means of abrogating the rule was by Constitutional amendment explicitly affirming an income-tax power,[5] and the Amendment was finally declared adopted in February 1913. In something of an attempt at saving face, the Court thereafter declared that the Amendment "conferred no new power of taxation but simply prohibited the previously complete and plenary power of income taxation possessed by Congress from the beginning from being taken out of the category of indirect taxation to which it inherently belonged."[6]

The principal questions which subsequently arose under the Amendment were concerned with definitions of income subject to taxation—whether the terms included any type of gain "derived from capital, from labor, or from both combined,"[7] and whether this definition included "profit gained from the sale or commission of capital assets."[8] Cash dividends, and dividends paid on stock in another company, have been held taxable as income,[9] but in 1920 the Court precipitated a furore by a 5–4 holding that stock dividends in the same company were not income until sold—thus, as Brandeis said in dissent, limiting the tax to income on income.[10] The 1920 rule was qualified in 1926 by a return to the general definition of income in earlier cases,[11] although another 1920 rule, exempting the income of Federal judges from taxation, was not overturned until 1939.[12]

Congress is held to have discretion to "condition, limit or deny deductions from gross income"[13] and may tax income even when derived from illicit activities (e.g., bootlegging).[14] The doctrine of tax immunities, developed in the nineteenth century as an accommodation of state and national sovereignties,[15] and subsequently contributing to increasingly criticized extensions of immunities,[16] was reversed by the Court in 1938[17] and 1939.[18] To preserve the sovereignty of government, the Court concluded, "It is not ordinarily necessary to confer . . . a competitive advantage over private persons."[19]

1. *Pollock v. Farmers' Loan & Trust Co.*, 158 U.S. 601 (1895).
2. *Springer v. United States*, 102 U.S. 586 (1881); *Veazie Bank v. Fenno*, Wall. 533 (1869); *Hylton v. United States*, 3 Dall. 171 (1796).
3. *Cf.* Swindler, *The Old Legality*, Ch. 1.
4. *Nicol v. Ames*, 173 U.S. 509 (1899); *Knowlton v. Moore*, 178 U.S. 41 (1900); *Patton v. Brady*, 184 U.S. 608 (1902); *Flint v. Stone Tracy Co.* 220 U.S. 107 (1911).
5. Swindler, *The Old Legality*, Ch. 8.
6. *Stanton v. Baltic Mining Co.*, 240 U.S. 103, 112 (1916). More honestly, the Court acknowledged in another case that the Amendment forbade application of the Pollock rule. *Brushaber v. Union Pac. R. Co.*, 240 U.S. 1, 18 (1916); and *cf. Peck v. Lowe*, 247 U.S. 165 (1918).
7. *Stratton's Independence v. Howbert*, 231 U.S. 399 (1913), construing the Federal Corporation Tax of 1909, 36 Stat. 111. *Cf.* also *Doyle v. Mitchell Bros.*, 247 U.S. 179 (1918).
8. *Cf. Lynch v. Turrish*, 247 U.S. 221 (1918); *So. Pacific R. Co. v. Lowe*, 247 U.S. 330 (1918).
9. *Lynch v. Hornby*, 247 U.S. 339 (1918); *Peabody v. Eisner*, 247 U.S. 347 (1918).
10. *Eisner v. Macomber*, 252 U.S. 189, 220 (1920). As late as 1943, the Court declined to reconsider the rule in this case. *Helvering v. Griffiths*, 318 U.S. 371 (1943). But any dividend which gives stockholders a different interest in the issuing corporation may be treated as income. *Helvering v. Gowran*, 302 U.S. 238 (1937).
11. *Bowers v. Kerbaugh-Empire Co.*, 271 U.S. 170 (1926). *Cf.* also *Metcalf v. Eddy & Mitchell*, 269 U.S. 514 (1926).
12. *Evans v. Gore*, 253 U.S. 245 (1920), overruled in *O'Malley v. Woodruff*, 307 U.S. 277 (1939).
13. *Helvering v. Ind. Life Ins. Co.*, 292 U.S. 371, 381 (1934).
14. *United States v. Sullivan*, 247 U.S. 259 (1927); and *cf. Rutkin v. United States*, 343 U.S. 130 (1952); *James v. United States*, 366 U.S. 213 (1962).
15. *Collector v. Day*, 11 Wall. 113 (1871); *Dobbins v. Erie County*, 16 Pet. 435 (1842).
16. *Cf. Comm. v. Schomber's Estate*, 144 F. 2d 998 (1944), cert. den. 323 U.S. 792 (1944); *D. D. Oil Co. v. Comm.*, 147 F. 2d 936 (1945); *Anderson Oldsmobile v. Hofferbert*, 102 F. S. 902 (1952), aff'd. 197 F. 2d 504 (1952).
17. *Helvering v. Gerhardt*, 304 U.S. 405 (1938).
18. *Graves v. New York ex rel. O'Keefe*, 306 U.S. 466 (1939).
19. *Helvering v. Gerhardt*, 304 U.S. at 410 (1938).

Amendment XVII. Popular Election of Senators

The Senate of the United States shall be composed of two Senators from each state, elected by the people thereof, for six years; and each Senator shall have one vote. The electors in each state shall have the qualifications requisite for electors of the most numerous branch of the state legislatures.

When vacancies happen in the representation of any state in the Senate, the executive authority of such state shall issue writs of election to fill such vacancies: *Provided,* That the legislature of any state may empower the executive thereof to make temporary appointments until the people fill the vacancies by election as the legislature may direct.

This amendment shall not be so construed as to affect the election or term of any Senator chosen before it becomes valid as part of the Constitution.

This Amendment, altering the original provision for legislative election established in Article I. §3, was one of the tenets of the Progressive Movement in the early part of the twentieth century.[1] Even before the adoption of the Amendment, many states in their primary laws had established a type of preferential vote which, while not always binding on members elected to the state legislature, tended toward making legislative election of United States Senators as much a reflection of popular will as the Electoral College balloting for President.[2] The use of the primary for selection of Senatorial candidates has been held invalid where either state law or party procedure discriminates against voters because of race.[3]

---

1. *Cf.* Swindler, *The Old Legality,* Ch. 10.
2. *Cf. State v. Blaisdell,* 118 N.W. 141 (1908); *State v. Frear,* 321 U.S. 649 (1910).
3. *Smith v. Allwright,* 321 U.S. 649 (1944); *Nixon v. Condon,* 286 U.S. 73 (1932).

Amendment XVIII
Prohibition of Intoxicating Liquor

[Section 1. After one year from the ratification of this article the manufacture, sale, or transportation of intoxicating liquors within, the importation thereof into, or the exportation thereof from the United States and all territory subject to the jurisdiction thereof for beverage purposes is hereby prohibited.

[Section 2. The Congress and the several states shall have concurrent power to enforce this article by appropriate legislation.

[Section 3. This article shall be inoperative unless it shall have been ratified as an amendment to the Constitution by the legislatures of the several states, as provided in the Constitution, within seven years from the date of the submission hereof to the states by the Congress.]

See Amendment XXI, repealing this Amendment; and for background on constitutional issues involving this Amendment, see Swindler, *The Old Legality*, Ch. 15.

Amendment XIX. Woman Suffrage

Section 1. The right of citizens of the United States to vote shall not be denied or abridged by the United States or by any state on account of sex.

Section 2. Congress shall have power to enforce this article by appropriate legislation.

The extension of suffrage to women—note the similarity in language of the Fifteenth Amendment—climaxed a struggle which began early in the nineteenth century and was carried on sporadically, both in England and America, until well into the twentieth. The major victory in this campaign came in Wyoming Territory in 1869, when equal suffrage was established by law; but only a handful of other states followed the example. The alternative to state-by-state reform of voting-rights laws was a single amendment to the Federal Constitution, which, like the Fifteenth Amendment, would build on the citizenship provisions of the Fourteenth, declaring the rights of citizens of the United States and thereupon prohibiting their infringement by the states. Thus incidentally, the rights of citizens of the United States, enforceable by the Federal Constitution as against the states, were further delineated. (See discussion of national citizenship under the Fourteenth Amendment.)

Although this Amendment, like the Eighteenth, was challenged in the courts as being a subject beyond the power of government to deal with, the argument was rebuffed. In essence, it was contended that because of its character the Amendment invaded a subject area which was exclusively within the jurisdiction of the states: "so great an addition to the electorate, if made without the state's consent, destroys its autonomy as a political body."[1] The Court answered simply by pointing to the language of the Fifteenth Amendment.[2] (See the discussion of the doctrine of *ultra vires* with reference to judicial review in Article III *supra*.) More recently, against a novel contention that in exempting women who did not vote from the poll tax there was a denial of equal protection, the Court observed that the Amendment could be read to apply to both sexes insofar as it swept aside all inconsistent laws, Federal or state.[3]

The right to vote is still subject to state regulations so long as the laws of the state do not conflict with the provisions of the Fifteenth and Nineteenth (and now the Twenty-sixth) Amendments as to sex, race, color or previous condition of servitude.[4] Early in the history of the present Amendment, a South Carolina court construed the new constitutional rule not in itself to confer a right to vote but only to prohibit discrimination on account of sex.[5] However, since the consensus of state construction has been that the effect of the Amendment was to nullify or expunge any reference to males from state electoral laws, any electoral disqualification on account of sex was in fact invalidated.[6]

1. *Leser v. Garnett*, 258 U.S. 130 (1922).
2. *Id.*, at 136. *Cf.* also *United States v. Reese*, 92 U.S. 214 (1876); *Neale v. Delaware*, 103 U.S. 370 (1881); *Myers v. Anderson*, 238 U.S. 368 (1915); *Gwinn v. United States*, 238 U.S. 347 (1915).

3. *Breedlove v. Suttles,* 302 U.S. 277 (1937).
4. *Tedesco v. Board of Elections,* 43 S. 2d 514 (1949), app. dism. 339 U.S. 940 (1949); *Smith v. Blackwell,* 34 F.S. 989 (1940), aff'd. 115 F. 2d 186 (1940).
5. *State v. Mittle,* 113 S.E. 335 (1922), error dism., 260 U.S. 705 (1922).
6. *Heyward v. Hall,* 198 S. 114 (1940); *Foster v. College Park,* 117 S.E. 84 (1923); cf. *Graves v. Eubank,* 87 S. 587 (1921).

Amendment XX
The "Lame Duck" Amendment

Section 1. The terms of the President and Vice President shall end at noon on the 20th day of January, and the terms of Senators and Representatives at noon on the 3d day of January, of the years in which such terms would have ended if this article had not been ratified; and the terms of their successors shall then begin.

Section 2. The Congress shall assemble at least once in every year, and such meeting shall begin at noon on the 3d day of January, unless they shall by law appoint a different day.

Section 3. If, at the time fixed for the beginning of the term of the President, the President elect shall have died, the Vice President elect shall become President. If a President shall not have been chosen before the time fixed for the beginning of his term, or if the President elect shall have failed to qualify, then the Vice President elect shall act as President until a President shall have qualified; and the Congress may by law provide for the case wherein neither a President elect nor a Vice President elect shall have qualified, declaring who shall then act as President, or the manner in which one who is to act shall be selected, and such person shall act accordingly until a President or Vice President shall have qualified.

Section 4. The Congress may by law provide for the case of the death of any of the persons from whom the House of Representatives may choose a President whenever the right of choice shall have devolved upon them, and for the case of the death of any of the persons from whom the Senate may choose a Vice President whenever the right of choice shall have devolved upon them.

Section 5. Sections 1 and 2 shall take effect on the 15th day of October following the ratification of this article.

Section 6. This article shall be inoperative unless it shall have been ratified as an amendment to the Constitution by the legislatures of three-fourths of the several states within seven years from the date of its submission.

The original Constitution, interestingly enough, had not fixed the date when a new Presidential term should begin or end. The old Continental Congress had set March 4, 1789, as the time for the business of government under the new Constitution to begin. Although George Washington did not take office for his first term until April 30, the second Congress passed a statute making March 4 following the quadrennial election as the official date for the beginning of a new Presidential term. While this date could theoretically have been modified by a new statute, the related problem of moving up the date for the beginning of the new Congress had to be dealt with by amendment.

Amendment XXI. Repeal of Amendment XVIII

Section 1. The eighteenth article of amendment to the Constitution of the United States is hereby repealed.

Section 2. The transportation or importation into any state, territory or possession of the United States for delivery or use therein of intoxicating liquors, in violation of the laws thereof, is hereby prohibited.

Section 3. This article shall be inoperative unless it shall have been ratified as an amendment to the Constitution by conventions in the several states, as provided in the Constitution, within seven years from the date of the submission hereof to the states by the Congress.

The third section of the Amendment as proposed misread the zeal of the public for repeal, for adoption was effected within eleven months, between February 20 and December 5, 1933. Aside from the precedent—not uncommon in state constitutions—of excising from the Federal Constitution a provision which had previously been incorporated into it, although there had been other proposals to repeal other Amendments, the effect of the

Twenty-first Amendment was not to restore the precise *status quo ante* the Eighteenth. Section 2 confirmed as constitutional law a legislative policy which had only been tentatively recognized prior to 1919. Under the Webb-Kenyon Interstate Liquor Act of 1913,[1] Congress had prohibited the importing of alcoholic beverages into "dry" states, and the constitutionality of the statute had been upheld in 1917.[2] However, the Court did not deal definitively with the question of whether the constitutional power ultimately lay in the plenary power over commerce, or whether there was an implied power in Congress to "federalize" certain state laws in order to make them effective against other states.[3]

After 1933 the Court was disposed to assert both state and Federal authority over intoxicants and the traffic therein. State laws were sustained in the face of charges that they discriminated against interstate commerce and the due-process and equal-protection clauses of the Fourteenth Amendment: licenses in favor of domestic liquors,[4] or laws retaliatory to laws of other states discriminating against out-of-state shipments,[5] and similar borderline matters were decided on the merits without attempting to develop a general rule of constitutional construction. Federal interests, in any case, are held to be paramount to local interests where interstate shipments traverse a state[6] and are defined under the commerce clause rather than under this Amendment.[7] The old "unbroken package" doctrine has been applied, under both the commerce clause and the export-import clause, to bar state taxes on imported liquors prior to retail distribution.[8]

---

1. 37 Stat. 699; *cf. Georgia v. Wenger*, 94 F.S. 976 (1950), aff'd. 187 F. 2d 285 (1951), cert. den. 342 U.S. 822 (1952).
2. *Clark Dist. Co. v. Western Maryland R. Co.*, 242 U.S. 311 (1917).
3. *Cf.* generally *Leisy v. Hardin*, 135 U.S. 100 (1890), and *In re Rahrer*, 140 U.S. 545 (1891); and subsequently, *Finch Co. v. McKittrick*, 305 U.S. 395 (1939); *Duckworth v. Arkansas*, 314 U.S. 390 (1941); *Carter v. Virginia*, 321 U.S. 131 (1944).
4. *Young's Market v. State Board*, 299 U.S. 59 (1939); *Mahoney v. Triner Corp.*, 304 U.S. 40 (1938); *Brewing Co. v. Liquor Comm.*, 305 U.S. 391 (1939); and *cf. United States v. Frankfort Distillers*, 324 U.S. 293 (1945).
5. *Finch & Co. v. McKittrick*, 305 U.S. 395 (1939).
6. *Ziffrin, Inc. v. Reeves*, 308 U.S. 132 (1939); *Duckworth v. Arkansas*, 314 U.S. 390 (1941); *Carter v. Virginia*, 321 U.S. 131 (1944); *Cartlidge v. Rainey*, 168 F. 2d 841 (1948), cert. den. 335 U.S. 885 (1948).

7. The Federal Alcohol Administration Act of 1935, 49 Stat. 977, 27 U.S.C. 201, was held valid as against an argument that this Amendment vested in the states complete control over commerce in liquor. *Arrow Distillers v. Alexander*, 109 F. 2d 397 (1940), cert. den. 310 U.S. 646 (1940).

8. *Dept. of Revenue v. Beam Distillers*, 377 U.S. 341 (1964); *Hostetter v. Idlewild Liquor Corp.*, 377 U.S. 324 (1964). Cf. also *Seagram & Sons v. Hostetter*, 384 U.S. 35 (1966). Federal power is exclusive over liquor imported into national parks or other Federal premises within a state. *Collins v. Yosemite Park Co.*, 304 U.S. 518 (1938).

Amendment XXII
Limitation of Presidential Terms

Section 1. No person shall be elected to the office of the President more than twice, and no person who has held the office of President, or acted as President, for more than two years of a term to which some other person was elected President shall be elected to the office of the President more than once. But this Article shall not apply to any person holding the office of President when this Article was proposed by the Congress, and shall not prevent any person who may be holding the office of President, or acting as President, during the term within which this Article becomes operative from holding the office of President or acting as President during the remainder of such term.

Section 2. This Article shall be inoperative unless it shall have been ratified as an amendment to the Constitution by the legislatures of three-fourths of the several states within seven years from the date of its submission to the states by the Congress.

Amendment XXIII
District of Columbia Franchise

Section 1. The District constituting the seat of government of the United States shall appoint in such manner as the Congress may direct:
A number of electors of President and Vice President equal to the

whole number of Senators and Representatives in Congress to which the district would be entitled if it were a state, but in no event more than the least populous state; they shall be in addition to those appointed by the states, but they shall be considered, for the purposes of the election of President and Vice President, to be electors appointed by a state; and they shall meet in the district and perform such duties as provided by the twelfth article of amendment.

Section 2. The Congress shall have power to enforce this article by appropriate legislation.

Amendment XXIV. Abolition of Poll Taxes

Section 1. The right of citizens of the United States to vote in any primary or other election for President or Vice President, for electors for President or Vice President, or for Senator or Representative in Congress, shall not be denied or abridged by the United States or any state by reason of failure to pay any poll tax or other tax.

Section 2. The Congress shall have power to enforce this article by appropriate legislation.

Prior to this Amendment, the Court in 1937 had upheld a Georgia poll tax against a charge that it violated the equal-protection clause of the Fourteenth Amendment.[1] In 1966, subsequent to this Amendment but without direct reference to it, the Court held that the equal-protection clause invalidated any state poll tax which abridged a voter's right to exercise his franchise.[2] A similar property-tax qualification, limiting school bond elections to property owners within the school district, was also invalidated on equal-protection grounds.[3] Thus, construction of other clauses in the Constitution have prepared the setting for the anti-poll-tax orientation of the present Amendment.

1. *Breedlove v. Suttles,* 302 U.S. 277 (1937).
2. *Harper v. Virginia Board of Elections,* 383 U.S. 663 (1966); and cf. *Harman v. Forssenius,* 380 U.S. 528 (1965).
3. *Kramer v. Union Free School District,* 395 U.S. 621 (1969); *Phoenix v. Koldziejski,* 399 U.S. 204 (1970); *Cipriano v. Houma,* 395 U.S. 701 (1969).

Amendment XXV. Presidential Disability

Section 1. In case of the removal of the President from office or of his death or resignation, the Vice President shall become President.

Section 2. Whenever there is a vacancy in the office of the Vice President, the President shall nominate a Vice President who shall take office upon confirmation by a majority vote of both Houses of Congress.

Section 3. Whenever the President transmits to the President pro tempore of the Senate and the Speaker of the House of Representatives his written declaration that he is unable to discharge the powers and duties of his office, and until he transmits to them a written declaration to the contrary, such powers and duties shall be discharged by the Vice President as Acting President.

Section 4. Whenever the Vice President and a majority of either the principal officers of the executive departments or of such other body as Congress may by law provide, transmit to the President pro tempore of the Senate and the Speaker of the House of Representatives their written declaration that the President is unable to discharge the powers and duties of his office, the Vice President shall immediately assume the powers and duties of the office as Acting President.

Thereafter, when the President transmits to the President pro tempore of the Senate and the Speaker of the House of Representatives his written declaration that no inability exists, he shall resume the powers and duties of his office unless the Vice President and a majority of either the principal officers of the executive department or of such other body as Congress may by law provide, transmit within four days to the President pro tempore of the Senate and the Speaker of the House of Representatives their written declaration that the President is unable to discharge the powers and duties of his office. Thereupon Congress shall decide the issue, assembling within forty-eight hours for that purpose if not in session. If the Congress, within twenty-one days after receipt of the latter written declaration, or, if Congress is not in session, within twenty-one days after Congress is required to assemble, determines by two-thirds vote of both Houses that the President is unable to discharge the powers and duties of his office, the Vice President shall continue to discharge the same as Acting President; otherwise, the President shall resume the powers and duties of his office.

Although this Amendment had been prompted by the known history of heart trouble in President Lyndon B. Johnson when he succeeded John F. Kennedy in 1963, its first practical application occurred in 1973 when Vice President Spiro T. Agnew resigned his office, necessitating the nomination of a successor.

Amendment XXVI. Minimum Voting Age

Section 1. The right of citizens of the United States, who are eighteen years of age or older, to vote shall not be denied or abridged by the United States or any State on account of age.

Section 2. The Congress shall have power to enforce this article by appropriate legislation.

In the Voting Rights Act Amendment of 1970,[1] Congress established a minimum voting age of eighteen for all persons in both state and Federal elections, as well as abolishing literacy tests for a five-year period in state and national elections and abolishing residence requirements in national elections. The Supreme Court in the case of *Oregon v. Mitchell*[2] upheld all of the provisions in the statute except the voting-age limit in state elections, where a 5–4 majority denied the power of Congress to legislate on the subject. Three months later, on March 29, 1971, Congress submitted this Amendment, in language similar to the suffrage provisions of the Fifteenth and Nineteenth Amendments. Within ninety days it was adopted, on June 30, 1971.[3]

1. 84 Stat. 314, 42 U.S.C. 1973.
2. 400 U.S. 111 (1970).
3. On the subject of residence requirements, *cf. Dunn v. Blumstein*, 405 U.S. 330 (1972); and *cf. Evans v. Cornman*, 398 U.S. 419 (1970); *Carrington v. Rash*, 380 U.S. 89 (1965).

Amendment XXVII. Equality of Rights

[Section 1. Equality of rights under the law shall not be denied or abridged by the United States or any state on account of sex.

[Section 2. The Congress shall have power to enforce, by appropriate legislation, the provisions of this article.

[Section 3. This Amendment shall take effect two years after the date of ratification.]

As the present volume went to press, this Amendment, submitted on March 22, 1972, had been ratified by more than half of the states, and although a counter-current then set in, there was still prospect of adoption in the reasonable future. Such an Amendment had been vociferously advocated for years, without any of the scores of bills on the subject reaching the floor of either House of Congress.[1] Under the pressure of women's "liberation," however, Congress submitted the proposed Amendment in the face of arguments that it already had plenary authority to legislate on the subject under the equal-protection clause of the Fourteenth Amendment. The Court, too, had indicated a disposition to treat the equal-protection clause as self-executing in this subject area.[2] The Equal Employment Opportunity Act of 1972[3] and the Higher Education Act of 1965[4] were also precedents for Congressional initiative even before this Amendment was drafted.

1. *Cf.* Swindler, *The New Legality,* p. 376.
2. *Cf. Phillips v. Martin-Marietta Corp.,* 400 U.S. 542 (1971).
3. 86 Stat. 103, 5 U.S.C. 5108.
4. 79 Stat. 1219, 20 U.S.C. 403.

Table of Cases

Index